ANGELS

AND THE NEW SPIRITUALITY

ANGELS
AND THE NEW SPIRITUALITY

DUANE A. GARRETT

BROADMAN
&HOLMAN
PUBLISHERS

Nashville, Tennessee

Published by:
Broadman & Holman Publishers
Nashville, Tennessee

Design: Steven Boyd

4261-76
0-8054-6176-0

Dewey Decimal Classification: 235.3
Subject Heading: Angels
Library of Congress Card Catalog Number: 95-12467

Library of Congress Cataloging-in-Publication Data
Garrett, Duane A.
    Angels and the new spirituality / by Duane A. Garrett.
    p. cm.
    ISBN 0-8054-6176-0 (Hardbound)
    1. Angels—Biblical teaching. I. Title.
  BS680.A48G37 1995
    235' .3—dc20
95-12467
CIP
99 98 97 96 95 5 4 3 2 1

To my mother, Frances Black Garrett,
and the memory of my father, Robert Lee Garrett.
Two people who never suffered fools gladly.

Contents

Preface . . . . *ix*

1. Secret Things
   An Introduction to the World of Angels. *1*

2. Something of an Angel Light
   Angels in the Bible *10*

3. Auld Hornie, Satan, Nick, or Clootie
   Satan in the Bible. *27*

4. To Which of the Angels?
   Christ and the Angels in the Bible *50*

5. Nobody in Particular
   A Brief History of Angelology, Part 1. . . . . *58*

6. O World Unknowable
   A Brief History of Angelology, Part 2. . . . . *86*

7. Precisely Where Angels Dwell
   Major Questions about the Angels. *102*

8. Bats Not Angels
   New Age Angels, Part 1 . . . . *127*

9. Spirits from the Vasty Deep
   New Age Angels, Part 2 . . . . *141*

10. Golden Opinions from All Sorts of People
    Jews, Roman Catholics, Protestants, and the Angels. *161*

11. More Things in Heaven and Earth
    Anecdotes about Angels *178*

12. Improbable Fiction
    Angels in Evangelical Novels *190*

13. The Great Enemy of Truth
    The Powers and Spiritual Warfare *205*

14. Familiar Spirits
    Concluding Thoughts on Angels and the New Spirituality. *234*

    Notes *241*

    Selected Bibliography *256*

Preface

WRITING A BOOK IS LIKE A VISIT TO A LARGE, UNEX-plored museum. With every turn and every new display, the inquisitive visitor says, "I never knew that!" or "I never saw anything like that before!" If the displays are well-planned, the explorer will even come away with his or her understanding of the world changed.

That has been my experience in researching and writing this book. I have encountered teachings, legends, and ideas that I never imagined. I have discovered "new" religious trends that strangely repeat old religious habits and ideas, often in ways that the participants themselves do not realize. I have had to think again about my view of the world, God, and the angels. I hope this will be your experience as well.

Just as no worthwhile museum is the achievement of one person's work, so this book has come about through the help of many friends. First among these is Vicki Crumpton, who gave encouragement and insights to the project from beginning to end. Others who have helped significantly are Mike McGough, John Korner, and my sister-in-law, Janelle Garrett. Kathy Seidler deserves special mention: she spent countless hours working interlibrary loan to find the books I needed. I also wish to thank Richard Blackaby, who as president of the Canadian Southern Baptist Seminary was always an encouragement in this project. As with all my writing and everything else I do, deepest gratitude goes to my wife, Patricia Garrett, for her patience and support.

CHAPTER ONE

*The secret things belong to the L*ORD *our God,*
but the revealed things belong to us and to our children forever,
to observe all the words of this law.
DEUTERONOMY 29:29

Secret Things

An Introduction to the World of Angels

PERHAPS YOU HAVE HEARD THE STORY OF ARCTIC EXPLORERS making their way north during a polar spring. They pulled their sledges over frozen hills until they came to a spot where the ice was flat enough and the area sheltered enough to make a campsite for the evening. They pitched their tents, had their meal, and bedded down for the night.

The next morning, they discovered that the ice where they had camped had broken loose and was adrift at sea. All around them, instead of mountains of white, there was only the black water of the ocean. They did not know where they were or how to deal with this new situation. Their world had changed, and they had not even realized that it was happening.

Change a few details, and this is my story and the story of many Christians in my generation. I grew up in a world where everyone was a Baptist, Methodist, Lutheran, Roman Catholic, or Jew. While we had our differences, certain presuppositions were universal. God was Creator and

Judge. We were distinct from Him and our environment was His creation. God was righteous, and we either had to find forgiveness and eternal life or face eternal damnation. The great enemy of Christianity was atheism, that final destination of a road paved with secularism, scientific skepticism, and humanism. For Christians, the challenge was to convince people that spiritual things mattered and that they should take God into account.

Angels? For us they were, well, like an old aunt who wears funny hats. They were kind of an embarrassment. We hoped that the skeptic would not bring up the subject. They were such an easy target for ridicule—all that fluttering about with their halos and harps and white robes.

But suddenly I find that the world that I thought I knew has disappeared. People around me no longer pretend to share the Judeo-Christian worldview. They buy crystals for spiritual power and find solace in the chants and prayer songs of Native Americans. They read their horoscopes before business decisions. They embrace reincarnation. They blur the distinction between God and creation and believe that all is one. They abandon the secular city for a spiritual quest in the mountains of Peru. They do not need to be convinced of the reality of the spiritual dimension. They desert university research positions, offices on Wall Street, and country club parties to find solace for the soul. The prospect of discovering significance in atheism and materialism is too bleak to endure, and they are determined to find something that is sacred and that transcends this fleeting life. And they love the angels.

All of this leaves me bewildered. I think I know what to do with reincarnation, pantheism, crystals, and the like. I do not fully understand the attraction of these things, but I do know that they have nothing to do with Christianity and the Bible.

But what about angels? After all, they are in the Bible. They were at the resurrection of Jesus. I know I am supposed to believe in them. But who are they really? What do they do? Where do they come from? Why do so many people outside the church find them so attractive? Why are magazines, television shows, and movies suddenly fluttering with a virtual flock of angels? Why are they popping up in the books that do endorse reincarnation and crystals? How do I separate the good from the bad in this sudden craze over angels? Most difficult of all, why have I not paid attention to angels before? Have I been missing something?

The Perplexing World
of the New Spirituality of Angels

A woman named Elizabeth, so the story goes, visited the island of Páros while on a tour of Greece. After a brief stay she checked out of her hotel but had misgivings about departing Páros. As she boarded the ferry, her anxiety became so severe that she forced her way through the crowd, got off the boat, and went back to the hotel. The next day she took a long walk and came to rest under the shade of a tree in front of a closed-up house. An older woman soon arrived, and Elizabeth guessed that she was the owner. Embarrassed at being found trespassing, she spoke to the old woman, and for some reason chose French: "Pardon, Madame. . . ." It turned out that the older woman was herself French and that her name was Nicole. She invited Elizabeth in for some water. Not only that, but she had seen Elizabeth on the beach the day before and had felt a need to talk to her.

Nicole was bitterly unhappy. Her husband, a Protestant minister, had abandoned her for another woman. Her anger and hurt were all the worse for the fact that the other woman had been her friend. Nicole asked Elizabeth about God. Elizabeth spoke to her of God with more fervency (and more fluency in French) than she knew she possessed. At the end of the conversation, the two women knelt and prayed for the ability to love and trust again. Elizabeth left Páros the next day, but a year later she received a letter from Nicole. Now dying of cancer, Nicole thanked Elizabeth for their time together. It had been a miracle for her, since she was now free of anger and at peace with God.

I did not hear this story firsthand; it is one of hundreds (or thousands) of miracle stories that one finds in the many books and newsletters about angels. This particular account comes from *A Book of Angels* by Sophy Burnham.[1] I cannot vouch for accuracy of the story since I do not know either Sophy Burnham or Elizabeth. On the other hand, I have no reason to say that it is not true. I simply tell it to you as I read it, and if you wish, you can get Burnham's book and read it for yourself in more detail.

Although it does not include a specific reference to an angel, the providential events and the outcome of spiritual healing particularly impressed this story upon me. I suppose this is because I can easily imagine this story being recounted in a church—in my own church, for example—and can see in my mind the people nodding with approval, saying "Amen," and afterward going up to Elizabeth to tell her what a blessing the story had been, how they appreciated her for coming, and how they felt more people needed to hear this story.

I ought to mention one other aspect of the story. Elizabeth's words to Nicole apparently did not stem from or reflect what we might call Christian orthodoxy. Her opening words to Nicole were, "I cannot tell you what God is, but I can tell you how to find it." Then, according to Burnham, "They spent the rest of the afternoon talking feverishly about meditation and the spiritual path, about forgiveness and prayer, and suffering, and love, about the writer Kazantzakis, the Buddha, Christ."[2] Kazantzakis, by the way, is Nikos Kazantzakis, a Greek writer who explored various philosophical and spiritual ideas, who was drawn toward heroic pessimism and nihilism, and whose most famous works include *Zorba the Greek* and another book not likely to be included in offerings of the Evangelical Book Club, *The Last Temptation of Christ.*

And this is the world of angels, as they appear in the many books and movies and television specials you perhaps have seen. It is a world of spiritual ambiguity. It is a world in which the believing Christian or even the honest seeker falls into a vertigo of disorientation. People speak of angels who come from heaven and help people, of lives that are transformed, of God and the Bible, but so much of it is like a song played slightly off-key. You think you recognize it, but you are not sure. It is like watching a football game in which both teams are wearing the same uniform. It would be so much easier if one side simply shouted out, "We serve God!" and the other side shouted, "We don't believe in the Christian God!"

But they do not. Two people will with equal fervor speak rapturously of the glory of angels, and both will describe in stirring detail story after story of angel encounters and angelic acts of charity. It is only after you have probed a little that you discover that the two people are pushing radically different agendas and beliefs.

One European Roman Catholic group that is dedicated to the angels follows seven guiding principles. Outside its affirmation of the role of Mary in the life of the church, virtually any Christian could endorse its list of guidelines. One would never guess that this group is immersed so deeply in superstition and mind-control that it earned not one but two official Vatican rebukes.

On the surface, the new love of angels brings us back to God, to spirituality, and to wholesomeness. Beneath the halos and wings, however, we find a confusing maze of contradictory beliefs, superstition, and legend, as well as biblical faith.

A World of Confusion

Some angel stories and ideas are touching. But we also read of angels who take dogs to heaven and pompous angels who want to be our saviors and claim to be of "superuniverse status." We encounter an endless number of cute puns and are reassured at every turn that we are good people who deserve to be happy. We are encouraged to imagine that we have angel wings and can flutter them around. We wade through the most astonishing mystical jargon about the "fourth-dimensional consciousness" and the "burden of the ego" and "planetary vibrations." We conclude that not only the angels but also the people who follow them are not of this planet.

Not to worry, though. I have waded through the swamps for you. Some time ago, my wife was looking at one of the many angel books I was reading and commented, "Duane, you have an amazing tolerance for stupidity." "You have to have that," I replied, "if you want to be a theologian." In the pages that follow, I will point out the major swamps without making you go too deep into the muck. But I will also try to point to a higher ground, where the terrain is firm and the view is spectacular—the mountains of God where the real angels dwell. But we will never appreciate the mountains until we have smelled the swamps.

Deep Truth and Secret Knowledge

In the beginning, THE ONE began to sing, and each note became a shining light, and each light became an angel. The first twelve notes of the song were the angels of the twelve celestial dispensations. First came Sophroniel, patron of all wisdom and prudence, who spread pure wisdom to all the angels after him. Then came Ahabiel, the embodiment of love, who radiates compassion much as an irrigation system radiates water, drenching the entire cosmos. Then came Aretiel, angel of beauty, who—

Perhaps I should tell you that I am making all of this up. But it is pretty good stuff. It is at least as good as a lot of the books by ancient and modern writers that claim to tell us what angels are and where they came from and what their names are and what they do.

They claim to have discovered a hidden world that contains all we need to be happy and loving and to live forever—the world of the angels. For centuries the knowledge of this undiscovered land lay in the lore of the past and in the minds of the angels. Now, however, it appears that the angels have broken through and have begun to tell us not only the hidden, esoteric truths but also truths about ourselves.

This is nothing new, of course. Centuries ago mystics told of a secret knowledge or *gnosis* that only the initiates could grasp. Secret books gave the names of demons and the angels who could thwart them. Rituals, magic, and taboo have long been the key to the door of enlightenment. Angels appeared as saviors, teachers, and friends.

Make no mistake about this: the current interest in angels is not just about angels. It is a manifestation of an entirely new spirituality. It is an expression of a world that is yearning for more than science, government, and a consumer economy can offer. More than that, it is an approach to religion and the quest for personal worth that is leaving Christians bewildered and leaving them behind.

Yearning for a Special Friend: Guardian Angels

Few things attract more interest than the notion that you have your very own private guardian angel. This is a supernatural being, but he is one that is close and comfortable. He is not someone to fear; unlike "God," he is not the omnipotent and sometimes angry judge of the universe. In fact, the angel does not judge at all. His only job is to help and protect and love his charge.

For reasons we will explore later, people want such a little god of their own so badly that they no longer care whether they are being rational or not. Where I live, near Calgary, Alberta, there is a woman who claims to have a remarkable gift. She says if you tell her your full name, she can go into a meditation, focus on a candle, and have a vision of your guardian angel. She will get a message for you from the angel (usually a few pages long) and sketch a picture of the angel, which is yours to keep. You thus get to find out what your guardian angel looks like and have a direct word from him or her as well. She charges about $200 for the service.[3]

What could be more comforting in an age of broken families, economic uncertainty, rising crime, and loss of personal worth? *Love yourself unconditionally,* our angels tell us, *because we love you and we are always with you.* Angels make no demands except that we accept ourselves, take us nowhere but to the path of greater strength and self-fulfillment, and predict nothing for our planet except the dawn of a new age of understanding and spirituality. What is there not to like? How could it possibly hurt to have a picture of your angel as a reminder of your spiritual friend? Even if it is not—well—*true,* at least it is something warm to hold on to. And many people are willing to pay more than $200 for something that good.

The Stuttering Voice of the Christian Church

Surprisingly, Christian theology (including that of a very conservative stripe) has for a long time passed over the subject of angels in embarrassed silence. Theology books break this silence only long enough to say a few words about angels as a kind of aside and then quickly abandon them to languish in isolation. Certainly the angels are not integrated in any meaningful way into many major systems of theology—systems that can exist perfectly well without them. Karl Barth lamented this state of affairs succinctly: "Angels are not desired in Dogmatics. But a kind of internment camp (or is it a nursery?) is opened for them in which they are tolerated."[4]

This silence is now broken, but the message from the church is a babble of confusion. Some Christians place angels at or near the center of their faith. While they still give verbal affirmation to the central place of Jesus Christ, angels dominate their day-to-day religious life. They like nothing so much as trading stories of how angels rescue people, and they listen with rapt attention to the revelations of their own or another's guardian angels.

Other Christians pay a tremendous amount of attention to spirits. Not to angels, mind you, but *devils.* For them, the Christian life can be described best in a single word: *war!* We are on one side and the hordes of Satan are on the other. Our main task in life is to fight the good fight. The angels may be real, but in *this* world, you are much more likely to meet a demon. And you had better be ready because you can bet that they will be ready.

Other voices call out from the pulpits of the churches too. Some say that there are no angels. Some say that angels are real but that you cannot really know anything about them. Some say that angels and devils are not real persons, but that they are not just creatures of imagination either; they are real *in us* and our *institutions.* Some not only affirm that angels and devils are real persons but they also will happily tell us more about angels and their private lives than we could ever ask or imagine. Some are more than happy to let their imaginations run free and only occasionally come back to earth for orientation.

Not only do opinions differ wildly, but much angel lore is misleading. Some opinions about angels contain hidden implications and agendas. Some ideas come from movements, books, or individuals for whom the word "strange" seems to have been invented. If we are not careful about where we turn, we may wind up deep in a theological jungle.

We do not help ourselves by dodging the question of angels. There *is* something wonderful about these mysterious, holy beings. Can it be that our lives lack depth and holiness because we have neglected them? Of this I am sure: the modern church's failure to include the angels in its message has contributed mightily to the present confusion, and we will never be able to address the new spirituality of angels until we take angels themselves seriously. Perhaps then we will be able both to help people and to give the angels reason to rejoice.

Where Do We Go from Here?

As we enter the world of angels, I want to give you a map. Too often in the angel books I have read, the author talks on and on about who the angels are, what they do, and so forth, but never bothers to explain to the reader the source of all this surprising and detailed knowledge. It comes from an amalgamation of biblical teachings, mysterious speculations by Jewish and Christian sects, and other more recent mystical writers. Rather than just mention these groups and their books in passing (and leaving you wondering who or what they are), I want to give you something of the layout of the land. When you know what these books are and their perspective, you will be in a much better position to understand what is going on in the world of angel speculation. After that, we will move on to deal with questions of who the angels really are.

We will begin with the Bible, which I consider to be the only sure guide to the nature of the angels, but we cannot stop there. Some people have had some very important things to say about angels, and it would be arrogant of us to think that we can start from scratch and ignore how others have worked this ground. I have found that those who claim to use only the Bible in their studies of angels fool themselves no less than everyone else. They unknowingly incorporate a great deal of traditional lore without understanding where it comes from or what it means.

Also, we need to know what people are saying *today*. That, after all, is what affects the spiritual lives of thousands who learn about angels from popular books, from *Time* and *Newsweek*, and from television. Along the way, please be on the lookout for similar ideas that cross the centuries. You may be surprised at what an ancient mystic, a medieval spiritualist, and a modern guru have in common. You might learn from the past where the present is now and where it is going.

After we have looked at the Bible, we will survey angels through the ages in religious literature, and we will try to answer some basic questions about them. Then, we will look at the various expressions of interest in angels today and evaluate them. To sum it all up, we will explore what is wrong and what is right about bringing angels into our worldview.

I need to introduce you to two new words at the outset. I am sure you have not heard of them because I made them up. I had to do that because I know of no English words that expressed the concepts I had in mind. These are *angelphilia* (pronounced "angel philly ya") and the related word, *angelphile* (pronounced "angel file"). *Angelphilia* is an extreme interest in or devotion to angels (it may be excessive), and an *angelphile* is someone who is in that condition. (For those of you who know Greek: Yes, I know that "angelophilia" would be more correct, but "angelophilia" sounds to me like the name of an Italian shoe salesman, and I dislike it.) We will describe some of the great angelphiles of the past and present and explore the world of angelphilia.

In short, we will seek out the *facts*, the *fantasies*, and the *fanaticism* about angels. There is plenty of all three. But in the end, I hope you will have something even better: *faith*.

CHAPTER TWO

And yet a spirit still, and bright
With something of an angel light.
WILLIAM WORDSWORTH, "SHE WAS A PHANTOM OF DELIGHT"

Something of an Angel Light

Angels in the Bible

THE BIBLE WILL NOT TELL YOU EVERYTHING YOU EVER wanted to know about angels. On many questions we can only infer the answers, and on others we are in the dark altogether. Even so, the Bible does tell us a great deal, and its teachings correct many of the excesses and errors of angelphiles.

Messengers and Protectors

The word *angel* comes from the Greek *angelos*, which means "messenger." The Hebrew word for angel, *malakh*, also means messenger and is sometimes used to refer to human messengers. Angels certainly perform this work, but they are more than a heavenly messenger service.

The Original Quicksilver Messenger Service

Frequently angels do manifest themselves in order to deliver some message. They never have been so busy at this as they were around the time of the birth of Jesus. The angel Gabriel appeared suddenly to the priest Zechariah to tell him that his wife, Elizabeth, would have a son. This was not altogether a happy encounter for Zechariah. When he doubted the angel's word, Gabriel immediately struck him mute (Luke 1:8–23). Next, Gabriel made his way to Nazareth to tell Mary that she, though a virgin, would bear a son and call him Jesus. Possessing perhaps more sense and less impertinence than Zechariah, she humbly submitted (Luke 1:26–38).

The next visitation came to Joseph, who was understandably perturbed to hear that his fiancée was pregnant (he knew that he did not do it). An anonymous angel told him that her pregnancy was a work of God, and he was reassured. Joseph, unlike Zechariah and Mary, saw the visitation in a dream (Matt. 1:18–25).

Next came the actual birth of Jesus. An angel, during the dark of night, appeared in all his heavenly glory to a group of stunned shepherds and announced that the Messiah had been born. A whole army of angels then joined him, and the shepherds had the rare experience of hearing a heavenly choir firsthand (Luke 2:8–15).

The angels were still not done. Joseph had another dream. This time, an angel warned him that Herod was seeking to kill Jesus and that they should flee to Egypt. Still again, an angel told Joseph when Herod died that it was safe to go home (Matt. 2:13–20). We might also include in our survey the warning to the wise men that they should not go back to Herod after their visit with the Holy Family (Matt. 3:12). In the events surrounding the birth of Jesus, nothing significant transpired without some angel involvement.

The Bible describes other angel announcements. The first significant Gentile conversion to Christianity occurred after an angel encounter. An angel told the Roman centurion Cornelius to send for Simon Peter and pay close attention to his message (Acts 10). In Genesis 16, an angel found the runaway slave Hagar in the desert, told her to go home, and promised her that her son, Ishmael, would become a great nation. The Book of Numbers tells us that the prophet Balaam, while on a journey to deliver curses against Israel, found his way blocked by an angel. He could not see the angel, but his donkey could and refused to budge. At last the Lord opened his eyes so that Balaam became at least as spiritually sensitive as his donkey. In the encounter, the angel told him that had the donkey not refused to move, he would have struck Balaam dead (Num. 22:22–35).

A few salient points come out of this survey of angelic messages. First, angels are more likely to make themselves visible for significant events, such as the birth of the Messiah. Second, they may appear in a number of ways, including a visible manifestation to a man or woman, an appearance in a dream, or even by showing themselves to an animal but not a person. Third, angel appearances may well terrify those who see them. In many of the above occurrences, the angels begin their messages with "Fear not!" People fear angels with good reason. Zechariah lost the power of speech in a moment and Balaam came closer than he knew to being cut down in his path. Fourth, angels make their appearances when they choose. In every case, the human involved was not asking for or expecting an angelic visitation. This last detail is important. Today, as we shall see, many people want to find a method of invoking an angel.

Jail Breaks

Angels can bring more than just messages. In 1 Kings 19:5–7, the prophet Elijah found himself on the run from Jezebel and without food. Taking a nap, he was awakened by an angel and found before him a freshly prepared meal. And in 2 Kings 6, when hostile Syrian soldiers surrounded Elisha's hometown, his servant reacted in a way that was understandable if less than heroic: "Alas! What shall we do?" (v. 15). Elisha prayed that the servant's eyes would be opened, and then he saw that "the mountain was full of horses and chariots of fire all around Elisha" (v. 17).

In the famous episode of the fiery furnace (Dan. 3), Shadrach, Meshach, and Abednego expected to become instant toast when they were thrown into the oven. Instead, they found themselves unharmed, and the watching king saw standing with them in the furnace a fourth figure who had "the appearance of a god." Years later, Daniel's enemies condemned him to a night entombed with a group of hungry lions. When he was released the next morning, he reported, "My God sent his angel and shut the lions' mouths" (Dan. 6:22).

Angels pulled off a couple of jail breaks in the Book of Acts. In 5:17–24, they broke the apostles out of the prison in a way that could make Houdini envious. The prison doors remained locked and the guards never left their posts, but the angels spirited their apostolic charges away without ever being noticed. The same thing happened again when Peter was in jail. An angel whisked him away so quietly and with such ease that Peter himself could not believe it was happening until he was standing outside (Acts 12:6–12).

But the angels did not always effect such dramatic rescues. Paul spent years in prison after his arrest in Jerusalem. While en route as a prisoner to Rome, however, his ship foundered in a storm and was left drifting with dwindling supplies. An angel appeared on the scene to assure him that he would make it safely to Rome (Acts 27:21–25).

A particular phrase the Bible uses to describe help from the angels is that they will "go before you." When Abraham sent his servant to find a wife for Isaac, he promised him that "he will send his angel before you, and you shall take a wife for my son from there" (Gen. 24:7). The same expression occurs in Exodus 23:20, where the angel of the Lord "goes before" the nation of Israel during the Exodus.

Angels can deliver people from trouble. Here again, however, their methods vary. People may or may not see them, and sometimes no one is more surprised at what they do than the beneficiary of their activity. Their work can be as delightfully ordinary as making lunch for a hungry prophet or as supernatural as saving men in the middle of a blazing furnace. They help people who serve God and especially those who are persecuted for their integrity, but two equally deserving people may not receive the same kind of help.

Angels as Executioners

The Bible often describes angels not as helpers but as agents of judgment. Describing the plagues on the Egyptians, Psalm 78:49 says, "He let loose on them his fierce anger, wrath, indignation, and distress, a company of destroying angels." Isaiah 37 describes a similar situation, in which the angel of the Lord struck down the Assyrian army while it was preparing a siege against Jerusalem.

Gnashing Teeth

Angels frequently appear in passages that describe the final judgment. In his explanation of the parable of the weeds, Jesus stated that in the last day, "The Son of Man will send his angels, and they will collect out of his kingdom all causes of sin and all evildoers, and they will throw them into the furnace of fire, where there will be weeping and gnashing of teeth" (Matt. 13:41–42). So also in Matthew 16:27, Jesus said that "the Son of Man is to come with his angels in the glory of his Father, and then he will repay everyone for what has been done."

The most dramatic examples come from the book of Revelation. There, angels serve as the agents of every act of punishment on wayward humanity. In Revelation 8, they sound seven trumpets that signal the wrath of God, and in chapters 15 and 16 they pour plagues out on earth from seven bowls.

Judgment is one angelic role that, as we shall see, has altogether escaped contemporary angelphiles. In most recent books, angels are sweet, compassionate beings who love unconditionally and never do anything that might hurt someone. If some of these books are to be believed, the angels care very little about moral issues and would not think of being involved in punishment.

Turnabout Is Fair Play?

As a curious turnabout, Paul also told us that we shall one day judge the angels (1 Cor. 6:3). He gave no details about the nature of this judgment. The word *judge* could mean "rule" in accordance with normal Hebrew usage, and the point may simply be that angels will be subordinate to us in the hereafter. If some final judgment is in view, Paul likely meant that we will judge fallen angels. In context, he wanted to dissuade the lawsuit-happy Corinthians from taking one another to court, and he told them that people who someday will judge angels ought to be able to solve their own petty disputes without recourse to secular courts. For our purposes, the subordinate role of the angels stands out here. Although they may be agents of wrath, their work is always in the control of God.

Observers of Human Nature

In Dickens' *Pickwick Papers*, Mr. Pickwick calls himself "an observer of human nature." This job description especially suits the angels as well.

In 1 Corinthians 4:9, Paul said that the apostles, like a parade of condemned prisoners marching through the streets of Rome, were a spectacle before both humans and angels. Paul's point was not so much to reveal some hidden truth about the work of angels as to say that the apostles, in all their humiliation and suffering, were on exhibition before anyone and everyone. Still, the notion that the angels are "wondering spectators of the vicissitudes of the church militant"[1] is implicit.

More difficult is 1 Corinthians 11:10, where Paul said that a woman should have a symbol of authority on her head "because of the angels." I have no intention of getting into the questions of whether women should wear veils and why Paul made an issue of this. I am sure that wiser heads, be they veiled or unveiled, can deal with that.[2] My concern is with why he felt that the angels were involved in this matter.

The solution is not, as some have suggested, that the "angels" are really demons and that they might lust after unveiled women or that "angels" is a euphemism for "God." Instead, Paul had at least two reasons for alluding to the angels here. First, he related the role of women in the church to the natural order of human society as God ordained it at the creation. In a word, each sex has its purpose and role (vv. 8–9). Inasmuch as the angels were present at the creation, Paul wanted the churches to display to the angels a society that reflects rather than violates the creation order. Second, Paul believed that angels are present at Christian worship, and he did not want the churches to present an affront to them. In this sense, it is safe to say that Paul would have regarded any impropriety in worship as an offense to the angels.

Other texts also allude to the angelic role of watcher. Christ, in his incarnation, was "seen by angels" (1 Tim. 3:16). In 1 Timothy 5:21, Paul charged Timothy "in the presence of God and of Christ Jesus and of the elect angels" faithfully to fulfill the work of a pastor. Hebrews 13:2 exhorts us to show hospitality on the grounds that some "have entertained angels without knowing it." In Revelation 3:5, Jesus promises to acknowledge faithful saints by name in the presence of the angels.

Finally, 1 Peter 1:12 adds an important bit of information on the place of angels as observers. The text states that angels eagerly desire to understand the mystery of the gospel of Jesus Christ. This implies not only that the angels look upon what is happening on earth but also that they do not fully understand the work of God. This counterbalances the tendency of some to treat angels as near omniscient spiritual guides.

The notion that the angels observe human affairs gains added force in light of the New Testament teaching that God gave the Law to Israel through the agency of angels (Acts 7:53; Gal. 3:19). The Old Testament itself does not mention the role of angels in the giving of the Law, although it does describe thunder, clouds, and lightning at Mt. Sinai, and the Greek versions of Deuteronomy 33:2 and Psalm 68:18 interpret these phenomena to be angelic.[3] Since angels assisted in the giving of the Law, it is not surprising that they should be watching the affairs of people to see how close they come to following it.

In summary, angels do observe what goes on here. Their presence, though unseen, should serve as a further incentive to behavior that honors Christ and gives evidence of having been touched by God. At the same time, they do not know all and are themselves subordinate beings.

Angels in Visions and Prophecies

The Bible often associates angels with visions and prophecies. In Genesis 28:12–17, Jacob had his famous dream at Bethel in which he saw a stairway leading into heaven with angels ascending and descending. He heard a word from God to the effect that he was the heir of the covenant to Abraham and Isaac, woke up, and exclaimed, "This is none other than the house of God!" To Jacob, the vision meant that the spot where he slept was the place where heaven and earth intersected. He saw it as the gateway through which the angels came to do their work on earth. Seeing the angels, moreover, reinforced his conviction that the voice he heard was the voice of God. Beyond that, angels played no particular role in this vision.

Angelic Interpreters

Sometimes the angels act as guides for the prophets in explaining and interpreting visions. Zechariah, for example, saw a series of visions and each time an angel served as his interpreter. For example, in Zechariah 6:1–8, he saw four chariots coming out from between two mountains, and said to his angel, "What are these, my lord?" The angel explained that these are four "winds" that go out and patrol the earth for the Lord. Much the same occurs in Daniel, where the prophet saw "a man dressed in linen" who had a face "like lightning" (Dan. 10:5–6). This "man," obviously an angelic figure, explained to Daniel in detail about things to come in the history of his people (Dan. 10:10–12:4).

Sometimes the angels themselves appear in visions with bizarre but highly symbolic features. The most famous example of this is in Ezekiel 1, in which the prophet saw the chariot of the Lord. The vision included the "wheels within wheels" that are covered with eyes, a shining blue dome, and a brightly shining figure seated above the dome. Within the vision are four living creatures, each of whom has four faces (of a man, an ox, an eagle, and a lion). Each has four wings, and their legs and feet are straight, like those of an ox.

Every aspect of this vision carries meaning, although the symbolism is at times difficult and the interpretation is open to dispute. In my opinion, the four creatures symbolize the Lord's dominion over creation (with the man's face representing humanity, the highest of all creatures, the ox being the strongest domestic animal; the eagle being the mightiest bird, and the lion being the most ferocious of the wild animals). For our purposes, however, it suffices to note that angels can take on very strange appearances in order to convey some concept to the prophet or reader.

The Book of Revelation contains a great deal of this. Here too, four angels take on the appearances of man, ox, eagle, and lion, although each figure has one face and not four (Rev. 4:7). John also saw four angels who hold back the four winds, an angel who rises with the sun, and an angel with a rainbow over his head and legs like pillars of fire (7:1–2; 10:1–2). Throughout the prophecy, angels act as guides to the apostle as well. In Revelation 22:16, Jesus states that He sent His angel to declare His message to the churches.

Sometimes an angel acts out a role in order to convey some information. In Ezekiel, the prophet sees an angel ("a man clothed in linen") who goes through Jerusalem and puts a mark on the forehead of everyone who grieves over the idolatry that has invaded the city, while six other angels go and strike down those who have no mark (9:2–6). The action implies that God will sweep away idolaters in judgment but will spare the faithful. In Ezekiel 40–43, the prophet saw a vision of a new, ideal temple (a symbol of purified worship), and an angel guided him through the precincts. The angel carried a measuring rod with which he measured every structure in the vicinity, and Ezekiel dutifully reported to us all the measurements. We can make of this what we will, but a similar thing happens in Revelation 21:15–17, in which an angel measured the New Jerusalem and gave the dimensions to John.

The Seraphim

Isaiah gave us an intriguing portrait of angels in the visionary sixth chapter of his book, where he saw the Lord "high and lifted up" and surrounded by seraphim. This is the only place in the Bible where the term *seraphim* occurs as applied to angels. The text describes the seraphim as having six wings each. With two they covered their faces, with two they covered their feet, and with two they flew. They sang a simple song of "Holy, holy, holy is the LORD of Hosts; the whole earth is full of his glory."

The wings over the face represent humility in the presence of God. Even the angels are unworthy to be in God's presence with bare faces and to look directly upon Him. The wings that covered the feet likewise imply proper demeanor before God. Commentators often remark that in Hebrew, the word "feet" can be a euphemism for the sexual parts, but that is not exactly the point here. Rather, the angels have their wings draped down over their bodies as a covering that extends from head to toe, so to speak. Again, the message is that God is the great King, and no one appears before Him in an unseemly manner or without proper attire. The fact that they flew with two wings indicates that they were in active service of God and in ready attendance for any command. All in all, the picture is one of complete subordination and respect, an attitude that they reinforce with their refrain that God is "holy."

Seeing all this, Isaiah bemoaned his own unworthiness. He expressed chagrin at being "a man of unclean lips" and yet standing before God. An angel brought a live coal, touched his lips with it (remember, this is a vision!), and declared him cleansed. We should not make anything of the fact that an angel brought the coal to him. The angel was merely serving as a minister of God. If we can say this with no disrespect, the angels in this vision are little more than props. Their function is to emphasize the holiness of God to Isaiah and the reader. This explains why Isaiah's message to Jerusalem must be one of judgment (6:9–13), because the city had violated that holiness.

Of more interest to us is the question of whether seraphim are a special or exalted order of angels. That is a possibility, but I doubt it. Hebrew scholars disagree among themselves about the meaning of the term *seraph* (*seraphim* is the plural form). The word sometimes refers to venomous snakes, as in Numbers 21:6, where God punished Israel with *seraphim* snakes. These snakes were not angelic, but poisonous. On this basis, some believe that the angels Isaiah saw had a serpentine appearance. The text, however, states that they flew and implies that they had hands (Isa. 6:6), but it says nothing about them being snake-like.

The word *seraph* comes from the root *saraph*, which means to "burn." This probably explains why it is used of venomous snakes, since their bites give their victims burning pain. As used of the angels whom Isaiah saw, the term probably means that when Isaiah saw them, they seemed to glow like a fire. Many descriptions of angel encounters in the Bible mention that angels have glowing faces or bodies (Dan. 10:6). That being the case, *seraph* is probably not a designation or rank at all, but only a description of how they looked to Isaiah.[4]

Because of that, and because the Bible nowhere else speaks of an order of seraphim, we should hesitate about setting the rank of the seraphim somewhere in our angelic hierarchy. It may be that Isaiah would have described any shining, angelic figures as seraphim. In a later chapter, we shall return to the question of whether there are angelic orders about which we have knowledge.

The Angel of the Lord

Within the Bible itself, the most pressing angel question is the identity of the "angel of the Lord."

A Subordinate Messenger of God?

Frequently, the angel of the Lord carried out what we might call normal angel activities. In Genesis 16:7–9, the angel of the Lord found the runaway Hagar and sent her home. In Numbers 22:22–35, the angel of the Lord confronted the greedy Balaam on his way to do a job as a rent-a-curse prophet against Israel. And in Judges 13, playing a role similar to that of Gabriel in the birth of John the Baptist, the angel of the Lord appeared to the wife of Manoah and told her that she would give birth to a son, Samson.

In some passages, the angel of the Lord obeyed God and did His work in subordination to Him. Second Samuel 24:15–16 states that the Lord sent a plague on Israel as punishment for David's census of the nation. When the angelic agent of the plague came near the threshing floor of Araunah the Jebusite, the Lord repented and told the angel to cease. The end of verse 16 specifically calls this angel "the angel of the Lord."

In Zechariah 1:12, the angel of the Lord interceded for Judah: "O Lord of hosts, how long will you withhold mercy from Jerusalem and the cities of Judah, with which you have been angry these seventy years?" This attitude of prayer, to which the Lord replied (v. 13), implies that the angel of the Lord functions in a subordinate role.

All New Testament texts either explicitly give the "angel of the Lord" a subordinate position or at least say nothing to indicate that this angel is more than just an angel. In Matthew 1:20, an angel of the Lord told Joseph to take Mary as his wife. Again in 2:13 and 19, an angel of the Lord warned the holy family to get out of the country and told them when it was safe to return. In Acts 12:7, an angel of the Lord got Simon Peter out of jail, and in verse 23 of the same chapter an angel of the Lord killed Herod. In these texts, the New Testament does not use the definite article ("the") with "angel of the Lord."[5] In other words, the New Testament uses "angel of the Lord" as a generic term and not as a reference to some specific angel. It never implies that any "angel of the Lord" is God Himself.

God Himself?

In many Old Testament passages, however, the angel of the Lord is a specific figure and appears to be God. The classic text is Exodus 3:1–6.

> Moses was keeping the flock of his father-in-law Jethro, the priest of Midian; he led his flock beyond the wilderness, and came to Horeb, the mountain of God. There the angel of the LORD appeared to him in a flame of fire out of a bush; he looked, and the bush was blazing, yet it was not consumed. Then Moses said, "I must turn aside and look at this great sight, and see why the bush is not burned up." When the LORD saw that he had turned aside to see, God called to him out of the bush, "Moses, Moses!" And he said, "Here I am." Then he said, "Come no closer! Remove the sandals from your feet, for the place on which you are standing is holy ground." He said further, "I am the God of your father, the God of Abraham, the God of Isaac, and the God of Jacob." And Moses hid his face, for he was afraid to look at God.

The passage first tells us that "the angel of the LORD" appeared to Moses in the bush, but then the text says that "God called to him out of the bush" and further identifies Himself as "the God of your father." Moses, too, "was afraid to look at God." Just who is it that appeared in the burning bush? Was it the angel of the Lord or the Lord Himself? Or are they one and the same?

Other passages also merge the angel of the Lord and God. Judges 6:22 records that Gideon, after his encounter under the oak at Ophrah, "perceived that it was the angel of the LORD" and cried out "Help me, LORD God! For I have seen the angel of the LORD face to face." Elsewhere, the Bible implies that one could not look upon God's face and live. Would Gideon have had such fear had he believed that the angel of the Lord was only an angel? It is hard for us to say.

Equally curious is the exchange between the angel of the Lord and Manoah and his wife in Judges 13:15–19. In this text, Manoah asked the angel of the Lord his name, and the angel replied that it "is too wonderful" for Manoah. The angel also told Manoah to offer a sacrifice to the Lord.

At first glance, we might think that the angel of the Lord disassociated himself from the Lord by telling Manoah to make his sacrifice "to the LORD." But why did the angel of the Lord refuse to give his name and say that "it is too wonderful"? The ineffable name properly belongs to God. Why does the text point out that Manoah did not yet realize that this was the angel of the Lord, as if that were somehow significant? Moreover, Manoah himself identified the angel of the Lord with God in verses 21 and 22: "The angel of the LORD did not appear again to Manoah and his wife. Then Manoah realized that it was the angel of the LORD. And Manoah said to his wife, 'We shall surely die, for we have seen God.'" His wife did not disagree with him but said that they would be safe because he accepted their sacrifice (v. 23). Overall, the line between the angel of the Lord and God is noticeably blurred.

We see the same thing back in Zechariah 3:1, in which the angel of the Lord stood watching as Satan accused the high priest. Verse 2 then reads, "And the LORD said to Satan, 'The LORD rebuke you, O Satan!'"

Why would the Lord say, "The LORD rebuke you!"? Also, the context implies that the angel of the Lord was speaking and not just standing there mute, but verse 2 simply calls the speaker "the LORD." We cannot escape the sense that in this text, the angel of the Lord is the same as, but also is different from, God.

Two interpretations of this problem are possible. One is that the angel of the Lord so speaks and acts for God that whoever has seen this angel has in effect seen God. In the words of Karl Barth, the angel is "a perfect mirror of God."[6] The angel is not God, but one can truly say that when the angel has been present God has been present. Thus, the angel of the Lord is still only an angel.

The other interpretation is that the term "angel of the Lord" is used in two different ways. It can refer either to an ordinary angel or to God Himself (a theophany). When the angel of the Lord is an appearance of God, it is often called the *Logos* ("Word"). Christian theology also calls the Logos the "Second Person of the Trinity." The Logos is one person of the Godhead; the other two are the Father and the Holy Spirit. Also, the Logos directly interacts with humans; he is God revealed. The Logos eventually came to earth as a human in the incarnation as Jesus Christ.[7] To me, this is the better interpretation.

An aside: sometimes preachers call the Logos the "preincarnate Christ." While what I am saying here basically agrees with that, I do not like the term "preincarnate Christ." Jesus Christ is not only God; He is also human. Although the Logos has existed for all eternity, Jesus of Nazareth did not exist until He was born some two thousand years ago. In the words of the creed, He is "truly God and truly man in one person." As the Logos, He can rightly say, "Before Abraham was, I Am."

But the human side of Jesus no more had a "preincarnate" existence than does anyone else. Therefore, we might argue that the angel of the Lord was the Logos, but we should avoid the term "preincarnate Jesus Christ." The designation "preincarnate Christ" makes it seem as though the *humanity* of Jesus of Nazareth existed before He was born, which is not true.

To return to the question at hand: it appears to me that at least some (but by no means all) of the appearances of the angel of the Lord in the Old Testament must be manifestations of the Logos. Two factors weigh heavily for me here.

First, several texts in the Old Testament simply use language that cannot, by any interpretive stretch, be put in the mouth of an angel. The classic case is Exodus 3:1–6, cited above, where the angel of the Lord appeared and said, "I am the God of . . . Abraham." I find it hard to believe that any angel, no matter how closely he identifies with the work of God or reflects God, could say such a thing.

Second, it is striking that none of the appearances of the angel of the Lord in the New Testament has any trappings of deity. When the angel appeared to an individual in the Book of Acts, he might speak with authority but he never called himself by any name of God. If it was legitimate for an angel to do this in the Old Testament, why not in the New Testament? To me, the most reasonable explanation is that in the Old Testament, the Logos alone, and not the angels, took on the identity of God. After the Logos became incarnate as Jesus Christ, any appearance He made would not be in the form of an angel but as the risen Christ.

Also, the people in the New Testament who saw angels never were under any illusion that they were anything other than angels. Peter, for example, after an encounter with the angel of the Lord, simply responded, "The Lord has sent his angel and rescued me" (Acts 12:11). By contrast, they recognized an appearance of Christ Himself (as in Acts 9:17) as distinct from an appearance of an angel. This means that in the New Testament an angel could appear and that people did not in any way suppose the angel to be a manifestation of God.

For our purposes, it is important to realize that many references to the angel of the Lord in the Old Testament may not be to what we call an angel at all but to the Logos. This should make us all the more careful about making assertions concerning the Bible's teaching on angels.

In the Courts of the Lord

Many passages describe angels in the courts of the Lord. In Revelation 5:1–2, John saw "the right hand of the one seated on the throne," and it gave a scroll to an angel standing nearby; the angel called out and asked who was worthy to break the seals on the scroll. In Revelation 21:12, angels guarded the gates of the New Jerusalem.

Children's Angels

Sometimes the angels that are near God perform a special function. In Matthew 18:10, Jesus said that the angels of little children "continually see the face of my Father in heaven." The precise meaning of this eludes us.[8] It may imply the existence of "guardian angels" either for individual children or collectively for all children (more on this subject later). If "guardian angels" are meant, we have to wonder why these angels are in the Father's presence rather than down on earth, watching over their accident-prone little wards. Of course, it is possible that angels can do their work on earth while beholding the face of the Father in heaven. The text may mean that these angels have immediate access to God and represent children before God, but the notion of angelic intercessors is not entirely at home in the Bible.

Certainly the main point, apart from trying to figure out the role of the angels here, is that children are very important to God. The Father allows angels who are important to Him to come close to His presence. Remember that the seraphim of Isaiah 6 covered their faces in the presence of God, but that the angels of the children continually look upon His face. The presence of children's angels before God, whatever it is they actually do, says less to us about the work of these angels than it does about the love of the Father for children.[9]

Hallelujah!

Whatever else the angels in courts of the Lord do, they spend a lot of time praising God. In Revelation 5:11, thousands upon thousands of angels sang "Worthy is the Lamb." The four creatures of Revelation 4 did not cease singing "Holy, holy, holy." Psalm 103:20 calls upon the angels to "bless the LORD." The angelic praise of God teaches us that the adoration of God surpasses every other activity in importance and intrinsic goodness. It also shows us something of what is in our future.

Just as the angels devote themselves to the praise of God, we too should worship only God and never the angels. According to Colossians 2:18, the adoration of angels typifies cultic religion. In Revelation 22:8–9, the apostle John impulsively fell down to worship his angel guide but received an immediate rebuke: "You must not do that! I am a fellow servant with you and your comrades the prophets, and with those who keep the words of this book. Worship God!"

Satan in the Audience

In 1 Kings 22:19–22, the "hosts of heaven" stood before God in His courts, and it is evident they are not all the good kind. When the Lord called for someone to entrap Ahab in a foolhardy expedition, a "lying spirit" came forward and offered to entice him into battle.

The most dramatic portrait of angels in the courts of the Lord comes in Job 1–2, where Satan, along with all the other "heavenly beings," presented themselves before the Lord. Satan and God immediately engaged in a debate over the virtue of Job, the question being whether

Job's obedience was from the heart or whether he behaved himself only so that God would continue to protect him and his money. We will look at these chapters in more detail later in this book. At this point, we should notice that not only elect angels but also fallen ones come and stand before the Lord. The fallen ones, in particular Satan, use the occasion to find fault with God's people.

The Angels and Sex

The Bible gives us one last detail about angels, almost as an aside, and really not in a discussion in which angels are the issue. When the Sadducees tried to outwit Jesus with what they felt was a knockdown argument against the plausibility of the resurrection, He gave them a bit of insight into the nature of the resurrection and to angels as well. The question concerned a very unfortunate but happily hypothetical woman whose husbands habitually died before giving her any children. The question was, in the resurrection whose wife would she be? For the Sadducees, this hypothetical problem only pointed out the absurdity of the notion of a resurrection.

Jesus responded that eternal life is an added bonus that comes from knowing God. On the matter of marriage, He informed His opponents that "in the resurrection they neither marry nor are given in marriage, but are like the angels in heaven" (Matt. 22:30). What does this tell us about the angels?

Two possibilities exist. Either the angels have gender but never marry, or they do not have gender and therefore marriage and sexuality is not an issue. The text tells us no more than this, but it seems to imply that gender is not an issue for angels. That being the case, I presume that the meaning is that they are genderless. This issue, too, will resurface in our study of angels, and we will go into more detail later.

What the Bible Does Not Tell Us

We have now completed our survey of angels in the Bible. We have seen that they are messengers, helpers, executioners, and guides into prophecy. They spend much time observing what happens on earth. We have learned that the angel of the Lord in the Old Testament is more than an angel but is often the Logos. We have even picked up a few tidbits and implied concepts, such as that angels have no gender or at least never marry.

What should be apparent is that the Bible in fact tells us very little about the angels. We do not know where they came from. We can be sure that they are not eternally old and that they are creations of God, since the Bible tells us that only God Himself innately possesses immortality (1 Tim. 6:16). Colossians 1:16 tells us that God created all things. Also, angels are everywhere subordinate to God.

When were they created, and why? On this, Scripture is silent. We do not know if the angels were created before or after the material universe in Genesis 1. The Bible does not describe their creation or give a reason for their creation.

How many of them are there? We can be sure that there are "myriads upon myriads," but we have nothing like an exact number. Do they have organization and ranks? We shall consider this question later, but for the moment we should notice that no text of the Bible gives us an angelic table of organization. We have already seen that the notion that seraphim are a high ranking class of angels is probably misguided.

Also, the Bible does not give us a history of angels. This will take on more significance when we consider the question of Satan and demons, but for now, it is noteworthy that the Bible does not give us anything of their story. Apart from two angels (Michael and Gabriel), the Bible does not even give us any names.

I find myself drawn to the conviction that the secret things belong to the Lord our God. For us, it is sufficient to know that He is our God, and we should obey Him (Deut. 29:29). If more angelic details were necessary or helpful, I am sure we would have that information. But like specific information on the end of the world, detailed knowledge of angels may be more than we can handle. And excessive curiosity can be very dangerous. We should keep that in mind as we proceed.

⊚

CHAPTER THREE

And thou! whatever title suit thee,
Auld Hornie, Satan, Nick, or Clootie.
<small>ROBERT BURNS, "ADDRESS TO THE DEVIL"</small>

Auld Hornie, Satan, Nick, or Clootie

Satan in the Bible

IF WE MET THE DEVIL, WOULD WE KNOW HIM? PERHAPS, or perhaps not. Perhaps those who think they know the most about him would be the most easily deceived by him. Those who look for angels must of necessity consider the fallen angel, but they do not agree among themselves as to *if* he is, *who* he is, or *what* he does. But those who desire to know angels should get to know him as well. After all, it is no good getting up close and personal with an angel if your angel-friend just might be Old Scratch. Some dismiss him altogether. Even if there is a devil, they say, we do not have to worry about him. We can focus all our attention on the good, loving angels, and the bad ones will at least have the decency to leave us alone.

Some profess that he is actually a good angel who has suffered twenty centuries of bad press and malicious gossip. Even if he does tempt, it is only to add steel to our character. No real harm in that, or at least none is intended, they say.

Some people not only claim that he is evil but think that they know a great deal about him. They know how and why he fell into sin and can recognize his tricks in the blink of an eye. They know all about his demonic hordes as well.

Where does the Bible stand in all of this? On some points, it leaves us in no doubt. On others, it gives at best a partial answer or is altogether silent. We can know something of the nature of his game but many aspects of demonology, like the tree of the knowledge of good and evil, are off limits.

The Roles of Satan

"Satan" appears frequently in the New Testament and in a few rare but significant places in the Old Testament. One scholar argues that there is no "Satan" in the Old Testament at all, but that the Hebrew term *satan* can describe any one of the angels who has the task of resisting somebody. Thus, the angel of the Lord was an "adversary" to Balaam in Numbers 22:22 (the Hebrew word used here—*satan*—means "adversary").[1] God often raises a human "adversary" (*satan*) to a person, as in 1 Kings 11:14.

Elsewhere in the Old Testament, however, we find that there is a specific, individual heavenly adversary. In the Book of Job, Satan (actually "the *satan*" or rather "the adversary"—a specific person but not a proper name) stood in opposition to God. We cannot see this as simply an angel with a temporary task of opposing Job; rather, this being permanently opposes God. He is *the* adversary. We see the same in Zechariah 3. It seems clear that "Satan" was not originally used as the name for the devil, but that eventually the devil came to be known as "the satan" (that is, the adversary) and the name Satan finally stuck. Surprisingly, therefore, we do not even know his original name.

The Devil Made Me Do It

In the Bible, the Devil appears early as tempter. In the garden of Eden, he persuaded Eve that the forbidden fruit would do her no harm and that God really wanted to keep her from gaining the hidden knowledge that He possesses (Gen. 3). In the Book of Job, he did not tempt the righteous patriarch directly but battered him with personal disasters in an effort to coerce him to curse God (Job 1–2). In 1

Chronicles 21:1, he "stood up against Israel" and "incited" David to conduct a census of the nation, an act for which he and his people would suffer mightily.

After the temptation of Eve, the clearest portrayal of Satanic temptation in the Bible comes in Matthew 4 (see also Luke 4), where the devil tempted Christ to abandon His calling and take the easy road to messianic success. Here, Satan quoted Scripture, offered inducements, and appealed to pride in an effort to turn Jesus away from the road to the cross. Not surprisingly, after that experience Jesus regarded any effort to turn Him from His task, even if it came from His most loyal follower, as ultimately satanic in origin (Matt. 16:23).

Jesus and the apostles consistently described Satan as an enemy. He prowls about like a lion, looking for someone to devour (1 Pet. 5:8). He murders without a thought and is what we might call a pathological liar (John 8:44). Like a bird going after seed, he snatches away the gospel message before people can understand and receive it (Matt. 13:19). He fills the heart with folly and madness, so that some people under his influence even try to fool God (Acts 5:3). He seizes upon the sexual needs of Christian men and women as a way of disrupting their lives (1 Cor. 7:5). If someone allows anger to persist, Satan uses that as an opportunity for creating trouble (Eph. 4:26–27). Should members of a church offend and fail to forgive one another, he can use that, too, to his advantage (2 Cor. 2:10–11). He does not possess overwhelming power or persistence, however; if resisted, he runs away (James 4:7). If all else fails, he resorts to persecution and affliction to discourage the church (Rev. 2:9–13). We should bear in mind, however, that temptation is primarily something we do to ourselves (James 1:14).

The Devil and TV Evangelists

Habitual liar and tempter that he is, Satan uses deceit above all else as the means to bring people down. He disguises himself as an angel of light (2 Cor. 11:14). This ought to get the attention of anyone who wants to study angels. It especially should give pause to someone who has had or wants to have a personal angel encounter. We should no more accept without question messages from the angelic realm than we should allow ourselves to be the gullible dupes of any self-styled prophet or TV evangelist. If an angel from heaven gives us secret knowledge that contradicts what we have in the Bible, we should run away (Gal. 1:8).

Satan is not above using signs and wonders to add credibility to his message. Although Christ and the apostles performed miracles themselves, they did not present those miracles as the final test of religious truth. Miracles can be a sign of antichrist-religion (2 Thess. 2:9; Rev. 16:14).

Giving the Devil His Due

Anyone who makes an offering to an idol or a pagan god gives a sacrifice to the devil. The Old Testament frequently forbids making sacrifices to demons (Lev. 17:7; 2 Chron. 11:15; Ps. 106:37). At the same time, it always speaks of an idol as a "nothing," as the mere work of men's hands, and as something that neither sees nor hears nor acts. Viewed this way, idol worship is not so much demonic as it is stupid.

Paul explains this dual approach to idols. On one hand, an idol is a nothing. Neither food sacrificed to an idol nor the idol itself has any significance. On the other hand, behind the idols stand the false teaching, depraved character, and dark forces of demons and demonic religion (1 Cor. 10:19–20). Christians, therefore, should not treat idols as objects with great spiritual power, whether beneficent or malevolent. Should they do that, their attitude would be little different from their pagan counterparts. Nevertheless, Christians should avoid idols and contact with idols because they are defiled with demonic ideals.

Possession

Few things disgust and frighten people more than demonic possession. While the devil as tempter might be the object of comedy—a suave, sophisticated devil or a figure in a red suit prodding people with his pitchfork—demon possession rarely strikes people as funny.

The Bible describes a number of cases of demonic possession but actually says very little about the matter. The Old Testament has next to nothing on the subject. It describes how "an evil spirit from the Lord" tormented Saul and it mentions that David played the lyre to soothe his nerves (1 Sam 16:14–16). It also refers to mediums and wizards but says little about whether they are controlled by evil spirits.

By comparison, the New Testament describes a tremendous number of cases of demonic possession. Indeed, compared to what we see in the rest of the Bible, demons seemed to have taken possession of people with astonishing frequency during the ministry of Jesus. So common are the occurrences that Luke 8:2 mentions just in passing that seven demons departed from Mary Magdalene when Jesus healed her.

We can propose several explanations for this. First, demon activity was more common when Jesus was on earth because of the spiritual conflict surrounding the incarnation. Second, demon possession is still very common, but we do not recognize it as easily as Jesus did. Third, Jesus happened to come during a time that was politically, socially, and religiously unstable when people embraced strange new types of spirituality. Thus, demon possession was more common. On the third view, demonic activity waxes and wanes in different times and different places in proportion to the behavior of society. Personally, I think there is truth in all three explanations.

The Gerasene (or Gadarene) demoniac serves as the archetype for possession and exorcism in the Bible. As described in Luke 8:27–39, the man wore no clothes, dwelt among tombs, had superhuman strength, and was subject to wild outbreaks of frenzy. At the same time, he somehow recognized from afar the significance of Jesus and ran to meet Him. An uncounted "legion" of demons possessed him, and Jesus, bypassing the man's consciousness, could speak directly to them. The demons were in terror of Jesus and made no real effort to combat Him. For some reason they abhorred the thought of not having a body to inhabit and begged permission to enter pigs (although they soon found out that pigs are less willing than humans to host demons).

We can draw a number of conclusions from this. Demons are real, personal beings and not just mythological symbols of evil and sickness. They can possess people, but they are completely helpless before Christ. They tend to travel in packs and for some reason would rather be inhabiting a body than floating free (Luke 11:24–26). They can cause strange and even inhuman behavior in the people they possess.

This agrees with Luke's other accounts of demon possession. In 9:42, a demon-possessed boy would suddenly go into convulsions and fall to the ground. In 4:41, demons who encounter Jesus could not refrain from shouting out, "You are the Son of God!" The text implies that, being spiritual entities, they could not fail to acknowledge the presence of God among them.

Luke 22:3 tells us that Satan entered Judas Iscariot as he went to betray Jesus. This tells us less about the character of demon possession than it does about the enormity of Judas's act. As I. Howard Marshall says, "The reference to Satan . . . shows how more than human decisions were involved in the passion of Jesus; the early church could see no other explanation of what happened."[2]

In Matthew 9:32, people bring to Jesus a man whom the verse describes as a "demon possessed deaf person" (translating literally). The text does not say that the demon specialized in making people deaf or even that the demon possession and the deafness were related, although the probable implication is that they were. Matthew 12:22 similarly speaks of a blind and mute demoniac. The Book of Matthew mentioned the deafness of these demoniacs for a reason: it shows the severity of their demonic affliction. The purpose is not to give us a tool for categorizing demons and the troubles they cause nor to say that deafness is always a work of demons, but rather to demonstrate that Jesus' miracles were undeniable. Someone could question whether a man really had a demon, but no one could deny that he had been deaf. For this reason, on both occasions Matthew pointed out that Jesus' enemies explained His miracles by saying He operated in the power of Satan himself. They could not possibly deny that He had healed the man.

In Luke 13:11–16, Jesus healed a woman who had been crippled and declared that Satan had "held her in bondage" for eighteen years. In this case, we have no reason to think that the woman was demon possessed at all. He called her illness a "bondage" from Satan because all disease and death ultimately comes from the sinful condition. Satan, as tempter, is the lord of sin.

An exorcism involving Paul calls for special comment. In Acts 16:16–19, a slave girl with "a spirit of divination" followed Paul through the city of Philippi shouting, "These men are slaves of the Most High God, who proclaim to you a way of salvation." Paul finally had enough of this uninvited and deranged escort and he turned and rebuked the spirit in the name of Jesus. It immediately left the girl. The owners of the girl, who had made a lot of money from her powers, hauled Paul off to jail. As far as they were concerned, he had ruined her.

A few insights into the demonic come from this. First, many an alleged prophet, fortune-teller, or channeler may be demonic. In the Greek text, verse 16 actually says that the girl possessed a "python spirit." The python was associated with the oracle at Delphi, the most famous shrine of ancient Greece and a sanctuary of Apollo.[3] Apparently the girl had a spirit that people associated with the prophetic voice of Delphi;

that is, in the minds of the locals she was a legitimate prophetess (it may be that she did not behave in an obviously demented manner until the encounter with Paul). The point here is that genuine spiritual or prophetic powers can have a demonic origin.

Second, demons recognize the true servants of God. As with the demonic acclamation that followed Jesus, I doubt that the girl's shouting after Paul represented some kind of demonic scheme to undermine Paul's ministry. Rather, I think that the spiritual power in Paul attracted the demon like a fish to a lure.

Third, this text tells us that Paul did not view exorcism as a major part of his ministry since he only drove the demon from the girl out of sheer exasperation after "many days." This contrasts with the attitude of the disciples in Luke 10:17–20 (an attitude Jesus mildly rebukes) to the effect that authority over demons is the highest form of spiritual victory.

The New Testament mentions one other exorcism of significance to us—an abortive exorcism. Acts 19:13–16 describes how a group of itinerant Jewish exorcists tried to use the name of "Jesus whom Paul preaches" to expel a demon. The demon gave the sardonic reply, "Jesus I know, and Paul I know; but who are you?" and attacked the men, who fled leaving behind both clothing and dignity. Exorcism is not a matter to be taken lightly, and the name of Jesus is not a magic charm.

Disciplinary Demons

Several passages tell us that God uses demons for disciplinary functions with His own people. Thus, God may allow demons to torment believers who fall into sin, or He may use them to goad obedient Christians to stay the course. In 1 Corinthians 5, Paul confronted the moral negligence of the church in Corinth. A man was having sexual relations with his father's wife, and the church had done nothing to stop it. Paul ordered the church to come together and "hand this man over to Satan for the destruction of the flesh, so that his spirit may be saved in the day of the Lord" (v. 5).

It is difficult to know precisely what handing someone over to Satan entails. It may have been simply a matter of expulsion from the church. If so, then the point is that outside the shelter of the church, the individual is more exposed to the attacks of the Evil One. Also, the phrase "destruction of the flesh" describes the idea of putting an end to sinful lusts, but it implies physical suffering as well.[4] The purpose is that in the end, the man will be redeemed and not face damnation. Paul implied that demonic punishment might drive the believing sinner to repentance. In the same way, Paul turned Hymenaeus and Alexander over to Satan so that they would "learn not to blaspheme" (1 Tim. 1:20).

If this seems harsh, Paul also experienced something of the same thing himself. In 2 Corinthians 12:7–9, Paul mentioned how God sent him "a messenger of Satan" to torment him and thus prevent him from falling into pride over the revelations he had received. Three times he asked the Lord to remove this "thorn in the flesh," but God refused with the reply, "My grace is sufficient for you."

Christians have wondered and debated over Paul's "thorn" for centuries. Was it a literal demon? Was it a spiritual or psychological struggle in Paul's own soul? Was it persecution or a persistent (human) enemy? Or was it a chronic illness or physical weakness? Some see here an allusion to Paul's vision problem (as implied in Gal. 4:13–15). Others believe it was temptations, and still others believe it was the Jewish opposition that dogged him at every step.[5] For our purposes, the answer does not matter. The important thing is that Paul associated the thorn with Satan and believed that it was a goad to drive him to deeper reliance upon Christ and less pride in himself.

Subordinate Demons

The above passages imply something about Satan that current Christian discussions of the demonic altogether miss. Satan and his horde are fully under God's authority. Put another way, they can do nothing without God's permission. This does not mean that the devils are willing servants of God, but it does mean that they are not free to do whatever they choose.

In Job 1–2, Satan could not harm Job or any of his possessions without explicit permission from God. In 1 Samuel 16:15, an "evil spirit from God" (that is, working under God's authority) tormented Saul. In 1 Kings 22, the Lord sent a "lying spirit" to the false prophets. In the passages we have just seen, Satan can torment believers only after they have been given over into his authority.

Second Samuel 24:1 and 1 Chronicles 21:1–2 are parallel passages that teach us something about the relationship of Satan to God. Both describe David's disastrous attempt to take a census of the nation. The Chronicles version ascribes this event to the machinations of Satan, who "stood up against Israel" and incited David to take the census. The Samuel version, however, states that "the anger of the Lord was kindled against Israel, and he incited David" to number the people. Some scholars believe that the difference between the two versions reflects the writers' respective theological biases or that the Chronicles version comes from a time when belief in Satan was more widespread. Even so, the two complement each other in a way that agrees with the rest of the Bible. Satan opposed Israel and tried to bring it down, but he could only act when God permitted. Looked at from the opposite perspective, God used Satan as His cat's paw when He wanted to punish Israel.

Satan may be a powerful enemy, but he is an enemy who is and always has been on God's leash. The Bible contains no hint of dualism. This is the notion that two opposite and equally powerful forces, one good and one evil, vie for control of the world. It is something like the *Star Wars* notion of the good side and the dark side of the "Force." Many Christians are practical dualists: while they might theoretically affirm the sovereignty of God, they actually conceive of the world as a cosmic struggle between God and Satan. They even speak of Satan "defeating" God and His purposes here and there. While the Bible describes Satan as an enemy, he is an enemy who has to ask permission to do anything and who, however unhappily, obeys God. This will be of significance when we consider the matter of "spiritual warfare."

The Fall of Satan

In the Bible, Satan appears early and without explanation. In Genesis 3, just after God created the universe and set Adam and Eve in the garden, Satan appeared as a serpent. (It is true that some people do not think that the "serpent" of Genesis is the same as Satan, but we need not go into this. We can simply accept the Bible's interpretation of itself at face value—see 2 Cor. 11:3.) We find it hard to accept this abrupt and unexplained appearance by the prince of darkness. Why did God let him in the garden? Why is he evil? Where did he come from? Throughout most of the Bible, Satan is simply there, and we are to accept his existence as a brute fact. Not surprisingly, many people find this hard to handle. They want to know more of his personal history and cannot leave the deeper questions about the origin of Satan unanswered. And many believe that the Bible does answer these questions.

The most common view today among Christians is that Satan fell in an act of rebellion, long before the creation of humanity, when he decided to try to take over heaven. John Milton elaborated on this notion in his imaginative epic poem, *Paradise Lost.* This is not the only view, however. One ancient tradition states that his fall came after the creation of Adam and Eve: Satan refused to degrade himself by serving a creature of material flesh and so came to oppose God.[6] The idea is that he considered serving a creature of the dust, a creature that has all kinds of disgusting bodily functions, beneath his dignity and so he rebelled.

The origin of demons, too, is uncertain. Many teach that one third of the angels joined Satan in his rebellion and that these are the demons of today. One writer calls this the "scriptural identification" of demons,[7] but biblical evidence supporting this hypothesis is paltry to say the least.

Perhaps the most ancient opinion is that demons are the offspring of the "sons of God" and "daughters of women" of Genesis 6:1–2. This view asserts that some angels had sexual relations with human women before Noah's flood and that their demigod offspring are the restless spirits of earth who yearn for physical bodies. If true, this would explain why the New Testament presents demons as anxious for a body to possess. If their mothers were human women, they might feel at a loss without human bodies. On the other hand, although the Bible may well teach that angels once cohabited with human women (more about this idea later), it does not say anything about their offspring becoming demons.

In discussions of the origin of Satan and the demons, people usually cite four texts from the Bible: Isaiah 14:4–21, Ezekiel 28:11–19, Luke 10:18, and Revelation 12. We must look to these passages to determine what, if anything, they tell us about Satan's fall.

Isaiah 14:4–21

On the surface, it would not appear that Isaiah had the devil on his mind when he composed this song. Old Testament scholars call this kind of poem a "taunt song" because it is the sort of song you sing when you want to deride your enemies. Self-evidently, the enemy that Isaiah has in mind is Babylon. Isaiah names Babylon in 14:4, and the song comes in a larger context that prophesies the fall of Babylon (Isaiah 13:1–14:23).

Babylon held a special place in Isaiah's heart. From the beginning of his ministry, he knew that Jerusalem was so deep in sin that God was sure to destroy it and take His people into exile. That certainty was part of his original commission (Isa. 6).

At first, he probably thought it likely that the superpower of his day, Assyria, would swoop down and carry away pitiful little Judah. The piety and prayer of Hezekiah forestalled that event, however, and around the year 701 B.C. God thwarted the Assyrian threat (Isa. 36–37). But this only delayed the sentence of death that hung over Jerusalem; it did not remove it. The rising power of Babylon was replacing Assyria as the mother of all empires, and Isaiah knew that Babylon would be the agent of Jerusalem's doom. Ironically, Hezekiah sealed the fate of his nation when he showed off the riches of Jerusalem to envoys from Babylon (Isa. 39).[8]

Isaiah therefore wrote his prophecies against the backdrop of certainty that Jerusalem would fall to Babylon, and he naturally had considerable interest in what would become of Babylon itself. No doubt it came as great comfort to Isaiah and his Jewish readers that God would bring the cruelty of the Babylonians back upon their own heads. In chapters 13 and 14, as well as in other passages, Isaiah proclaimed that vindictive Babylon would itself be humbled.

In 14:12–15, however, he seemed to be talking about more than just Babylon:

> How you are fallen from heaven, O Day Star, son of Dawn! How you are cut down to the ground, you who laid the nations low! You said in your heart, "I will ascend to heaven; I will raise my throne above the stars of God; I will sit on the mount of assembly on the heights of Zaphon; I will ascend to the tops of the clouds, I will make myself like the Most High." But you are brought down to Sheol, to the depths of the Pit.

When did Babylon ever ascend to heaven? When did it ever set its throne above God's? Many claim that this is obviously not just Babylon but is Satan himself. They say that the passage describes the original act of rebellious pride that brought about the fall of one who had formerly been a great and beautiful angel. The sublime heights of the throne room of God had not been enough for Satan. He wanted more, even the very place of God. Since he could not have it, he became wicked, disgraced, and depraved. The King James Version, which has "Lucifer" where the NRSV has "Day Star," appears to support this interpretation.

But we need to exercise caution here. First of all, the Bible nowhere uses the name "Lucifer" as a moniker for Satan. Actually, the Hebrew word that is translated "Day Star" or "Lucifer" only occurs here. It means "morning star" (that is, the planet Venus) or "crescent moon."[9] The name "Lucifer" is derived from the Latin words for "light bearer" and has no special significance, least of all as a designation for Satan. People began to use the name "Lucifer" for Satan on the basis of this text, but that does not mean that the word had this significance for Isaiah or his original readers.

Also, we cannot settle the interpretation of this passage with simple logic that goes like this: "The passage says that the 'Day Star' ascended to heaven and tried to take God's throne. Babylon never did this. Therefore, the 'Day Star' must be Satan." We have to look at the historical setting of Isaiah's song before we can make assumptions about what he may or may not have meant.

Isaiah has shaped the images and legends of the ancient world to make a point in this song. In one story, a god named Athtar takes the place of the high god Baal as part of a general revolt by the other gods. It seems that the Canaanites linked Athtar to Venus, the "Day Star" of Isaiah's song. The Canaanite myth is not altogether like the poem we see here in Isaiah, but, being part of the cultural world of his readers, Isaiah may have used a familiar element in the story to paint a picture of Babylonian arrogance. Also, Isaiah spoke of the heights of "Zaphon" in our text. This was a mountain in north Syria where, according to Canaanite mythology, the gods assembled; it was similar to Mt. Olympus of Greek mythology. Thus, when the "Day Star" aspires to take his place at the peak of Mt. Zaphon, he wants to be the ruler in the assembly of the gods.[10]

Isaiah frequently made use of the characters and stories of his world in order to communicate effectively. In 27:1, Isaiah mentioned the creature "Leviathan," and in 51:9 he spoke of the monster "Rahab." These dragon-like creatures inhabited the world of Canaanite and Babylonian mythology, and Isaiah used the language of the myths to give added power to his message. His audience knew these stories well. Isaiah did not imply that the Canaanite myths were true; he used them to portray vividly events like the fall of Babylon and the Exodus from Egypt.

When someone today says, "That lineman is as big as Godzilla," he does not mean that Godzilla is a real monster. Although there is more to Isaiah's use of ancient mythology than this modern example implies, I think you get the point.

In addition, ancient people often associated their city with a specific god, and they linked the political success of the city to the prowess and power of their special god. The Athenians believed that the goddess Athena cared especially for their city. In Babylon, Marduk was the great patron god. Hammurabi honored him as the god of Babylon, and closer to Isaiah's time, Nebuchadnezzar II devoted his military conquests to him.[11] For the Babylonians, the rise of their empire would also have implied the ascent of their god over the gods of all other nations, and Isaiah's song might taunt that belief.

To come to the point, Isaiah 14:12–15 is not a song *about* a god or an angel. It is a song which *metaphorically portrays* the city of Babylon as a god. The song describes the religion and arrogance of an ancient city, not the pride and fall of an actual angel. If there is any literal angelology here, it is more likely that Isaiah meant that the angel (or god) of Babylon tried to claim world authority for himself. A primordial fall of Satan was not in view.

One could always reply that Isaiah 14:12–15 looks back to the fall of Satan as the archetype for arrogant sin against God. In one sense, that may be true since all sin ultimately comes from rejection of God's authority. We should not suppose, however, that Isaiah gives us some secret insight into the sin of Satan. If anything, it leaves us with more questions than answers. If this is the fall of Satan, then when did it happen? Why did Satan turn against God? Why did God allow it to happen at all since He should have foreseen it? Can good angels still turn against God today? We find none of the answers to these questions in this text. All in all, it is best simply to accept Isaiah's clear signals that Babylon and not some supernatural being was the focus of his attention.

Ezekiel 28:11–19

After Isaiah 14, the second most commonly cited text alleged to describe the fall of Satan is Ezekiel 28:11–19. This passage calls the king of Tyre "the signet of perfection, full of wisdom and perfect in beauty" (v. 12) and claims he was "in Eden" until sin was found in him and he was expelled (v. 13).

The questions here are much the same. If this is just the king of Tyre (a Phoenician trade center on the Mediterranean coast, north of Jerusalem), why is he described in such exalted language? Was Tyre (or the king of Tyre) ever "full of wisdom and perfect in beauty" or "blameless" in God's sight? Did the king of Tyre ever walk in Eden adorned in precious stones (v. 13)? Again, the apparent conclusion is that this must be Satan prior to his fall.

But is this the correct interpretation? Probably not. First, there is again the pesky little problem that Ezekiel explicitly told us that he was talking about Tyre and its king. If this text really means to describe Satan's fall, Ezekiel presumably would have told us. Statements to the effect that the king of Tyre was "perfect in beauty" are better taken as exaggeration for effect than as literal reality (this kind of exaggeration, technically called hyperbole, is common in the Bible).

Second, the passage does not fully correspond with what we know of Satan. In Genesis, Satan appeared in Eden in snake form and was never anything but a tempter. In Ezekiel, the "king of Tyre" dwelt in Eden in a state of glory under vestments of "every precious stone." Ezekiel never implied that the person he described tempted Adam and Eve. To the contrary, God drove him out as soon as iniquity was found in him.

Other incongruities appear as well. The king of Tyre dwelt in "Eden," but his home was also called "mountain of God" (v. 14), a description not appropriate for Eden. This implies that we should not take either "Eden" or "mountain of God" too literally. Rather, these terms metaphorically represent the fabulous wealth of Tyre. Also, the king fell into sin because of the "abundance of trade" (vv. 16–18). This is appropriate as applied to Tyre (a seafaring, trading state) but makes no sense as applied to Satan. Similarly, verses 17 and 18 say that other kings and peoples watch the king of Tyre fall to disgrace. This again makes perfect sense as applied to Tyre (which Babylon and later Alexander the Great defeated) but does not fit what we know of Satan.

The word "cherub" poses a problem. The NRSV states that the "king of Tyre" had a cherub assigned to him (v. 14), and that this cherub in turn drove him out of Eden after his sin (v. 16). The King James Version, by contrast, says "Thou art the anointed cherub that covereth" (v. 14) and "I will destroy thee, O covering cherub." In other words, depending on how you translate it, the king of Tyre either *was* a cherub or *had* a cherub assigned to him as his personal guardian. The Hebrew is very difficult and one can make a case for either translation.

The "cherub" appears at various points in the Old Testament as a kind of watchdog angel. In Genesis 3:24, a cherub guarded Eden to prevent Adam and Eve from gaining reentry. Four cherubim attended the chariot of the Lord in the fantastic vision of Ezekiel 1 (see also Ezek. 9:3 and 11:22). In the Book of Psalms, God sat enthroned above the cherubim or rode the cherubim (18:10; 80:1). In all these texts, the cherubim attended God as a kind of honor guard, or they protected Eden for Him.

Elsewhere, the cherubim are little more than artistic motifs that symbolize God's protection over sacred things. Two statues of cherubim with outstretched wings covered the atoning seat over the ark of the covenant (Exod. 25:20). Cherubim decorated the curtains of the tent of meeting (Exod. 26:1), the walls of Solomon's temple (1 Kings 6:29; 2 Chron. 3:10–14), and the doors of Ezekiel's ideal temple (Ezek. 41:25).

In this text, Ezekiel combined all kinds of biblical references and cultural notions in order to paint a picture of the king of Tyre as someone who had it all. From Genesis, he took the story of Eden in order to make the point that Tyre was a virtual paradise until greed and violence called down God's punishment. Just as Adam lost Eden, so God would turn the king of Tyre and his people out of their idyllic kingdom. From traditional ancient Near Eastern thinking, he spoke of God dwelling on a high mountain (just as we saw in the Isaiah text). From the sanctuaries of ancient Palestine, he took the familiar image of guardian cherubim that stand near the throne of God. In Israel, these guardian cherubim were overlaid in costly materials and were woven with striking colors into the curtains of the sanctuary. Recalling Israel's and perhaps other similar temples, as well as the literal wealth of Tyre, Ezekiel spoke of the king of Tyre as covered in gold and precious jewels (v. 13). He described the king as if he were inside a lavishly furnished sanctuary.

The precise meaning of "stones of fire" (v. 14) eludes us. It could be a highly poetic way of describing jewels and again make the point that the king of Tyre had wealth all around him. On the other hand, it could be literal stones of fire, that is, burning coals, such as were found at the altars and incense burners of ancient temples. If that is the case, then once again Ezekiel drew on the religious language of his day to portray the king of Tyre in the most exalted of settings. He walked amidst the burning coals in the sense that his palace was so splendid as to be like a temple with its altars and smoking boxes of incense.

Ezekiel had another reason for associating the king of Tyre with the trappings of the temple. Hiram, king of Tyre, provided the expertise and much of the material for the construction of Solomon's temple (1 Kings 5:1–7:48). Hiram also built other grand temples to Melqart and Astarte in Tyre itself. To the priest Ezekiel, the phrase "king of Tyre" would call to mind "temple" in a free association game.

In summary, if we take the text to mean that the king of Tyre *had* a guardian cherub appointed to him, then the king's palace is described as if it were a lavish temple filled with gold and jewels, and with cherubim standing watch over it all. Drawing upon the story of Eden in Genesis, however, Ezekiel promised that just as the cherub ejected Adam from his paradise, so also the cherubim would remove the king of Tyre from his.

If we take verse 14 to mean that the king himself *was* a cherub, the point is not that he literally was an angel but that he was like an expensive, jewel-encrusted, golden cherub-statue that adorned an ancient temple. This would explain the peculiar language of verse 13 ("worked in gold were your settings and your engravings"), where it sounds as if the king is a statue. Remember that this is a metaphor. The king was in an ideal situation, but he lost it by profaning his sanctuaries (v. 18). The point would be this: although you live in a paradise, as if you were a cherub in God's temple, you are losing it all because of your sin. I think that this is the better interpretation.

In either case, once again we see a prophet using the religious images of the ancient Near East as metaphors for a human condition. Ezekiel did not recount literal history in the angelic realm.[12] And again, even if we choose to believe that the fall of Satan is a kind of archetype for what we find in Ezekiel 28, so many unanswered questions remain that we have really gained very little real knowledge about angelic history.

Luke 10:18

Did the Son of God witness Satan's sin and subsequent tumble into the nether regions? No doubt He did, but it is another question whether He actually told us anything about it. Yet some readers feel He did just that in Luke 10:18: "He said to them, 'I watched Satan fall from heaven like a flash of lightning.'"

Jesus had sent out His disciples to take His work of preaching and wonder-working to all the villages of Jewish Palestine. He had told them what to carry and what to do and had even instructed them in how to respond when people rejected their message (10:1–12). He had grieved over those who would not listen (10:13–16).

When the disciples returned, and Jesus talked to them. They report that the mission had been a great success—even the demons submitted to them (v. 17)! Jesus responded by telling them He watched Satan fall from heaven (v. 18) and affirmed that they had received great spiritual power (v. 19). He warned them not to focus on their newly found powers as demon-busters but to rejoice in the gift of eternal life (v. 20). He then thanked God for revealing so much to His disciples (vv. 21–24).

What is the significance of Jesus' claim to have watched Satan fall from heaven? He could have meant the original fall of Satan and his expulsion from heaven. Or He could have meant that while the disciples were on their mission, He saw Satan fall from heaven. Or He could have had a purely symbolic meaning: "I watched Satan fall . . ." could simply be a way of saying, "Satan's kingdom is coming apart."

We have little reason to suppose that Jesus referred to the primeval fall of Satan. Such a reference would have no purpose here—the disciples were not asking about the fall of Satan; they were excited about their mission and the submission of the evil spirits. While we might come up with a reason that Jesus would suddenly throw out a remark to the effect that He saw the original fall, it was really a nonsequitur.

On the other hand, if by Satan's "fall" Jesus meant that the mission of the disciples had shaken the powers of darkness, His comment made perfect sense. He was giving them the strongest kind of affirmation and encouragement. In doing the work of preaching and performing miracles, they had broken Satan's power over people (metaphorically described as his place in heaven). He then told them that they had the authority to defeat all of Satan's powers (v. 19) but warned them not to make this the focus of their spiritual joy (v. 20). In short, this text tells us nothing about the original fall of Satan, but it does encourage us that we can have a hand in bringing down Satan now.

Revelation 12

At last, one might think, we come to a text that unequivocally tells of the fall of Satan. Here we have no Babylon or Tyre to distract us; the central figure is unquestionably Satan. Also, we do not have a historical setting, like the mission of the disciples, to confuse the issue. The scene is heaven, Satan and Michael are in combat, and a fall from heaven is clearly in view.

Thus, many see here a portrait of Satan's loss of virtue. Also, they believe, this text tells us what percentage of angels became demons. In verse 4, the dragon sweeps one third of the stars from heaven, which leads many to the conclusion that one third of the angels fell with Satan and became devils. Once again, however, we need to read the text carefully. What we think we see may not really be there.

First, we need to identify the major characters in this chapter. The dragon is Satan, and the seven heads, ten horns, and seven diadems represent the diversity of his earthly powers (v. 3); that is, many different governments and institutions in one way or another do his bidding on earth. The woman is Israel; the sun, moon, and twelve stars (v. 1) recall the dream of Joseph, in which the tribes of Israel appear as stars (Gen. 37:9). The male child whom the dragon seeks to kill, who is destined to rule with a rod of iron, and who is taken to the throne of God (v. 4–5) is Christ (Rev. 19:15). The "rest of her children" who "keep the testimony of Jesus" are Christians. These are the people of God viewed individually, whereas the woman is the people of God viewed ideally and corporately.

The events of the chapter are as follows. First, the dragon tries to destroy Christ at birth. This represents the hostility of the Satanic powers to the Messiah and to Israel as the "mother" of the Messiah, a hostility that culminated in Herod's slaughter of the innocents (Matt. 2). The child is born and goes up to the throne of God. Behind these events, as any Christian should recognize, is the death, burial, resurrection, and ascension of Jesus. Third, war breaks out in heaven and Michael expels Satan. Fourth, a furious Satan seeks to do as much harm as possible to the people of God on earth. We will address the significance of these events in a moment.

Already you should recognize that this cannot be the original fall of Satan. In this chapter, Michael expels the dragon from heaven late in human history, after the ascension of Jesus into heaven. This cannot be an expulsion of Satan after his original sin, which presumably occurred deep in the past, perhaps before the foundation of earth itself.

Similarly, the "third of the stars of heaven" that the dragon swept down with his tail (v. 4) do not tell us anything about how many angels followed Satan. The falling stars are not angels falling from grace. They represent the dragon's hostility to the woman and her child.

A clue to the meaning of the stars is in the imagery of this verse. The multiple heads, horns, and crowns on the dragon take us back to Daniel, where we see comparable visions. In the visions of Daniel 7, for example, the "leopard" has four heads and the "fourth beast" has ten horns. The heads and horns represent powers of various nations that exist under the empires that the leopard and the fourth beast represent. Thus, we can be confident that the horns and heads of the dragon in Revelation represent the powers of this world under Satan's domain.

In Daniel 8, however, we see a figure called a "little horn" who throws down and tramples on some of the stars of heaven (Dan. 8:10). The stars here are not angels and the "little horn" is definitely not Satan—it is a Greek king named Antiochus Epiphanes who tried to eliminate the Jewish faith in the second century B.C. He slaughtered a large number of Jews, profaned the temple in Jerusalem, and converted it into a shrine for "Jupiter Olympius." Daniel 8:10–11 described this man as a little horn who trampled down some of the stars of heaven and overthrew the sanctuary. Remember that "hosts of heaven" and "stars" often represent the children of Israel (Gen. 15:5; Jer. 33:22; Dan. 12:3).

In Revelation 12:4, similarly, stars are not angels that become demons. They represent the dragon's disdain for the people of God and for everything that is sacred. Just as Antiochus slaughtered the Jews and profaned the temple, Satan does the same on a grander scale. The number "one third" is arbitrary. It simply means that Satan will do a lot of damage, harm many people, and profane a great deal. As a poetic picture, it shows us something of the size and fury of the dragon, that he can bring down a third of the stars with the sweep of his tail. It has nothing to do with the number of demons that follow Satan.

Let us get back to the story. Recall that Michael expelled Satan immediately after Christ ascended to heaven. Satan's role in heaven is that of accuser, as we have seen in Job. Now, he suddenly finds himself *persona non grata.* Why? Implicit in the story is the death and resurrection of the Messiah, the Son of the woman.[13] Because the Son has laid His life down as a sacrificial lamb (Rev. 5:6) and has come back to heaven, Satan no longer has any grounds to slander the people of God. The power of sin is the Law (1 Cor. 15:56). It is the tool by which Satan accuses people before God.

Now that Christ has obtained forgiveness for His people, Satan does not have a leg to stand on. His days of accusing the children of God are over, and he has lost any claim to a place in the courts of the Lord. If there be any doubt that this is what this text is all about, a voice in heaven shouts that the "accuser" is cast out (v. 10). "It is God who justifies, who is to condemn?" (Rom. 8:33–34). That being the case, Michael summarily boots him out. The reason Michael in particular has this role is that he is the "prince" of Israel according to Daniel 10:21. He therefore acts as the champion of the "woman" who represents the Israel of God.

Cast down to earth, the dragon turns his attention to persecuting God's people. In this, John says that we can expect trouble and hardship. Satan knows that his days are numbered, that he has no grounds for dragging God's people into condemnation, and that all he can do is harm as many as possible (vv. 13–17). The message to us is to persevere. Our salvation is secure and our accuser has been expelled. We need only to be faithful through all the trials that come our way.

In summary, this text no more gives us a history of the fall of Satan than it gives us a tour of hell. For those, you need to go to fiction such as *Paradise Lost* and the *Divine Comedy*.

Demon Lovers?

We would be remiss if we failed to mention that the Bible does provide one fleeting, strange glimpse at what seems to be a bit of angelic history. In Genesis 6:1–2, we read that the "sons of God" saw that the "daughters of men" were beautiful and took them as wives. The text then tells us that the "Nephilim" lived in those days. These were the "heroes of old."

Three major interpretations of this passage prevail. Some say that the "daughters of men" were godless women of the line of Cain and that they brought down the moral standards of godly men, the "sons of God," who were of the line of Seth. Few interpreters defend this view today. Others say that the sons of God were men with great political power and that they abused their power by taking whatever women they wanted for themselves. They were "sons of God" in the same sense that the rulers are called "gods" in Psalm 82. In taking whatever women they wanted, they caused moral chaos. Finally, the oldest interpretation is that the "sons of God" were angels who took on human form and procreated with women. The earliest Jewish and Christian interpreters uniformly understand "sons of God" in this way. The New Testament, too, appears to interpret Genesis 6:1–2 as angelic activity (2 Pet. 2:4 and Jude 6).[14]

The Nephilim, unfortunately, are of little help to us. They were the offspring of the "sons of God" and "daughters of men," but we do not know exactly what Nephilim are. The name "Nephilim" appears in one other text, Numbers 13:33, which implies that they were large, powerful people (who may or may not have been thought to have superhuman strength). Whatever one may make of the Numbers text, however, the phrase "heroes of old" in Genesis 6:4 implies that by the time Genesis was written, the Nephilim of this text were of ancient, legendary status. Any of the above three interpretations could be satisfactory, but honesty requires me to observe that it is almost inconceivable that an ancient Semite would read "sons of God" as meaning anything other than "gods" (that is, supernatural beings— angels or the like). "Daughters of men," in contrast, naturally means "human women."[15] In short, the ancient Hebrew would take this to mean that angelic beings somehow took on corporal form as males and had sexual relations with women, and this is how the ancient Jewish interpreters all took it. This does not really contradict the teaching of Jesus that angels do not marry (and thus are presumably without gender), since clearly what the angels do here is illicit and represents an abandoning of their proper place. I suspect that the real reason modern people reject this interpretation is that they just find it too far-fetched. Sometimes even very conservative interpreters try to take the sting out of hard passages through a kind of demythologizing.

A note of explanation: some people may wonder that I am willing to see the "demonic" explanation of Genesis 6:1–2 when I question seeing Satan in Isaiah 14 and Ezekiel 28. The reason is twofold. First, I always think that we should take Scripture in its most normal sense and not assume that we know more about the topic than the original author. When Isaiah tells us in chapter 14 that he is talking about Babylon, I do not see that I have any grounds to claim that what Isaiah really means is that he is talking about Satan. But in Genesis 6:1–2, the most natural meaning to an ancient Hebrew reader would have been that supernatural beings cohabited with human women. So I presume that this is what the text means.

Second, I try to keep a healthy awareness of how little we really know about angels and demons. Many will argue that we know that this cannot be speaking of angels because angels do not have sex or bodies.[16] Mark 12:25 and parallel passages come into play here: angels "do not marry nor are they given in marriage." But who are we to say that angels could not have left their proper realm and assumed sexual, physical bodies? Do we really know that much about them? Were we present when God called them into existence? Sometimes it is good to step back and recall what we do not know.

We should not be alarmed if the Bible records that at one time angelic beings cohabited with human women. This seems to be a major reason behind the flood, which is not to be repeated. Also, the Bible nowhere warns us that such a thing might happen again—the *Rosemary's Baby* scenario. If anything, it implies that the angels who participated in such activity found themselves put away forever or at least until their final judgment.[17]

Also, I would add, we should not allow ourselves to construct a fantastic history of the angels on the basis of this meager evidence. We shall see how some of the ancient Jewish interpreters did just that. Even if the Bible tells us that angels once cohabited with women, it keeps the information to a minimum. It does not assert that their offspring became demons or give us any juicy details about how this all happened.

The Destiny of the Devil

This topic need not detain us long since the Bible is clear and to the point. The devil stands under condemnation (1 Tim 3:6). God is going to crush Satan under the feet of His people (Rom. 16:20). In the end, God will cast him into the "lake of fire," where he will be tormented "day and night forever and ever" (Rev. 20:10).

Behind this straightforward portrayal of Satan's destiny lies the fact that the Bible uniformly treats Satan as evil and an enemy of God. While this might seem self-evident from what we have already seen, many have a different interpretation. Various heretical groups through the centuries and to this day have taught that Satan is not evil at all. They see him rather as a good angel charged with the task of being chief prosecutor against people. When he accuses them, he is only doing his job. Even when he tempts people to sin, some say, he is only giving them tests so that in the end they will have stronger character.

Some scholars say that this is the original view of Satan, as reflected in Job 1–2. When Satan went before God to accuse Job, they argue, he was no more doing evil than the government's attorneys are doing evil when they prosecute a thief. In this view, the idea of Satan progressed through the centuries from prosecuting angel to rebellious enemy of God. Apart from the fact this historical reconstruction is of doubtful value (most cultures have the idea of evil spirits, not prosecuting attorney spirits), the text of Job 1–2 does not sustain it. Only through complete literary insensitivity can we fail to see the malice of Satan in these chapters. He maligned Job (and God) to God's face when he complained that God had surrounded Job with a defensive hedge (1:10). He was eager to damage Job as much as possible. Indeed, Satan did not prosecute Job at all—he did not accuse Job of anything, although he did accuse God of coddling Job. Rather, he wanted to drive Job into sin by doing him as much harm as possible.

Thus, the condemnation of Satan accords well with everything else we see of him. He is evil and he is hostile to God. Beyond that, what do we know of him? Do we know when and how he fell? Not really, except that we can assume that God did not create him as an evil being but that Satan somehow came to reject God's authority. Do we know how many demons there are, when they fell, or how they are organized? No, on all counts. Do we have any passwords, rituals, or prayers in the Bible that will protect us from him? No again, except that Jesus taught us to pray simply for protection from the Evil One.[18]

Well, then, what do we know of the devils? Enough. We know that in addition to our own proclivity to evil, supernatural beings seek to draw us down. We know that our anger, lust, grudges, and greeds all give opportunities for the Evil One to sift us like wheat. We know that evil spirits can control people in a way that is as frightening as it is tragic. But we also know that if we are in Christ, our accuser is cast down. We know that He that is in us is greater than he that is in the world. We know that his final destruction is as sure as our salvation. And we know to be careful and discerning, because when we first see him, we may not know him.

He is the reflection of God's glory and the exact imprint of God's very being, and he sustains all things by his powerful word. When he had made purification for sins, he sat down at the right hand of the Majesty on high, having become as much superior to angels as the name he has inherited is more excellent than theirs. For to which of the angels did God ever say, "You are my Son; today I have begotten you"? Or again, "I will be his Father, and he will be my Son"?

HEBREWS 1:3–5

To Which of the Angels?

Christk and the Angels in the Bible

THE NEW TESTAMENT EVERYWHERE PRESENTS ANGELS as subordinate to Jesus. We have already noticed that they proclaimed His birth (see for example, Luke 2:10). After His temptation and forty-day fast, angels came and ministered to Him (Matt. 4:11). At the other end of His life, they also appeared at His resurrection. In John 20:12, a weeping Mary Magdalene looked inside the tomb of Jesus to see two angels sitting there, who announced to her that she should not expect to find Him there since He was risen. In all their dealings with Him, angels were joyful heralds or obedient servants but, in contrast to their dealings with biblical prophets, they never gave Jesus instructions.

Jesus not only claimed to have authority over the angels, He was surprised that the disciples did not realize this. On the night of His arrest, when Peter tried to fight off the guards who had come to take Him away, Jesus responded, "Do you think that I cannot appeal to my Father, and he will at once send me more than twelve legions of angels?" (Matt. 26:53).

We have already seen that Jesus exercised authority over demons in His ministry. They cried out when they saw Him (Mark 3:11), and He could drive them out with a mere word (Matt. 8:16). He could even share this authority with His followers (Matt. 10:1). The New Testament frequently speaks of Jesus' authority over the angels and the "powers" (for example, 1 Pet. 3:22). The subject of Jesus and the powers takes us into an altogether different area, which we shall consider later.

The angels in heaven acknowledge that Christ alone is worthy of praise. In Revelation 5, the angels sing that only He has authority over human destiny (there portrayed as opening a scroll, v. 9) and that only He merits all honor and thanksgiving. "Then I looked, and I heard the voice of many angels surrounding the throne and the living creatures and the elders; they numbered myriads of myriads and thousands of thousands, singing with full voice, 'Worthy is the Lamb that was slaughtered to receive power and wealth and wisdom and might and honor and glory and blessing!'" (vv. 11–12).

Earth, Air, Water, Fire, and Angels: Colossians 2

Could Christians prefer praying to angels over calling on the name of Jesus? Apparently so. One early heresy taught that people should not call on Christ for help, but the angels. For this reason, the Council of Laodicea in the early fourth century forbade praying to angels.[1] But the problem goes back even to the earliest days of Christianity.

The Colossian church faced a strange amalgamation of heretical teachings. On the one hand, their conversion to Christianity naturally attracted these Gentiles to the Old Testament and to Judaism. Many wondered if they should undergo circumcision, the normal rite of proselytes. On the other hand, the pagan worldview they had known all their lives still held their minds in a firm grip.

In Colossians 2:8–23, Paul alluded to dangerous practices and beliefs that attracted these vulnerable converts. These include "philosophy and empty deceit," the "elemental spirits of the world," ascetic practices (in matters of food, drink, and conduct), circumcision, following a sacred calendar, self-abasement, giving heed to alleged visions, and worshiping angels. Some of these items reflect Jewish influence, as circumcision obviously does. Others reflect the pagan beliefs and practices of this era. What we see is a mixture of ideas from both worlds that seemed to offer the Colossians a higher spirituality but that in reality precluded a proper focus on Christ.

The phrase "elements of the world" (sometimes translated, "elemental spirits of the universe") in 2:8 has confounded scholars for years. Some take it to mean "basic teachings of the world," while others see a reference to demonic spirits and so translate it "elemental spirits" or the like. I am convinced that the phrase holds the key to this passage.

To begin with, we should *not* translate it as "elemental spirits" or understand it to mean demons or the like. The Greek word did not acquire that meaning until later times.[2] Also, while the word can mean "basic teachings" (Heb. 5:12), that rendition is not particularly helpful here. An ancient reader would have naturally taken this phrase to mean simply "the elements of the world" and we do better by sticking to that translation.

The ancients believed that the world was made of four elements: earth, air, fire, and water. Authors who lived and wrote either prior to or shortly after the time of Paul (men such as Ovid, Philo, Cicero, and Plutarch) tell us of the significance of these elements. It was not a simple matter of physics. They believed that if the elements got out of balance, then floods, earthquakes, or volcanoes were sure to follow. More importantly for our purposes, they asserted that the soul was made of "kindled air" and that it naturally strove to ascend to the heavenly realms beyond the moon. The goal of life was to enable this ascent to take place.

But there was a catch. If someone ate the wrong kind of food or handled the wrong kind of material, he or she could weigh down the soul with the heavier, earthly elements so that it could not ascend to heaven. That soul would be condemned to enduring the pain of thousands of lifetimes in all kinds of animals during cycles of reincarnation. Therefore, various ancient cults had regulations about what one could eat (meat and beans were often taboo), and they required people to abstain from anything that defiled (such as sexual intercourse). In addition, they thought that certain souls had already ascended to the rank of "heroes" or even beyond that to "spirits," and that these ascended souls could help others rise to the heavens.[3]

We can readily see how a form of Judaism might meld with this pagan thought in the minds of the Colossians. Like the cults, Judaism had its list of proscribed food. More esoteric forms of Judaism, such as that described in some of the Dead Sea Scrolls, also practiced rigorous forms of asceticism. Judaism followed a calendar of sacred days, and most important of all, certain sects of Judaism had more angels than you could shake a stick at.

Some of the Colossians may have identified the angels of Judaism with the ascended spirits of the cults, and then they could have fallen into a hodgepodge religion of Christianity, Judaism, and paganism. Their goal would have been to find a way to enable their souls to pierce the heavenly barrier and escape the material world of earth. Paul, of course, saw in this only superstition, false teaching, and a demotion of Christ from the One who is over all things to being merely an ascended spirit master. Curiously, this demotion is precisely how the New Age movement regards Him now.

Viewed in this light, Paul's concern about the "elements of the world," empty philosophy, prohibitions against eating various foods, and a religion focused on angels makes sense. He wanted the church members to know that Christ is over all things. No angel or spirit master could assist in the soul's ascent to heaven, and no elements could weigh the soul down. Ascetic practices ("Do not taste, Do not touch"—v. 21) have "an appearance of wisdom in promoting self-imposed piety" but they do nothing to deal with sin nor do they aid in the process of salvation.

Instead, the Colossians needed to learn that Christ alone possesses all the power of God and that they were baptized into Him and had abandoned the ways of the flesh. They had been forgiven of their sins in Him, and all spiritual powers are subject to Him. Those who have come to Christ have died to their former philosophies, including the "elements of the world" that governed their thinking, and they should acknowledge Christ alone as the agent of the salvation of their souls. In this work, angels have no role to play. Paul's message, in short, is that Christ is the very God and the only Savior, and that any "deep" teachings that go beyond Christ actually lead into oblivion.

Hebrews 1–2: To Which One of the Angels

The letter to the Hebrews began rather strangely. After opening remarks to the effect that Jesus is the ultimate revelation of God (1:1–4), the author went to great lengths to prove that Jesus is greater than the angels (1:5–14; 2:5–9). He cited the Old Testament, he reasoned, and he repeatedly emphasized that angels are mere subordinate creatures. Why this intense desire to show that Jesus is superior to angels?

Perhaps the original readers of the letter were drifting into some kind of cult that exalted angels. If so, they might have been in a situation similar to that at Colossae, where people looked to angels or ascended masters to help with the soul's trek to heaven. Another possibility is that Hebrews opposes some kind of angel-Christology; that is, perhaps the Book of Hebrews took a stand against a group that regarded Jesus Himself as an angel.

Unfortunately, nothing in the text supports either of these alternatives. The book never implies that the original readers were either worshiping angels or believed that Jesus Himself was an angel. Rather, the author moved beyond the discussion of angels fairly quickly—probably because he was confident that his readers agreed that Christ is above the angels and thus he needed not belabor the point any further.[4]

In order to understand the purpose of this chapter, we need to look briefly at what Hebrews is all about. This book is not easy to interpret. The writer moves back and forth between exposition, in which he teaches doctrine about Christ, and exhortation, in which he challenges the readers to perseverance and obedience. Hebrews tells us that Christ is superior to the angels, that He is a greater high priest than those of the priesthood of Aaron, and that the new covenant is superior to the old. In the exhortation, the book warns us not to reject the word spoken by the Son, gives examples of both faithfulness and unfaithfulness, and urges us not to fail to "enter his rest."

Doctrine provides the basis for exhortation. To put it another way, Hebrews is not a set of teachings with a few practical applications tacked on for good measure. Rather, it is exhortation bolstered by points of doctrine. The superiority of the Son gives us sufficient reason to continue to be faithful to Him.[5]

In Hebrews 1, the author begins to build his case. He uses a kind of argument known as *a fortiori* or, more simply, "from lesser to greater." In this kind of argument, one begins by making a simple argument that the audience will quickly affirm. That is then used as the basis for moving on to the greater, more important case. In effect the reasoning is this:

"Since you agree that 'A' is true, don't you think it reasonable that 'B' is true, too?"

In this case, Hebrews 1:3–14 forms the *basis* for the argument. This does not mean that it is not important, but that it is something we should easily understand and that prepares us to move on to the author's main point. The foundation for his argument, simply put, is this: Jesus Christ is superior to all angels.

The writer first stated that Christ is God made manifest, that He upholds the universe, and that He has made atonement for His people and has received subsequent exaltation (v. 3). He then made the point that Christ in His being and His title surpasses all angels (v. 4).

Our author first cited Psalm 2:7 ("You are my Son; today I have begotten you") and 2 Samuel 7:14 ("I will be his Father, and he will be my Son"), to the effect that Christ alone is called God's son. In both cases, he rightly applied the Old Testament texts to Jesus. The Psalms passage described the foolhardy conspiracy of the nations against God's anointed. This "anointed" is the Davidic monarch, and the ultimate Davidic monarch is the Messiah Himself. The Samuel passage explained God's promise to establish the line of David as the chosen, eternal dynasty. Although the other kings from David's line (Solomon, for example) in some measure fulfilled this promise, the ultimate realization came in the person of the Davidic Messiah, Jesus Christ.

Next (v. 6), he cited Deuteronomy 32:43 (in the ancient Greek version, which is somewhat different from most English versions) that all the angels should worship "the Firstborn" when He came into the world. Our author may have called to mind how the angels worshiped Jesus at His birth, or he may have spoken of how the angels will worship Him at His second advent.[6] By contrast, the angels serve as mere messengers and agents for God. To this end, Hebrews 1:7 cites Psalm 104:4 (again, from the Greek version).

The Book of Hebrews also points out that Jesus eternally reigns as King. The author cited Psalm 45:6–7 ("Your throne, O God, is forever and ever") as evidence. This psalm celebrates the royal wedding of a Davidic monarch, but once again Hebrews' interpretation of the passage is legitimate. The psalm uses the wedding of the king to portray how the nations will someday bow to the Davidic king, and the ultimate fulfillment is in the Messiah. By contrast, the heavens themselves will pass away (v. 10–12, citing Ps. 102:25–27).

Finally, in verse 13, Hebrews cited the passage that was nearest to the author's heart, Psalm 110 ("Sit at my right hand until I make your enemies a footstool for your feet"). One more time, he (correctly) took a psalm about the Davidic king and saw its ultimate fulfillment in the Messiah. Only Christ has been enthroned alongside the Father; angels merely do their bidding (v. 14).

What is the point of all this? We find out in Hebrews 2:2–3: "For if the message declared through angels was valid, and every transgression or disobedience received a just penalty, how can we escape if we neglect so great a salvation? It was declared at first through the Lord, and it was attested to us by those who heard him." The argument has moved from the lesser to the greater. If violating laws given by angels merited punishment (the lesser side of the argument), how much worse will be our punishment if we neglect the gospel brought by the Son (the greater side of the argument)? Having laid his foundation in chapter 1, he made the point that we must not neglect the salvation in Jesus Christ.

To understand this, we must realize that the readers undoubtedly associated the Law with angels. We have already seen several New Testament allusions to this. We have also noted how angels were often associated with the giving of revelation. The point, then, is that a revelation that came through angels (the Old Testament, in particular) had great authority. Those who failed to obey, as the Israelites of the Old Testament often did, were punished severely. Yet in Christ we have a far greater, more final revelation (Heb. 1:1–2). If an Israelite was stoned to death for gathering sticks on the Sabbath (Num. 15:32–36), how much worse will it go for us, if we turn our backs on the Son of God?

For our purposes, this text shows that the Bible regards angels as secondary, even incidental, figures in comparison to the Son of God. They have neither His power nor His position. They are servants where He is God. More than that, He excels them in love and humility, in that He allowed Himself for a time to become lower than the angels for humanity's sake (Heb. 2:9). Unlike angels, the Son of God knows what it is to be human.

The folly of the current craze over angels could not be more pronounced. People prefer lesser spirits to the creator of all spirits. They seek revelation from angels rather than learning from the final revelation in the Son. If we reject God, to which one of the angels shall we turn for help?

A Man of Sorrows, and Well Acquainted with Grief

The superiority of Jesus involves more than that He is God but that also He is man. Angels are not like us. They can have none of the sensory experiences that we experience every day. We know what it is like to be physical, limited, and mortal. We know what it is to smell Thanksgiving dinner cooking in Mom's kitchen, to feel a pain in the back, to have the exhilaration of running down a hill, and to be too sick to get up in the morning.

Whatever an angel is, one thing is certain: an angel is not human. To call upon an angel when you need food is to call upon someone who has never felt the pangs of hunger. To call upon an angel when you are sick is to call upon someone who has never known sickness. To seek an angel's comfort when mourning the death of a friend is to call upon one who has never known grief or death.

Jesus, on the other hand, has known what it was to breathe the quiet air of an early Galilean morning. He has felt what it is to work with His hands and no doubt experienced the frustration of a piece of wood that just would not fit where it was supposed to. He was carried in His mother's arms. He has felt the pain of an empty stomach and has heard the tempter's voice telling Him to take a moral shortcut to sate that hunger. He has heard the singing and the celebration of a wedding party, and He has been in a house of mourning, when a little daughter was taken by death. Jesus has wept.

For us, perhaps the final statement of Jesus' superiority to the angels is not just that all things were created by Him and for Him but that He is also one of us. I do not know if tears have ever stained an angel's face, but I know that they have stained His. Jesus did drink deeply from the cup of sorrow; it did not pass from Him. That cup has never been near an angel's lips.

CHAPTER FIVE

In Heaven an angel is nobody in particular.
GEORGE BERNARD SHAW

Nobody in Particular

A Brief History of Angelology, Part 1

WE HAVE NO HOPE OF MAKING SENSE OF ALL THE NOISE
about angels today unless we consider what people have said about them
in the past. People rarely break new ground in religion—and if they do,
we ought to know about that too. By investigating the beliefs of people
in the past, we can often ascertain where the religious movements of
today are going. This analysis will of necessity be brief. We will try to
point out the major teachings and will try to make sense of the enormous
diversity of opinions, practices, and options.

Polytheism

The gods of the ancient world fulfilled at least five functions. Some
served as "astral deities." They governed the sun, moon, and constellations. For example, Apollo, god of the sun, rode across the sky every
day in his flaming chariot. Second, they provided mythological expla-

nations for the seasons and changes of the agricultural calendar. Baal's death and resurrection explained the annual cycle of drought and rains. The Greeks interpreted the annual cycle of the withering of vegetation in autumn by the story of the annual four-month sojourn of Persephone in the underworld. Third, gods and goddesses protected hearth and home. Family members honored their private household gods and passed the images and stories of their gods from generation to generation. Fourth, the gods personified events, virtues, and evils as well as human passions and abilities.

Gods of war and love, of fortune, and of creativity populated the ever-expanding pantheons of ancient societies. In Greece, Athena gave a man wisdom, the Muses inspired him to poetic creativity, and the Fates determined his destiny. Finally, the gods and goddesses were patrons and matrons of city-states, and the gods themselves were in a hierarchy of powers that mirrored the hierarchical bureaucracy of the ancient city governments.[1]

Through the ages, people have also attributed all of the above characteristics and activities to angels. Some invoke angels as special, private protectors of an individual or home ("guardian angels"), and some claim that the angels, like the Muses, inspire great art. Mystical theology regularly asserts that angels govern the movement of the stars, as we shall see, and some say that special angels guard the trees and crops. Modern angelphile books often speak of the "angel of courage" or the "angel of healing" or the like. Virtually every aspect of polytheism has crept into Christian or quasi-Christian thinking under the guise of angels. Even the familiar image of the angel as a man or woman with a large pair of wings also comes from Greek and Roman religion. The temple of Artemis in Ephesus has a figure of an angel complete with wings and sword that could easily have come from any cathedral in Christian Europe.[2]

Jewish Angelology

The Dead Sea Scrolls

The Dead Sea Scrolls, documents found in caves near Wadi Qumran at the northwest corner the Dead Sea, are at the same time the most significant and the most overblown archaeological find of this century.

Their significance lies in the fact that they contain, among other things, copies and fragments of Old Testament books that are one thousand years older than any other manuscripts of the Hebrew Bible. On the other hand, the scrolls have spawned more than their share of outlandish theories and sensational (but false) stories in the media. Despite what you may have heard, neither Jesus nor John the Baptist nor any other person from the New Testament appears in the scrolls. Nor did the Vatican conspire to keep the contents of the scrolls secret.[3]

The scrolls are probably the remains of a Jewish sect called the Essenes. This group, and in particular the segment of it that lived in Qumran, was an extremist fringe of Judaism from around 150 B.C. to about A.D. 70. They had something like a monastic community at Qumran.

In addition to the Hebrew Bible and other religious books (such as *1 Enoch*, which we consider below), the Essenes possessed religious books distinctive to their movement. These documents contain the teachings and regulations of their community. In the texts, we see that they perceived themselves as a righteous remnant who set themselves apart from the decadent Judaism of their day. They believed that the end was at hand and that the struggle between light and darkness would soon reach its climax. They looked for two messiahs—one priestly messiah, the other kingly. They either practiced celibacy or allowed sexual relations only for the sake of procreation.[4] Also, many of them were very fond of angels.

The *Manual of Discipline* found in cave 1 at Qumran teaches that humanity is under the rule of two spirits—the Angel of Darkness (Belial) and the Prince of Lights (probably Michael). This was a modified, practical dualism. The Essenes still regarded God as the Creator of all and the only eternal being, but they believed that the real spiritual battle involved the Angel of Darkness and the Prince of Light. Humans were more or less passive objects in the struggle between these two nearly equal spiritual powers. Even so, the Qumran texts do not try to account for the beginning of sin itself, nor do they attribute all human sins to demonic influence. The documents predict that the elect will one day dwell in heavenly light but the wicked will suffer under punishment inflicted by the "angels of destruction."[5]

In some respects the Qumran texts have an orthodox view of angels. A group of psalm-like poems from cave 1 describes the angels as created beings who will live forever and who are subordinate to God, and they praise God for the forgiveness that allows people to share in the happy destiny of the angels.[6]

In other respects, their views may strike us as peculiar. The "Songs of Sabbath Sacrifice" from caves 4 and 11 and from Masada imply the existence of a heavenly temple in which angels serve as priests. These thirteen songs indicate that seven orders of angel-priests serve in the temple in heaven and that an archangel rules over each order. The angel-priests are modeled on the priests of the ancient Jewish temple. They wear the same priestly dress that their earthly counterparts wear.[7] It seems that the authors of these songs imagined that worship in heaven had to be very much like what they, as Jews, saw in their earthly temple. Perhaps the lesson here is that we need to be careful about attributing aspects of the world we know to the world of the angels. A Baptist who pictures choirs of angels singing "Just as I Am" while other angels move forward to rededicate their lives should perhaps reconsider his or her view of heaven.

Perhaps the most important document for our purposes is the *War Scroll*, a text that deals with the conflict between Michael, with his hosts of angels and saints (the Sons of Light), and Belial, with his hosts of devils and sinners (the Sons of Darkness). Human membership in the Sons of Light was basically limited to members of the Qumran sect, and they went forth to battle with the names of the archangels written on their shields. Edomites, non-Essene Jews, and the *Kittim* (Romans) received special mention as partisans for the Sons of Darkness. The opposing forces were equal in strength, but the sovereignty of God guaranteed victory for the Sons of Light. God had long ago decreed that this final battle should take place, and He predetermined its outcome.

Because the holy angels would be in their ranks, the human members of the Sons of Light needed to give strict attention to the matter of ritual purity. In a striking departure from Deuteronomy, which stated that the Israelites must remain pure because *the Lord* was in their camp, the *War Scroll* admonished the people to be aware that *the angels* were among them. Also, while the Old Testament frequently spoke of God going forth to fight for Israel, the real chief of the Qumran "Sons of Light" was Michael. The Old Testament, moreover, never portrayed Belial leading an army of devils against Israel.[8]

In an ironic note, many of the prophecies of the Essenes came to pass, but not in the way they expected. The Messiah did come in their time, but He was one Messiah, not two, and He was a servant and not a warrior. Their climactic war with the Sons of Darkness finally came about as well. The Romans invaded a rebellious Judah and slaughtered thousands of Jews, including the people of Qumran. The Essene sect disappeared from history.

Apocrypha and Pseudepigrapha

After the completion of the Old Testament, the Jews who lived in the centuries immediately before and after the life of Jesus produced a number of quasi-biblical books meant to encourage and enlighten the faithful. Some of these books are called Apocrypha by Protestants and Deutero-canonical by Roman Catholics. Among these are 1 and 2 Maccabees (the Eastern Orthodox Church also includes 3 and 4 Maccabees), Tobit, Judith, 1 and 2 Esdras, Ecclesiasticus, and several other books. In the past, some scholars claimed that the Jews in Egypt treated these books as part of the Old Testament Scripture, but this is not true. The Jews never regarded these books as canonical.

In addition, a large number of ancient Jewish books have survived that we call Pseudepigrapha. These books tend to be apocalyptic, although there are also books that are more legendary in nature. Many of these books falsely claim authorship by some ancient hero of the Old Testament. They provide a good glimpse into the Jewish world at the time of Jesus and the early church.

The Angel, the Demon, and the Fish Liver: Tobit. Angels appear a number of times in the Apocrypha. In 3 Maccabees, for example, two awesome angels rescue the Jews of Egypt from the plots of Pharaoh Ptolemy IV Philopator. One book from this collection, Tobit, especially concerns us.

The book of Tobit introduces the angel Raphael, who calls himself "one of the seven holy angels who present the prayers of the saints and enter into the presence of the glory of the Holy One" (Tob. 12:15, RSV). The book was written sometime in the second century B.C. by an unknown Jewish author.

Tobit, the hero of the tale, was a Jew of exceptional piety who lived among the exiles in Nineveh. Among his other labors of charity, Tobit took it upon himself to bury the body of any slain Jew he happened to come upon. One night, his son Tobias told him that a fellow Jew had been strangled and left in the marketplace, and Tobit immediately went to take care of the situation. That night, because touching the corpse had made him unclean, he slept outside. At this point, Tobit fell victim to a tragic turn of events when bird droppings fell into his eyes and he went blind.

Meanwhile, a young Jewish woman in Ecbatana named Sarah had troubles enough of her own. Seven times she had wed, and every time the jealous demon Asmodeus had come and killed her new husband on their honeymoon night before they could consummate the marriage. Her reputation in ruins, she contemplated suicide but prayed for deliverance instead. At this point, Raphael stepped in.

It turned out that Tobit had an investment in Ecbatana, and Raphael decided to send Tobias there to fetch the money. Raphael (in disguise as a human) volunteered to escort Tobias. On the way to Ecbatana, the pair camped by the Tigris River—a surprising thing to do, since Ecbatana was east of Nineveh but the Tigris was to the west. But something even more surprising happened next: a fish jumped up from the river and tried to swallow young Tobias. Raphael told Tobias to catch this man-eating fish, which he somehow accomplished. Raphael then instructed him to cut out the fish's heart, liver, and gall and keep them for the journey.

In Ecbatana, Raphael told Tobias that Sarah was just the girl for him. Tobias, however, had heard how she had been a fatal attraction for seven other men and politely declined. But Raphael persuaded him that she really was a wonderful girl and that Tobias could deal with the demon quite easily. All he needed to do was take some hot ashes of incense into the bridal chamber, lay them on the heart and liver of the fish, and the demon would flee. The marriage was arranged and sure enough, when Asmodeus smelled the bouquet of burning fish heart and liver, probably fairly pungent by this time, he fled to Egypt, where an angel bound him. This delighted Sarah's father, who had already dug grave number eight for his new son-in-law. Tobias picked up the money he came for and went back to Nineveh where, using the fish gall, he cured Tobit's blindness. The story thus came to a happy conclusion, and Raphael had earned his reputation among angelphiles everywhere as one of the greats.

Tobit may not qualify as what we have called "angelphilia." Raphael was a character in the story of Tobit, but not the central character. The book of Tobit does not delve into the mysteries of the angelic world nor profess to give secret knowledge. At the same time, it displays traits that do not bode well for a faith centered on God rather than on angels. Raphael guided and helped Tobias in a way that went far beyond anything we see an angel doing in the Bible, and the use of fish parts to ward off a demon could easily justify magic arts for many ancient (and modern) readers. The book of Tobit opens the door to a semi-pagan kind of faith, in which friendly angels substitute for the older household gods and offer protection from evil spirits.

The Books of Enoch. "Enoch walked with God; then he was no more, because God took him." (Gen. 5:24). With these few words, Genesis laid the foundation for what was to become a huge edifice of mystical and esoteric speculation. In the centuries before and after Christ, Jewish mystics speculated on the mysteries that this otherwise unknown figure, Enoch, must have discovered when "God took him." They circulated all kinds of legends, which were collected into three large books full of secret knowledge about the heavenly realm. The books are *1 Enoch, 2 Enoch, and 3 Enoch.* These three books do not make a series; they were written in different times and places, although each one draws on a common Jewish pool of legends about Enoch.

First Enoch was written in stages between the fourth century B.C. and the first century A.D. In this book, we read all about Jewish speculation concerning that embarrassing little episode in Genesis 6:1–2, in which angels get a look at human women and decide that they have been missing out on something good. *First Enoch* goes into astonishing detail about the angels' taking of human women and the aftermath. It tells us, for example, that about two hundred angels participated in this escapade, and it even gives us the names of the leading angels.

The chief of all the conspirators was Azazel, and the fallen angels not only took human women, but they instructed humanity in the black arts and warfare. The good angels complained to God about all the foul goings-on, and He commissioned angels such as Michael and Raphael to bring judgment down upon them and cast Azazel into a dungeon. Enoch, however, was so wonderfully pious that he interceded even for Azazel and the fallen angels. God drew Enoch to Himself and assured him that his piety did not go unnoticed, but He still commanded him to go back to Azazel and company and tell them that they could forget about any hope of escaping their fate.

The book also says that the offspring of this unnatural union are the demons: "But now the giants who are born from the (union of) the spirits and the flesh . . . . Evil spirits have come out of their bodies. . . . They will become evil upon the earth and shall be called evil spirits. The dwelling of the spiritual beings of heaven is heaven; but the dwelling of the spirits of the earth, which are born upon the earth, is in the earth."[9] As we have already seen, this is an alternative answer to the question of where demons come from. For his troubles and with Uriel as his guide, Enoch got to see the hellish dungeon where the fallen angels would be spending their time.

First Enoch also contains in chapter 69 a catalogue of fallen angels. This describes in some detail the supposed activities of the angels who came to take human women. For example, "The third was named Gader'el; this one is he who showed the children of the people (how to make) the instruments of death (such as) the shield, the breastplate, and the sword for warfare, and all (the other) instruments of death to the children of the people. Through their agency (death) proceeds against the people who dwell upon the earth from that day forevermore."[10]

Beyond this, *1 Enoch* for the most part details the history of Israel and the future judgment in various visions and parables. It also speaks of seventy "shepherds" who are the seventy guardian angels of the nations. These angels were supposed to discipline Israel, but they went too far in their hostility to Israel and so incurred the wrath of God.[11] The angels Michael, Raphael, Gabriel, and Phanuel will seize the kings of the earth and the armies of Azazel and cast them into the furnace of hell on the great day of judgment.

Second Enoch is a mystery from beginning to end. It exists only in Slavonic versions, but its original language was probably Greek or Hebrew. Its author may have been from either a Jewish or a Christian sect, and we do not know when or where the book was written, beyond that it was probably written somewhere between the first century B.C. and tenth century A.D. It exists in two versions, one considerably longer than the other, but we do not know which version was written first.[12] Still, for our purposes, it provides a useful insight into some early Jewish (or Christian?) speculations about the angels.

The book opens with Enoch traveling upward through the ten heavens. En route, he saw various angels going about their duties. He sees "the 200 angels who govern the stars" as well as those who govern the "treasuries of the snow and the ice."[13] Enoch also saw the 150,000 angels who accompany the sun in its trek across the sky and the weird flying spirits that dwell in the path of the sun (2 Enoch 12–13). In the sixth heaven, he saw the seven groups of angels who oversee the movements of the sun, moon, and stars and the changing of the seasons. Generally, the tone of the vision is highly mythological and astrological.

Eventually Enoch reached the tenth heaven, where Gabriel and Michael set him before the Lord. Then, the angel Vrevoil instructs him in all the things of heaven and earth and under the sea and in all languages. This is a lot to cover, but Vrevoil never stopped speaking for thirty days and nights. Enoch displayed tremendous energy himself in this encounter. He not only listened to all that Vrevoil had to say but he also stayed up another thirty days and nights to write everything down in a series of 366 books.

God also explained in detail the events of the seven days of creation to Enoch. He told him that Satan (called here "Satanail") fell at the end of the second day of creation (2 Enoch 29). He also noted that Adam managed to hold on to paradise for only a meager five and a half hours before his expulsion (2 Enoch 32:1—but 71:28 says that Adam was in paradise for seven years). Before Enoch returned to earth, an ice angel chilled his face to take away the heavenly glow that would have been intolerable for humans to behold (2 Enoch 37). The book concludes with a bizarre and scandalous account of the origin of Melchizedek, the priest-king of Genesis 14:18 and Psalm 110:4 (2 Enoch 71–72).

Third Enoch was written in Hebrew around the seventh century B.C. in Babylon. It is part of the Hekalot, a type of mystical rabbinical literature. Books of Hekalot present themselves as accounts of visions of God and falsely attribute these visions to great rabbis of the past. Some of the texts contain rituals for compelling the angel of the divine presence to appear. Some scholars believe that Hekalot is a Jewish version of Gnosticism, which we shall consider shortly.[14]

At the center of 3 Enoch is an angel whose name, Metatron, sounds uncannily like that of a comic book superhero. This, if nothing else, keeps me from taking 3 Enoch too seriously. The name probably comes from the Latin metator, or "precursor," a reference to the angel who went before Israel.[15] It also relates to the mystical Jewish numerology called Gematria. The numbers of the name Metatron add up to 314, the same as the number of Shaddai, a term for God.[16]

At any rate, the book tells how Rabbi Ishmael journeyed through the six palaces of heaven (one within the other) to the gate of the seventh, where the guardian angels blocked his path. He prayed for help, and God sent Metatron to let him in. Metatron described himself as having seventy names, corresponding to the seventy names of the nations of earth, and Ishmael recognized that he was the highest and greatest of all angels.

It turned out that Metatron was none other than Enoch, whom God exalted to heaven and made ruler of all angels. Metatron said that the angels were disgusted that one born of a woman and who came from a "white drop" (that is, semen) should rule over them but that God assured them that Enoch was worth more than all humanity put together. If that were not enough, Metatron continued, God enlarged Enoch-Metatron until he was as big as the whole earth and gave him 1,365,000 blessings, 72 wings, and 365,000 eyes. Metatron in effect became prime minister of heaven. Metatron even had a crown inscribed, "The Lesser YHWH"[17] (YHWH is the unspeakable name of God, although today people routinely pronounce it as "Yahweh").

Metatron then let Ishmael in on all the angelic secrets of heaven. He said that seven great princes rule the seven heavens. These were Michael, over the seventh and highest heaven, then Gabriel, Satqiel, Sahaqiel, Baradiel, Baraqiel, and Sidriel. No less than 4,960,000,000 angels attended to each of these angelic princes. Other angels include Rahatiel, who governs the constellations, and Kokabiel, who rules the stars and has 3,650,000,000 angelic subordinates.

The book goes to great lengths to communicate the vastness of the angelic realm. It states that God had 4,960,000,000 camps of angels, that each camp had 496,000 angels, and that every angel was as big as the Mediterranean.[18] Despite their great power, the angels were subject to some fairly strict discipline. "Whenever the ministering angels do not recite the song [of God's praise] at the right time or in a proper and fitting manner, they are burned by the fire of their maker,"[19] Metatron noted.

Angels and Wicked Women: The Testament of the Twelve Patriarchs. The Bible tells us that the twelve sons of Jacob fathered the twelve tribes of Israel. Other than Joseph and to a lesser extent Judah and Reuben, there is virtually nothing said about the men themselves or their legacy to Israel. The *Testament of the Twelve Patriarchs* seeks to remedy this. Probably written during the second century B.C. in Syria by a Jew versed in Greek culture, it purports to give the last testament and spiritual teachings of each of the twelve.

The testaments for the most part reflect orthodox Judaism, but they also show the influence of Greek philosophy and Jewish mysticism. They take the view that man (that is, the male) is basically good. Women, by contrast, are by nature evil, treacherous, and more easily drawn into promiscuity than men. In perhaps the most astonishing example ever of blaming the victim, the book alleges that it was really the women's fault that the angels of Genesis 6 fell into sin. The women charmed the angels into taking on human form and also lusted after their angelic bodies.[20]

We also learn here that humans are caught in a conflict between Satan and God. Satan corrupts the soul and takes it captive, but the Lord will wage war against Satan for those who repent and deliver their souls from captivity (*Testament of Dan* 1:7; 5:10). At death, the evil soul suffers under the evil spirit that it had served, but the good soul comes to know the "angel of peace" and enters eternal life (*Testament of Asher* 6:5).

Angels serve as instructors to the patriarchs in the testaments, and they are especially keen to point out how lustful and dangerous women are: "And the angel of the Lord showed me that women have the mastery over both king and poor man: From the king they will take away his glory; from the virile man, his power; and from the poor man, even the slight support he has in his poverty."[21] Also, angels serve as intercessors for people, and Michael is the chief intercessor.[22]

The angels dwell in all three heavens. The angels in the lowest heaven, in addition to teaching the patriarchs, also punish the injustice of humanity. The second heaven contains a vast army of angels who fight against Satan and who are ready to execute the last judgment. The archangels dwell with God in the third heaven, where they present "rational and bloodless" sacrifices to God. Angels who are simply called "thrones and authorities" dwell there too (*Testament of Levi* 3:1–9).

Magic Sashes and the Language of the Angels: The Testament of Job. We are all familiar with the sufferings of Job and the biblical book that goes by his name. The story must have also appealed to some unknown Jew around the first century, since he tried to interpret the story in another book called the *Testament of Job*. This book, although not as openly a work of angelphilia as, for example, *3 Enoch*, clarifies the difference between angelphilia and biblical faith in a marvelous way.

As Job tells the story, his original name was Jobab. He lived near an idol's temple, but he doubted whether this could be the true form of God. Then one night an angel appeared to him and told him about the true God. Job immediately decided to destroy the pagan temple, but the angel warned him that Satan would avenge himself upon Job by destroying his property, killing his children, and striking him with plagues. Even so, the righteous Job leveled the temple to the ground. Sure enough, Job says, Satan soon arrived at his door disguised as a beggar and promised to get even.

Job then described his wonderful piety and kindness as well as his fabulous wealth, and how Satan took his possessions away. His wife, after seventeen years of affliction, urged Job to speak some word against the Lord and put an end to this testing. Job recognized Satan behind her words and called him out; then Satan, weeping, confessed that Job's piety was more than he could take.

Three years later Job's friends showed up to challenge Job, but through unshakable faith in the resurrection Job rebuffed them and was vindicated by God. Restored to his former glory, Job says, he immediately took pains to provide for the poor.

In his dying days, Job provided an inheritance for his children. He gave a sash to each of his daughters and told them, "Place these about your breast, so it may go well with you all the days of your life."[23] Miffed at having received such a paltry inheritance, they asked Job what good the strings were. Job replied that when God told him to "gird his loins," he put on these sashes and immediately was cured of all his diseases and sorrows and that the sashes could protect people from the devil. Each of the three daughters then put on her sash and immediately spoke in the language of the archangels. The daughters also witnessed angels come in a shining chariot and take Job's soul off to heaven.

If you are at all familiar with the Book of Job, you have no doubt noticed many differences between this and the biblical account. For our purposes, however, several things stand out.

First, the Job of the Bible never knew anything about the involvement of Satan in his sufferings. Even at the end, God did not mention Satan's part in Job's suffering. In the *Testament*, by contrast, Job knew all about his sufferings in advance and even had a personal encounter with the devil. Second, the Satan of the biblical Job was completely under God's command. He could do nothing to Job without

God's permission. The Satan of the *Testament of Job*, however, acted independently of God. In keeping with the theology of dualism, Satan acted as a powerful adversary whom the righteous must conquer by displays of personal holiness. Third, the *Testament* endorsed a form of superstition whereby a magic charm could protect someone from the devil. The biblical Job had nothing of this. Fourth, the *Testament* treated familiarity with the angels as a sign of godliness. An angel instructed Job about everything that would happen to him. His daughters also displayed blessedness by speaking in the language of the angels and by having the privilege of observing them as they take their father's soul away. Finally, and most importantly, the Job of the Bible was not a spiritual superman who knew all the secret things of God or who made the devil weep with exhaustion. In the Bible, Job did all the weeping and even in the end he was left in the dark about many things.

I cannot overemphasize the importance of these distinctions or how clearly they separate biblical faith from angelphilia. In angelphilia there is secret knowledge; in the Bible there is faith, and the faithful have to live with some admitted ignorance about the ways of God and the angels. In angelphilia (as we shall see) there is a spiritual warfare in which the devil and God are nearly equals as they contend for human souls; in the Bible, the devil is malicious but always under God's control. The superspirituality of the angelphile is confirmed by encounters with familiar spirits; the biblical believer, like Job, looks only to God and does not aspire to angelic visions and languages so much as to faith, hope, and love (1 Cor. 13:1, 13). Angelphilia, especially that of the New Age variety, endorses a spirituality of sacred objects. The Bible rejects this entirely.

I do not wish to imply that the *Testament of Job* does nothing but promote angelphilia. To the contrary, it tries to promote many biblical aspects of piety also. But its subtle messages of superspirituality, angelic visions, hidden knowledge, and spiritual warfare foreshadow much of the error of the present day.

Arara, Arare: The Testament of Solomon. Solomon, son of David and king of Israel, possessed all the intelligence, power, and wealth anyone could desire. He was devoted to God, but he had his weaknesses too. He was quite human. Legend, however, was not content to leave him as merely a wise and powerful king. As the name of Solomon came down into Jewish, Christian, and Islamic lore, storytellers elevated him to the status of supersorcerer and master of the secrets of the universe.

Probably some quasi-Christian mystic wrote the *Testament of Solomon*; it has a number of clear Christian references. It may have been written by a Jew and then later edited by a Christian; we do not know. Some say that the book is Gnostic. It probably came from somewhere in the first to third centuries A.D., and the author, whoever he was, drew heavily upon the magical lore of the ancient pagan world as filtered through some strange deviations of Judaism and Christianity. In this book, we see angelphilia gone berserk.

The story goes like this.[24] The demon Ornias, Solomon tells us, was sucking on the thumb of a little boy who was the son of the temple construction foreman. As the boy continued to languish and lose weight, Solomon prayed for help, and the archangel Michael came to give him a ring that would allow him to bind all demons. With the power of this ring, Solomon trapped and interrogated the demon Ornias. He found out that Ornias dwelt in Aquarius. He could transform himself into a man who craves effeminate boys or into a winged creature or into a lion. Ornias also admitted that the angel Ouriel could thwart him.

Solomon then used Ornias to summon Beelzebul himself who, under the power of the ring, agrees to bring him all the unclean demons. What follows is a succession of demon interrogations, in which Solomon learns the names, astrological signs, and powers of the demons, and also the names of the angels who can defeat them.

Some of the characters on this list are quite colorful.

▼ Onoskelis, a female demon of the constellation Capricorn, who strangles or perverts men. Solomon imprisoned her and forced her to stand and continually spin hemp into rope.

▼ Beelzebul, who resides in Venus, causes men to worship demons, incites carnal desire in holy men, and starts wars. The Almighty God alone can thwart him, but anyone can chase away Beelzebul by using the spell called "the Elo-i" (Aramic for "my God"). Solomon made him cut stones for the temple.

▼ Lix Tetrax, who dwells in a star found at the horn of the moon when it is in the south. He starts fires and whirlwinds, and is defeated by the archangel Azael. Solomon made him hurl stones up to the workmen on the temple.

▼ Obyzouth, a female demon who strangles newborn babies. The angel Raphael can thwart her; women who are about to give birth should write her name on papyrus to chase her away. Solomon hung her by the hair on the temple.

▼ The thirty-six heavenly body demons, who take the forms of humans, bulls, dragons, birds, or other animals. Among their number are Oropel (who gives people sore throats but flees when the angel Raphael is invoked), Soubelti (who causes shivering and numbness but retreats at the name of Rizoel), and Rhyx Anathreth (who gives people gas, but who will desist from his foul work at the invocation "Arara, Arare").

At the end of the book, Solomon confesses that he fell madly in love with the "Shummanite" woman (the woman, Abishag the Shunammite, is mentioned in 1 Kings 1:3–4, but she is not associated with Solomon). In order to obtain her, he says, he sacrificed locust blood to Molech. The glory of God departed him, and he lost all control over demons.

Those who focus on the spirits naturally begin to associate every event, be it good or ill, with a spirit. From this arises the desire to know how to invoke the proper spirit for every need and also to learn the ritual that will thwart hurtful spirits. This is not just a phenomenon of the ancient world but is the dark underside of centering one's life on the spirits. I believe that this kind of religion will soon emerge from the present angelphilia.

The Kabbalah

The term *Kabbalah* refers to the esoteric teachings of Jewish mysticism as it existed from the twelfth century in the middle ages. It was similar to the earlier Gnosticism (which we look at below) and included "instruction on the mystical path" as well as "cosmology, angelology, and magic."[25] Developed primarily in Spain, the principal book of Kabbalah is the Zohar.

Emanations. In antiquity, people accounted for the existence of the universe in one of two ways. The first way, that of the Bible, is creation out of nothing by divine decree. God speaks, and the universe comes to be (Gen. 1).

The second is by theogony or emanations. The word *theogony* means "divine begetting" and implies that a god or gods generated the world through a process that was sexual or quasi-sexual. There may be a family tree in which a series of ancient, primordial gods begot generations of gods until a later generation in some way generated the world and humans. The notion of emanations is similar, although it may or may not make use of sexual imagery. It implies a process of emergence or "emanation." The idea is that a single, high god ("The Holy One" or the like) in some way produced one or more lesser entities (the high angels). These entities produced another, lower level of angels, and the process continued with more lower levels growing successively out of higher levels until finally the physical world of humans, animals, plants, and rocks emerged. It is a kind of evolution in reverse, and (in many different forms with many variations) it is at the base of all kinds of mythology.

Another fairly common feature of mythological thinking is dualism. As opposed to the biblical notion of a sovereign God who rules even the evil spirits, this idea is that two roughly equal spiritual forces struggle with one another over humanity. Typically described as light versus darkness (as at Qumran), this view heavily emphasizes the idea of war between the two sides. Although strictly incompatible with monotheism, it nevertheless appears in many mystical systems. A pure dualism will posit two equal and opposite forces, like the "Force" and the "Dark Side of the Force" in Star Wars. A practical dualism asserts the existence of a supreme God but still sees a spiritual struggle among angelic powers in dualistic terms.

The authors of the Zohar were strongly drawn to the idea of emanations, although their writings are inconsistent enough that it is impossible to say that they fully embraced the idea. They believed that the lower, earthly realm is a mirror of the upper, heavenly realm and that a kind of ladder of being stretches from God down to the lowest levels. In paganism, a notion of emanations will include a multitude of gods; in a monotheistic system, however, angels take the place of the lower gods. The Zohar claims that the angels were created first and are the "foundation of all the other created things."[26] This naturally leads to heavy emphasis on angels.

The Zohar also gave great attention to the "other side," that is, to evil and the devils. Man has a good inclination and an evil inclination. There are secrets of heavenly wisdom and secrets of hellish sorcery, and there are angels and devils. Sometimes people must even appease the evil side with gifts; the Zohar teaches that when an animal was sacrificed in the Old Testament, some of the parts went to the dark powers.

Behind this limited dualism is again the notion of emanations. Good and evil emanate from the love and justice of God. Because evil is ultimately an emanation from God, it is subordinate to God and finally serves the purpose of God (and so the dualism of the Kabbalah is practical and not pure).

Still, the demons are terrible and ferocious. The principal figures are a male devil (Samael) and a female devil (Lilith). In the various legends and stories of Kabbalah, the male represents ferocity and destruction, and the female represents passion, hatred, and lust. In some accounts, the male devil had sexual relations with Eve and the female with Adam.[27] The Zohar especially developed the character of Lilith. She is at times the prostitute who seduced the fool and finally destroyed him. She was also jealous of Eve and subsequently traveled through the earth looking for newborn babies to kill by administering the croup.[28]

The Angels of the Zohar. As in *1 Enoch*, the Metatron of the Zohar rules over all the troops of heaven. He is lord of the heavenly sanctuary where Michael serves as high priest. He rules the world with the help of seventy angelic princes. At the same time, he is also linked with the powers of darkness, and he can represent both life and death. He is identified with the Tree of the Knowledge of Good and Evil. He is life on one side and death on the other. In this capacity, he is also the counterpart to Samael.

Since he combines both human and angelic perfection, he has a mediatorial function. He knows all the secrets of the hidden wisdom, and he brings the light of this wisdom to men. Every night he takes the souls of the righteous to heaven where they praise the creator, and he is in charge of the resurrection. Since he was also the man Enoch, he exemplifies the glory of man. In the Zohar, the essence of humanity is the soul, which is the "pure radiance of the divine emanation."[29] Enoch-Metatron therefore represents the culmination of the human soul's spiritual ascent.

He is also the counterpart to the two fallen angels, Uzza and Azael. These are the beings, according to the Zohar, who cohabited with women in Genesis 6. They represent the reverse of Metatron, in that they are angels who descended to earth and corruption. Just as he holds the mystical secrets of heavenly truth and the spiritual ascent, so also they bring down the secrets of magic. By these, the initiate can bring down and control angelic powers. Metatron and the two fallen angels oppose one another, but they also complement one another in that together they hold all the secrets of Kabbalah.[30]

The Kabbalah represented something of the high-water mark of early Jewish mysticism, and it contained many themes that appear in angelphilia. These include doctrines of emanation and dualism, a developed mythology about angels and devils, secret knowledge (including both heavenly wisdom and magic), the notion of the ascent of the soul, and a kind of deification of humanity (as in the person of Enoch-Metatron). We will see many of these ideas elsewhere in angel lore.

The Talmud and Rabbinical Teaching

The orthodox rabbis of Judaism wanted to rescue their religion from the excesses and bad theology of rampant angelphilia. They opposed anything that robbed God of His sovereignty and that handed the universe over to angels, good or evil. Thus, we see among the orthodox rabbis a tendency to treat angels and devils more as metaphors and as object lessons in parables and less as real beings who make up a theological system.

The Talmud contains many legends and teachings on angels, but a movement away from the excess of the Pseudepigrapha was already underway. Among specific teachings is the idea that just as there are four winds, so four angels surround the throne of God. These are Michael, Gabriel, Uriel, and Raphael.

A number of stories about angels convey a hidden lesson. For example, one legend stated that on the day that Solomon married the princess of Egypt, the angel Gabriel stuck a reed into the sea about which a mud-bank formed. On this spot would one day stand the city of Rome. The point of the story is that when Solomon sinned by turning to a pagan princess for his queen, God began the task of preparing an enemy to destroy Jerusalem.

Another famous angelic illustration is the story that two angels, one good and the other evil, follow a man home from the synagogue on Sabbath-eve. If they found the Sabbath light burning and all prepared, the good angel would exclaim, "May it be his will that it might be like this the next Sabbath," and the demon must answer, "Amen!" The roles reverse, however, if the house is not properly prepared. The legend obviously exhorts the pious Jew not to neglect Sabbath preparations, and it illustrates how angels are on their way to becoming mere figures in parables and not real beings at this stage of Jewish religion.

Satan, too, undergoes demythologizing. He came to be identified with death and with the evil impulse in humans. Stories about him abound, but they were moral parables more than real teachings about Satan. For example, one legend states that when Israel received the Torah on Mount Sinai, the Lord summoned the angel of death (Satan) and told him he had sway over the other nations, but not Israel. The intent was to exalt the Torah as the guide to life.[31]

Later rabbis, after the completion of the Talmud, continued the movement away from the angels. For example, Moses Maimonides (1135–1204), in his *Guide to the Perplexed* affirmed the existence of angels but could also be ambiguous on the subject. He explained that "all forces are angels"[32] and even that imagination and intellect could be called angels. This calls into question whether angels are anything more than metaphors for powers. Modern Judaism, as we shall see, has all but abandoned the angels.

Early Christian and Quasi-Christian Angelology

Early Church

We cannot possibly survey all the references to angels in the writings of the early Christian church. There are just too many. We can outline, however, a few tendencies.

Some of the church fathers were wont to see angels where none were present. When interpreting the Bible, for example, they occasionally imported the notion of angels even where it was altogether inappropriate and in so doing missed the point of the text under consideration completely.

In Luke 15:1–7, some scribes complained that Jesus had no business hanging around with sinners and tax collectors, and He responded that a man who owns one hundred sheep will leave the ninety-nine in order to seek the one lost sheep. He concluded, "There will be more joy in heaven over one sinner who repents than over ninety-nine righteous persons who need no repentance" (v. 7). In saying this, Jesus did not imply that 99 percent of humanity needed no repentance, nor did He mean that the scribes with whom He spoke needed no repentance. He merely stressed that God regards seeking those who are lost in sin to be of surpassing importance and thus that it was entirely appropriate for Him to be in the company of "sinners" instead of the "righteous" scribes.

Many of the fathers, including Origen, Gregory of Nyssa, and Cyril of Jerusalem, took an altogether different tack. They took the ninety-nine sheep to be angels and concluded that the passage meant that the Son left the realm of the angels, who needed no repentance, to come and seek lost humanity.[33] Had Jesus had such an esoteric, theological meaning in mind, it no doubt would have been lost on His original audience of scribes and sinners. But context and Jesus' own words show that this was not His intent.

Still, it would not be correct to think of the fathers as angel-crazy. On the whole, they restrained their speculation and were aware of how little they really knew about angels and how hard it was to speak on the subject.[34] They developed the kind of restrained angelology that, in one form or another, has been the standard for most Christians. Augustine, in particular, described in the *City of God* the angelology that Western Christians have more or less followed ever since his time, but he did not give the matter an extravagant amount of attention.[35]

The church fathers did feel that angels were an important part of their confession, however. For one thing, belief in angels refuted the popular accusation that they were "atheists" (that is, that they rejected all the gods). They believed that angels were noncorporeal intellects whom God, out of His desire to see heaven populated with examples of His goodness and power, created to be His servants.[36] They believed that Satan and the demons fell because of pride. In fact, Anselm of Canterbury (1033–1109) felt this explained why God created humanity. God had to restore the number of the angels who had fallen, but he could not simply create more angels since their number was fixed. Therefore, He created humans, and the number of the elect would become like angels and fill the gaps in the ranks.[37]

Gnostics

The name Gnosticism, from the Greek *gnosis* ("knowledge"), implies that secret knowledge about the workings of the spiritual realms is the key to salvation.[38] Gnosticism teaches that the fundamental problem of humanity is its bondage to the material world. Matter is by nature evil, and the human spirit needs to ascend into the spiritual domain where it is free from the influence of flesh and matter.

Gnosticism was the first great heresy of the Christian faith. Its roots are obscure and much debated, but it borrowed heavily from Jewish speculation and mysticism, from Greek philosophy, and possibly also from Babylonian astrology and Persian dualism. It found fertile soil among the recently converted and sometimes poorly catechized members of the Christian church, however, and by the mid-second century A.D. it had flowered into a major threat to orthodoxy within the churches. Gnostics also were able to allegorize and otherwise twist the Bible—especially the creation narrative and John's Gospel—in order to read their teachings into Scripture. Until this century, what we knew of Gnosticism came primarily from the writings of Christian teachers who opposed and ultimately defeated it. With the discovery of the Nag Hammadi library in Egypt, however, we now have a considerable collection of ancient Gnostic documents.

Two Teams, Twelve to a Side. The Gnostics were not a unified group with a monolithic doctrine but included many sects with similar but not necessarily identical ideas; all held to some kind of process of emanation. For example, the Gnostic book *Baruch* asserts that originally three primal beings existed. These were the "Good" and Elohim (both males; Elohim is the Hebrew word for "God") and Eden (female). The "Good" remained isolated in highest purity, but Elohim (a kind of sky-god) and Eden (an earth-goddess) fell passionately in love and produced twenty-four angels (twelve on each side), who in turn created the world. Elohim gave humanity the spirit, which yearns for heaven, but Eden gave the earthly, passionate soul. Elohim with his twelve angels ascended to heaven to observe the new creation, but he was astounded to see above him the glory of the Good, whom he had not known. Elohim remained with the Good, and Eden, furious at having been abandoned, began to persecute the spirit within humans. On her side were the twelve evil angels (including Bel, Satan, Naas, and Babel), but on Elohim's side were angels such as Amen, Michael, Baruch, and Gabriel.

The two principals in the war over humanity were Naas and Baruch. Naas used various means to corrupt humanity, including having sexual relations with both Eve and Adam. Baruch, in turn, fought Naas through various heroes and prophets, including Hercules. At last, Baruch found in Jesus of Nazareth the one pure Man who could fully resist Naas. Unable to defeat Him, Naas crucified Him, but on the cross Jesus cried out, "Woman, you have your son!" and so gave His earthly, soul-dominated body to Eden while His spirit ascended to the Good and Elohim. Thus in heaven, according to the book of *Baruch*, there is a kind of trinity of the Good, Elohim, and the spirit of Jesus.[39]

The church father Hippolytus, from whom we have this account, pronounced it the most monstrous book he had ever set eyes on. Yet we see in *Baruch* certain Gnostic tendencies. It equates evil with the physical world and the appetites of the flesh. Sin in the Christian sense of rebellion against God is not an issue, nor is there any need for atonement. Jesus does not die on the cross—He abandons it. Most important for our purposes, the spiritual conflict on earth is fought among the angels. The high gods, the Good and Elohim, are at best distant observers. The reader of *Baruch* gains knowledge of the names of both the good and bad angels and thus presumably has the key to escaping the world of the flesh and ascending to the spirit.

Foolish Wisdom. Perhaps the "standard" Gnostic myth, however, is that recorded in the *Apocryphon of John*, a document as bewildering as it is grotesque. Written in the second century A.D., it falsely claims the apostle John as its author. According to the story, John one day encountered the Pharisee Arimanios, who accused Jesus of leading the people astray. Troubled, John went to meditate in a mountain and in a vision saw Jesus, who recounted all the goings-on in the heavens to him.

First, the book described the origin of all things. God is the Pneuma ("spirit") and the Eternal One. The book defined God with negative and enigmatic language since, in Gnostic thinking, it is impossible to make any meaningful affirmation about God. The following is typical. "It is neither corporeal nor incorporeal. It is not great and not small. It is not a dimension and not a creature, and none can grasp it. It is nothing that exists, but something that is more excellent."[40]

Next, the book described the "aeons" or emanations that proceeded from the Eternal One. First, the Eternal One generated "Barbelo," who is at the same time female and also androgynous. At her request, four other androgynous aeons came forth (Foreknowledge, Imperishable, Eternal Life, and Truth). These made up the first rank of aeons. She then produced Only-begotten, who is Christ. Only-begotten then produced the four great lights (Grace, Insight, Perception, and Prudence). Each of these in turn produced three more aeons (the first light, for example, produced Grace, Truth, and Form). Last of all the aeons was Sophia ("wisdom"). The entire group of emanations is called the Pleroma ("fullness"). From this, we can see that there is a kind of heavenly hierarchy that moves toward the apex, the Eternal One.

But now things began to go wrong. Sophia wanted to produce some aeons too, but did not have the consent of her partner. So she became pregnant on her own, but gave birth to a monstrous aeon, a dragon with a lion's face called Yaldabaoth (also called the "Demiurge"). Yaldabaoth immediately set out creating a dark counterpart to the Pleroma. He created twelve evil archons and ultimately had a hierarchy of 360 dark angels. In various ways, the story identifies Yaldabaoth with the Old Testament God of Israel. For example, to keep the powers under him from going over to the Pleroma, Yaldabaoth cried out, "I am a jealous God; thou shalt have no other gods before me."[41]

At this point, Yaldabaoth created man. Each of the angels of the dark realm had a part in making man, but they were unable to bring him to life. They could only give him "psychic" energy (that is, the power of the flesh and the appetites). Repentant Sophia, meanwhile, begged the Father of aeons for the means to recover her power from wicked Yaldabaoth. As a stratagem, the Father of aeons breathed spirit into Adam through the agency of Only-begotten,[42] and Adam came to life.

The dark aeons were enraged at their work having been co-opted, and they imprisoned Adam (who had originally been something like an angel) in the material world of flesh. Yaldabaoth also put Adam to sleep and created Eve and set them in paradise, which is the domain of "imitation spirit." Adam, however, ate from the tree of knowledge, which reminded him of his "perfection," the spark of divinity within. The dark angels, in fear and anger, then drove Adam and Eve out of paradise. Yaldabaoth was overcome with lust for Eve and defiled her, so that she gave birth to Cain and Abel. Yaldabaoth then planted a similar desire in Adam, and sexuality became another part of his plan to entrap humanity in this counterfeit realm.

This understanding of the human situation appears in various forms in the Gnostic literature. *The Apocalypse of Adam* tells us, for example, that Adam and Eve were originally great angels but that the Lord God who created them dragged them down into the dominion of death. Still, the knowledge of the divine status of humanity passed to Seth, and salvation was still possible. Someday the angels would receive the true Gnostics into the place where the spirit of eternal life dwells.[43]

The sum of it all is that only through knowledge of the Pleroma can one escape the bonds of the material world and make the ascent to the true realm of spirit. In the topsy-turvy world of the Gnostics, the Old Testament God, as creator of this material world, is evil; the tree of knowledge reminds us of our inner divinity and is good. Gnosticism cuts us off from God in two directions. The true God (that is, the God of the Christ) is so lofty and abstract that we can say nothing about Him; the God about whom we can speak, the God of the Bible, is an abortion of a deity.

The beings that can help us are the intermediate spirits of the Pleroma. The spirits that hurt us are the dark angels of Yaldabaoth. In short, our salvation (or damnation) is via the angels. In Gnostic thinking, death is the moment of liberation from the corruption of this material body, but only those who have true knowledge can escape. For those of us who have the impertinence to die without benefit of gnosis, there can only be further agony as we are entrapped by the seven dark archons (powerful angels) of the planetary spheres as we ascend from earth.

Angelic Orgies and Other Gnostic Notions. The Gnostics had five rituals: baptism, Eucharist, anointing, "redemption," and the "bridal-chamber." This last ritual, still a mystery to us, has intrigued many observers. The Gnostic *Gospel of Philip* regards it as the most sacred of all the rituals and the key to spiritual ascent, whereby one moves from being a mere Christian to a "Christ."

Gnostics believed (according to the *Gospel of Philip* 60–87) that demons come in both the male and female variety and that they in turn seduce humans of the opposite sex. Only those who have the power of "the bridegroom and the bride" can escape. It appears that the ritual of the bridal-chamber mystically returned the individual to the original state of androgyny that Adam and Eve had before they were separated into two people of opposite sexes. This ritual guarantees immortality and victory over the dark angels. Some interpret the bridal-chamber as a ritual marriage to an angel.

Although the bridal-chamber ritual probably did not involve actual sexuality, some Gnostic rituals may have been quite lewd. Epiphanius (315–403), bishop of Salamis, described the sexual rituals of the Egyptian

Gnostics, and if his account can be trusted, they were lurid beyond belief. The historian of Gnosticism, Giovanni Filoramo, considers Epiphanius' account reliable.[44]

We have not begun to map out all of the dark paths that cross the gloomy forest of Gnosticism. We have focused on the angelology of the Gnostics and indeed have only touched the surface of that. Still, we see the main outlines of a religion that perverts Christianity, debases the Old Testament, and proclaims secret wisdom even as it asserts that the high God is unknowable. Salvation no longer involves sin but breaking free from the illusion of the self and the material world that the self inhabits in favor of reunion with the divine Pleroma.

Gnosticism did provide a seductive, dualistic worldview. The two realms of the heavenly Pleroma and the hierarchies of Yaldabaoth stood opposed to one another. The lustful prison of the flesh separated humanity from the pure light of the Spirit. It answered some basic human longings, and its appeal was such that many adherents overlooked its self-evident absurdities.

Gnosticism as it existed in A.D. 200 has perished but, as we shall see, the notion that we need only learn the secret of our inner divinity, break the bonds of ego, and transcend this world has returned with a vengeance. Once again all of this is being accomplished, we are told, with the help of the angels.

Dionysius the Pseudo-Areopagite

The Bible tells us that Paul, during a brief stay in Athens, found himself so unsettled by all the idols he saw that he could not restrain himself from preaching to the natives. His converts were few, but among them was a "Dionysius the Areopagite" (Acts 17:34). We know nothing of him beyond his name, which implies that he was a member of the Athenian council of elders (the Areopagus). But around A.D. 500 a Syrian mystic wrote a series of short books that circulated under the name of *Dionysius the Areopagite*. These works falsely claimed apostolic authority and came to have great influence on the church. Whoever the author really was, his words show him to have been familiar with the Bible and Apocrypha as well as with the Neoplatonic philosophers Plotinus, an early opponent of Christianity, and Proclus. The Pseudo-Areopagite attempted to merge Christianity with a mystical, Neoplatonic religious philosophy.

This means that we have to take a one-minute tour of Neoplatonism. In brief, this system taught that divine light pours down from the realm of heavenly perfection and streams out into the void. At the top is God, or more accurately The One (who is not a person but an impersonal, immaterial, and incorruptible essence).

Beneath The One is a kind of ladder of existence, and this ladder goes all the way down to the depraved and irrational world of physical beings. From The One comes Mind, which is no longer one but two, because Mind includes the knower and the known. From Mind comes the World Soul, which is the power that moves the universe. Beneath the World Soul is Nature, which is where things really start to fall apart. Nature pervades the universe and, unlike The One, is full of plurality and individuality. Finally there is Matter, the primary evil.

A human is a microcosm of the whole system. The object of the game is to climb up the ladder by means of philosophy or mystical experiences. In doing this, a person can escape the perversity of physical existence. A side feature of this thinking is that the incarnation of God in Christ is not only impossible but an unimaginable scandal: God could not possibly take on human flesh.

Pseudo-Dionysius tried to reconcile Christianity with Neoplatonism, but "when a clash occurred, the neo-Platonic elements tended to prevail."[45] While he did not accept all aspects of Neoplatonic thinking, he blurred the Trinity in his desire to find The One and he uneasily fit the incarnation into his system and rarely mentioned it. Like many later mystical angelphiles, he held that "sin is largely negative, that there is nothing that is inherently evil, and that in all evil is some good."[46] The cross and regeneration had little or no place in his theology, and his writings probably would have had no influence had readers not been taken in by his pseudonym.[47]

Among Pseudo-Dionysius' writings is a study of angels called *The Celestial Hierarchies*. If any single work can be called the mother of Christian angelphilia, surely this is it. Medieval scholars such as Thomas Aquinas and Albertus Magnus, mystics such as John of the Cross and Emanuel Swedenborg, and angelic poets such as Dante and John Milton all drew upon this and the other writings of the Pseudo-Areopagite.

First and foremost, the Pseudo-Areopagite espoused a monistic theology in which God is the "Divine One."[48] Like many Eastern mystics and modern New Age gurus, he believed that true enlightenment comes when the soul recognizes the unity of all things in God. Also, like the Gnostics (but unlike most modern New Agers), he treated the material world as crude and innately antispiritual or even as evil. The purpose of the celestial hierarchies of angels, he asserted, was to further "the attainment of our due measure of deification."[49]

Commenting on how the Bible portrayed the angels in animal-like form, he was scandalized that anyone might think that heaven actually contained such creatures. For example, in Revelation 4:6–8 angels have the forms of a lion, an ox, an eagle, and a man. Pseudo-Dionysius argued that the Bible used animal imagery in order to help us understand that the spiritual world was of pure thought and untainted by the corruption of matter. He said that if the sages had portrayed the angels as shining men, we might be tempted to think that they actually have bodies. By portraying angels as beasts, he claimed, the text made us realize that in reality they were pure thought united to the oneness of God. The ugliness of the animals encouraged us to abandon all material attachments. Also, he confided, these images concealed the truths of divine enlightenment from the unwashed masses.[50]

Pseudo-Dionysius was not the only one to propose that the angels had a hierarchy of ranks. The bishops Ambrose and Gregory the Great and the Rabbi Moses Maimonides also set forth celestial hierarchies,[51] but Pseudo-Dionysius' pecking order is the most famous and most imitated. He says that there are three threefold orders of angels, or nine ranks of angels altogether. This number scheme is probably no accident; the Neoplatonist Proclus placed mediating gods in his hierarchy to The One in groups of three and nine. Pseudo-Dionysius' angels are, from greatest to least: Seraphim, Cherubim, Thrones, Dominions, Virtues, Powers, Principalities, Archangels, and Angels. These are arranged in groups of three each.

Pseudo-Dionysius gave us a pseudo-hierarchy. We have no basis for knowing whether this chain of command in any way reflects the real world of angels. But our guide did not stop here. He described each order and explained their names, but he did so in a manner that shed more light on his own religious philosophy than on the nature of angels. For example, in his description of the "Thrones" he said little more than that they were "exempt from and untainted by any base and earthly thing," that they were the "supermundane ascent up the steep," and that they "receive the Divine immanence above all passion and matter."[52]

In this, we see that the Pseudo-Areopagite was more a follower of Neoplatonism than of Christ. He demonstrated a disdain for the created world—"base and earthly thing" and "passion and matter"—notwithstanding the fact that God calls it "good" in Genesis 1. His language sounds strangely impersonal, and the phrase "ascent up the steep" is more at home in Gnosticism or Neoplatonism than Christianity. At the same time—and this is the odd part—he does not really tell us anything at all about the order of angels called "Thrones." In Pseudo-Dionysius, mystical philosophy masquerades as secret knowledge about angels. Subsequent theologians of the church, we should add, forgot all about the purpose behind the hierarchies of Pseudo-Dionysius and simply added the idea of a nine-fold hierarchy in three triads to their body of received instruction on the nature of angels.

The Celestial Hierarchies, therefore, is in a real sense not about angels at all. It draws the reader into what is purported to be angelic ranks in order to get him on the ladder of spiritual ascent. We should not, therefore, treat this as quaint speculation. Behind this apparently innocent and almost silly attempt to rank the angels is a system of belief that profoundly negates the self and the world.

☙

CHAPTER SIX

O world invisible, we view thee,
O world intangible, we touch thee,
O world unknowable, we know thee,
Inapprehensible, we clutch thee!
FRANCIS THOMPSON, "THE KINGDOM OF GOD"

O World Unknowable

A Brief History of Angelology, Part 2

THE ANGELPHILIA OF THE ANCIENT JEWS, CHRISTIANS, and heretical groups is illustrative in that these groups show us the paths that angelphilia tends to take. The study of angels that has taken place since the medieval era, however, has more directly influenced current thinking on angels. It is time for us to consider the teachings and contributions of the modern Western world on angels.

Thomas Aquinas

Thomas Aquinas (1224–74) is pivotal in the history of Christianity. It could be argued that from the death of the apostles until the Protestant Reformation, Aquinas influenced Christian thinking more than any other single man. And unlike many modern theologians, he was vitally interested in angels. In his massive *Summa theologica* alone, for example, he answered in detail a staggering 118 specific questions about angels.

Two major factors influenced Aquinas's discussion of angels. The first was Christian teaching as embodied in the Scriptures and the writings of the church fathers and councils. Unfortunately, this included the conjectures of Pseudo-Dionysius. The second was an Aristotelian approach to reasoning and philosophy. With these as his foundation, Aquinas proceeded to discuss angels in a manner that at first glance borders on omniscience.

In *Summa contra gentiles* 2.91, Aquinas developed eight proofs for the existence of angels. He argued, for example, that just as the human soul can exist apart from the body after death, so angels can exist without bodies. What becomes of humans as the result of the death of the body angels already are by nature. He also stated that a mind in a body is a lower, imperfect order of creation. Thus (since God's creation abhors a vacuum) a higher, more nearly perfect, noncorporeal order of minds must exist also. Similarly, he argued that perception through the senses makes for an imperfect form of knowing, since it suffers the limits of sensory perception. This again means that creatures capable of perception without use of the senses must exist lest God's creation be painfully incomplete.[1]

This is only the beginning of his angelic theology. Is an angel incorporeal? Do angels differ in species? Are angels incorruptible? Can an angel be in several places at once? Do angels know themselves and know one another? Do angels know the future? Can they know secret thoughts? Were they created before the world? Aquinas set out fearlessly to answer all these questions and many more in his treatise on angels in the *Summa theologica.*

As an example of his method, we can consider "Question LII: Of the Angels in Relation to Place." He examined whether an angel is in a place, whether an angel can be in several places at once, and whether several angels can be at the same time in the same place. He rejected the idea that an angel is not in any specific place. Against the argument that an angel has no quantitative size and therefore cannot inhabit a place, he responded that an angel can be said to be in a place by virtue of his exercise of angelic power on that place. Properly, he said, a place does not contain an angel but an angel contains a place. He then argued that an angel cannot be in several places at once but only in one place at a time since, unlike God, the angel can apply his power to only one place at a time. He finally contended that several angels cannot be in the same place at the same time. He cited the analogy of the human body, which can only have one soul, and not two, and noted that it is impossible that two complete causes bring about at the same time one event. He rejected the idea that possession of a single body by several demons proves that several angels can be in one place at the same time since "the soul is of [the body's] form, while the demon is not."[2]

Aquinas's discussion of angels naturally reflected his own era and the traditions he received. He accepted, for example, the traditional hierarchy of nine ranks of angels. Like many before him, he claimed that angels move the heavenly bodies since otherwise the stars would rest in their "natural place." A more curious case is what he regarded as the three influences on people, namely, God, guardian angels, and the "celestial bodies" (that is, the stars). He contended that God's influence on a person can never fail but that the influence of an angel or a celestial body can. He distinguished between the influence of an angel and the influence of the stars by asserting that the celestial bodies work on a man "by means of some passion, as when a person is led to choose something by means of hatred, or love, or anger" but that a person "is disposed to an act of choice by an angel by means of intellectual consideration, without passion."[3] As always, Aquinas carefully reasoned out his answers, but for those of us who have no faith in the powers of "celestial bodies," the whole exercise loses its significance. We should note that Aquinas did not believe in astrology.

If we dismiss Aquinas as "prescientific" and therefore having nothing to say to us, however, we miss the insights of a man who profoundly wrestled with issues that confront us to the present day. For example, Thomas so formulated his doctrine of angels that he avoided entirely any kind of *monism*. This is the notion that "all is one" and it was near the center of heated academic debates in his day;[4] in our day it has reappeared in a very different guise in the angelphilia of the New Age movement. As we shall see, monism has devastating consequences on our view of God (He is obliterated), ourselves (we become "God"), creation (it is illusory), and morality (it is insignificant).

Aquinas also refuted any notion of emanation. He observed that it takes away God's omnipotence in creation. If God only created one or a few angels, and these angels then produced other angels or powers, and still other beings proceeded from the lower angels, then God is no longer God. God no longer directly created all things, from highest angel to a frog on a rock. Aquinas explained that angels have the power to move things but not to create them,[5] and in so doing he repudiated Neoplatonic thinking and upheld the biblical doctrine of creation.[6]

Aquinas also helped us understand the differences between God, ourselves, and the angels. Using a word you probably would not hear even on "Jeopardy," he said that angels are *aeviternal*. You and I and the physical world are *temporal*. We change both in ourselves (we can grow, go bald, or be burned to ashes) and in our actions (we can move to a different location or scratch our ears). God is *eternal*. This means more than that He exists forever; He is completely above time and change. Angels are *aeviternal*. They do not change in their nature but do change in their actions (they do not die or grow senile, but they do, for example, move from one place to another).

How, then, might we evaluate Aquinas? An obvious problem is that people and books that were authoritative to him may be at best quaint for us. Many of the issues he raised we are happy to leave at rest, and many of the arguments he put forward depend on presuppositions we cannot accept. The greatest problem with Aquinas, however, is that he missed how angels function under Christ. We shall return to this issue when we treat Karl Barth's interpretation of angels.

On the other hand, the sheer intellectual power of Aquinas—in combination with his faith and devotion—means that he has something to teach us. If nothing else, he helps us learn how to think about God, ourselves, and the angels. In the next chapter of this book, when we wrestle with key angel questions, we will find his guidance invaluable.

John Calvin

Widely regarded as one of the finest interpreters of the Bible in the history of Christendom, John Calvin lived from 1509 to 1564. He spent much of his adult life as a pastor in Geneva, Switzerland, and passed on to posterity numerous Bible commentaries and his major theological work, *The Institutes of the Christian Religion*. In this work, he makes a few comments on angels.

To begin with, he believed in angels and stated that they are "heavenly spirits, whose obedience and ministry God employs to execute all the purposes which he has decreed." He noted that in Scripture we learn "how they watch for our safety, how they undertake our defense, direct our path, and take heed that no evil befall us." He rejected the view of the Sadducees, that angels are not real beings but mere "manifestations which [God] gives us his own power."

On the other hand, he rejected every attempt to go beyond what is written in Scripture on the subject of angels: "Wherefore, if we would be duly wise, we must renounce those vain babblings of idle men, concerning the nature, ranks, and number of angels, without any authority from the Word of God." He dismissed Pseudo-Dionysius as "nugatory wisdom."

He was similarly cool to the idea of a guardian angel. "Whether or not each believer has a single angel assigned to him for his defense, I dare not positively affirm." He *did* affirm that the Bible speaks of angels watching over God's people, but he does not see this as confirming the idea of a single, lifelong companion. "If anyone does not think it enough to know that all the orders of the heavenly host are perpetually watching for his safety, I do not see what he could gain by knowing that he has one angel as a special guardian."[7] He also had little use for angel names, orders, and ranks.

John Milton

Angels and devils play a major role in the great poetry of Western Civilization. In the *Divine Comedy*, Dante travels through hell, purgatory, and heaven in an allegorical pilgrimage of the soul. His Satan is remarkable for dwelling at the center of hell, not in sulfurous flames, but in a frozen lake. Goethe's *Faust* explores the depths of human experience with the dubious aid of Mephistopheles. Surely no epic of literature, however, focuses as totally on the realm of angels and demons as does John Milton's *Paradise Lost*.

You do not need me to tell you that Milton is a great poet, and indeed my assessment of his work as an artistic achievement should not be of interest to anyone. Nor is there any point to analyzing Milton's theology as it is revealed in the poem. That is, at any rate, a difficult thing to do since "poetic license" covers all with a blanket of ambiguity. I do, however, want to observe in Milton how the very process of imagining angels and devils distorts any meaningful angelology.

John Milton (1608–74) lived through the most turbulent religious era of English history. Educated at Cambridge, his life's ambition was to achieve immortality as a poet. His father was a Protestant, and in his youth he subscribed without reservation to the teachings of the *Book of Common Prayer.* An ardent supporter of Cromwell and the Puritan party, he sacrificed his eyesight to the work of writing pamphlets in defense of their policies. The downfall of the Commonwealth left him not only a political outcast but sightless as well. During these dark years, he dictated *Paradise Lost* to his daughters.

His religious life was remarkable in itself. He maintained the astonishing habit of rising every morning at four o'clock to study the Hebrew Bible (after the onset of blindness, it was read to him). His Christian life, however, was not altogether consistent. He abandoned the Calvinism of the Puritans for an Arminian theology (which stresses the free will of man) and, more importantly, embraced a heterodox view of God. Instead of seeing the Son and Holy Spirit as coequal with the Father, he viewed them as lesser beings. Specifically, Milton embraced Arian theology (which regards the Son as a creature). He had once considered entering the clergy, but by the end of his life he had abandoned church entirely.

Paradise Lost sets out to "justify the ways of God to men" (*Paradise Lost* 1, 26).[8] It begins with a jolt. We find ourselves in hell alongside Satan and all the demons just expelled from heaven. They rouse themselves from the agonies of the inferno and begin to set things in order. He calls them into council, where he and the other arch-devils debate their next move. Should they have another go at open combat with the angels and try to storm heaven's gate? At length they determine instead to do an end run against heaven; they will strike God at His weakest point, the newly created man, and by corrupting him, "waste his whole creation, or possess all as our own" (2, 365–66).[9]

Along the way we learn that, prior to their incarceration in hell, Satan and his hordes had turned against God on the day He announced that they should all accept the authority of the Son over them. The two sides then prepared for battle (they wore full armor and carried spears), with Michael leading the angels and Satan leading the demons. Tumultuous warfare ensued, albeit in the awkward circumstance that both sides were immortal and thus neither could gain a really meaningful victory— although the angels had the advantage of moral purity. As the first day's battle ended and night fell (for there is night in this heaven), both sides retired to their camps.

Satan then devised a secret weapon. His demons hastily mined the soil of heaven for bronze and iron, found other minerals for powder, and the next day confronted the angels with blasts of artillery! The bewildered choirs of loyal spirits tumbled back helplessly against the wicked onslaught until at last they hit upon a crude but effective counterattack. The angels picked up the mountains of heaven and began hurling them at the rebel foe, which was more than enough to offset the temporary advantage of Satan's prototype cannons. So it would have gone on forever, with one side and then the other gaining brief but meaningless success. God, however, finally sent the Son, mounted in His chariot, to confront the Satanic hordes. Immediately all conflict ended, and a rout ensued. The demons could not for a minute stand before the Son, and they tumbled helter-skelter into the fires of hell, where we found them at the beginning of the poem. (This story of the rebellion is given in a flashback related to Adam by Raphael during a leisurely conversation in Eden.)

Back in hell, you will recall, the devils decided to attempt to corrupt humanity rather than risk open combat against heaven again. But there is a problem. Hell is locked tight and surrounded by a great chasm that can be crossed only at great risk. Satan rose to the occasion, however, and volunteers that he alone must take the risk and make the journey:

> But I should ill become this Throne, O Peers,
> And this Imperial Sov'ranty, adorn'd
> With splendour, arm'd with power, if aught propos'd
> And judg'd of public moment, in the shape
> Of difficulty or danger could deter
> Me from attempting.

(2, 445–50)[10]

Against great peril he makes the journey and through trickery gains access to Eden. To make a long story short, he then draws Eve and Adam into sin, and they lose paradise.

What do we make of all this? At the outset, it is obvious that Milton's angels and devils are remarkably human and his heaven is surprisingly earthy. It is enough that they fight with spears and shields, that they encamp at night, and that they hold council meetings of the ranking demons or angels. Things get totally out of hand when they start shooting cannons and throwing hills at one another. Each side, like any army, passionately believes in its side and rallies when it hears good news. Except for their immortality and their ability to fly, you would never know that they were anything other than human.[11]

Then there is the troubling feature of Satan's heroics. People who know a great deal more about this poem than I argue that it is entirely misguided to take Satan as the hero of the epic, notwithstanding the tendency of some pesky critics to do just that. Scholars observe, for example, that Satan shows heroic fortitude and selflessness only early in his career, well before the full corrupting force of his fall from grace takes effect. As the book progresses, Satan and his hordes undergo moral decay until all become snakes![12]

Even so, the fact remains that in a fair part of the book Satan looks heroic and behaves in a heroic manner. We cannot fail to notice Satan's willingness to put himself at peril in the effort to break himself and his followers out of hell. Regardless of what the "correct" interpretation of the poem is, we see in Milton's devil something more than the one whom Jesus called simply the "father of lies" (John 8:44). The mere fact that Milton apologists have to prove that Milton's Satan is the villain tells us something. (Shakespearean scholars rarely have to prove that Lady Macbeth or *Othello's* Iago are villains.)

Simply put, these very human spirits have little relation to the angels and demons of the Bible. As humans, we cannot tell a story that is anything other than a human story. In the very act of imagining spirits and inventing stories about them, we humanize them and so construct idols. These angels look less than angelic and these demons look better than demonic. We create spirits in our own image: this is the very essence of myth. As we are mixtures of good and evil, so are they. *Paradise Lost* is such a work; it is no more a story of real angels than Ovid's *Metamorphoses* is a story of real gods.

I have derived great pleasure from the *Iliad*, the *Odyssey*, the *Aeneid*, and even from more modern myths such as *The Lord of the Rings*. I cannot say the same for *Paradise Lost*. I do not reject it because I think it is a bad poem or because its author was an Arian or even because one can make a case that Satan is the hero (actually, I think one can make a better case in the other direction). I reject this work because I believe that it is fundamentally impious to subject God, Christ, and the angels to this kind of fantasizing (and fundamentally misleading to do the same with the devil). It is all well and good for

Homer and Virgil to invent incidents and conversations involving the Olympian gods, but it is entirely inappropriate to apply such reverie to the God of the Bible. To do so simply reduces Christianity to epic myth.

Therefore, whatever its value may be to world literature, I do not believe that *Paradise Lost* aids or illuminates the Christian faith.[13] Still less do I regard it as an accurate portrayal of angels. Tragically, many Christians, whether they have read the poem or not, look to this account as the orthodox version of the fall of Satan and of humanity.

Emanuel Swedenborg

Angelphiles everywhere know the name of Emanuel Swedenborg. The Swedish-born scientist-turned-mystic (1688–1772) wrote some thirty volumes of theology under the guidance of angels with whom he claimed to have daily conversations.

He was a man of extraordinary talent and energy. An accomplished mathematician, engineer, and researcher, he developed Sweden's mining industry, studied cosmology and sensory perception, produced Sweden's first scientific journal, and speculated about the possibility of flying machines and submarines. But he also had a religious background (his father was a Protestant minister), and in 1744 he had a personal crisis when he began having bizarre dreams, many of a sexual nature, and he felt profound guilt over his intellectual pride. He gave up science and devoted the rest of his life to spiritual pursuits.

His experience was more than a typical act of "getting religion," however. He claimed to have experienced a vision of God so powerful that it opened up his senses to the heavenly realms. Thereafter, he could see and converse with angels as easily as another person could see and hear the world. He believed that this revelation to him was the actual fulfillment of the promise of the Second Coming. "Unlike the first advent, which required God's personal presence, the second coming could be made through the human mind of Emanuel Swedenborg."[14]

The theology that came out of this experience did not accord well with traditional Christianity. He rejected the received understanding of the Trinity (one God eternally in three persons) and instead held that "In the Lord is the Trinity—the Divine Itself, the Divine Human, and the proceeding Divine Holy—and these are one. Before the world was created this Trinity was not."[15]

Swedenborg also took a different view of redemption. He believed that humanity suffered under the oppression of "hells." These were communities of the spirits of evil men, and they sought to dominate people. He believed that Jesus allowed into Himself temptations from these evil spirits but resisted them entirely. By doing this, He ended their power. This allowed divine power to break into human existence, and it became a great wall between humanity and the hells and so enabled people to escape the power of the evil spirits. People are therefore at liberty to obey God, and their salvation depends on whether they are willing to accept the truth. Following the example of Jesus, people can achieve unification of their spiritual and material selves.[16]

Many of Swedenborg's theories, with their combination of mysticism and eighteenth century science, are as peculiar as they are quaint. He taught that angels have many of the same characteristics as humans (eating, breathing, reading, enjoying marriage and sexuality, and so forth), and that godly people enjoy all these things after death too.[17] Elsewhere, however, he conceived of angels as something like bubbles in the sky. "[A]ll parts of the bodies of angels and spirits, external as well as internal, are held together in connection by atmospheres, the external by air and the internal by ethers. Without the surrounding pressure and action of these atmospheres the interior and exterior forms of the body would evidently dissolve away."[18] ("Ether" is a hypothetical substance that scientists once believed was the medium for light as it traveled through space. All attempts to prove its existence failed, and Einstein's special theory of relativity finally proved it to be unnecessary.) Also, apparently not content with the Genesis 1 version of things, Swedenborg taught that God did not create rats, scorpions, foxes, tigers, bats, crocodiles, frogs, snakes, owls, or the like. They come from hell.[19]

Swedenborg's ideas once had quite a following. His admirers have included Helen Keller, Ralph Waldo Emerson, and William Butler Yeats. By now, of course, his books are largely forgotten (and not very easy to find), and his movement is all but defunct. This is an unfortunate end for what was supposed to be the Second Coming.

Swedenborg serves as a warning to us of the danger of angel-inspired religion. Just as he claimed to have daily conversation with angels and to receive regular revelation from the heavens, so too today a new group of angelphiles claims new angelic revelations, as we shall see. "But even if we or an angel from heaven should proclaim to you a gospel contrary to what we proclaimed to you, let that one be accursed!" (Gal. 1:8).

Karl Barth

The great Swiss theologian Karl Barth (1886–1968) has given us the most important and exhaustive study of angels from a neoorthodox Protestant perspective. From the outset, he lets us know what are the bounds of his angelology: "The first of these clarifications must necessarily consist in the proposition that the teacher and master which we must keep in this matter can only be the Holy Scriptures of the Old and New Testament, that we must not accept any other authority, that we must respect what it says and what it does not say."[20] In this respect, he stands shoulder to shoulder with Calvin.

Over against Barth stood Thomas Aquinas, whom he censured even while praising his intellectual precision. Above everything else, Barth wanted a Christian faith that is dynamic in its focus on the Word of God, powerfully transforming all that it contacts. The last thing he wanted was a static, edifice-like theology that impresses all with its logical acuity but lacks power. He saw such a system in Aquinas, whose work reduced angelology to absurdity "by its very exactitude."[21] For Barth, Aquinas gave us an angelology that tells all about who they are and what is the nature of their being and yet misses the main thing—their role in the saving event in Christ.

Barth wanted an angelology that did not mix biblical theology with philosophy. He pointed out that the Bible "tells us nothing, for example, about the much ventilated question of the 'nature' of angels, whether they are persons, or what is their relationship to the physical world and to space, their number and order, their creation, their original unity, their ensuing division into angels and demons, and many other things which later there was both the desire and a supposed ability to know."[22] To try to move beyond the Bible and answer these questions is to miss the point entirely.

The point, for Barth, is that the angels themselves stand upon the once-for-all event of the work of God in Christ. Apart from Christ, angels as such have no significance in the Christian faith. At the same time, the fact that the Bible speaks so frequently of angels forces us to address the issue. Modern theology prefers to pass over them in silence. For Barth, ever the biblical theologian, this was an impossibility.

Barth focused on the distinction between heaven and earth. For him, this was not a static hierarchy in which earth is the lowly, dirty, inferior sphere of existence whereas heaven is the high, pure, immaterial sphere of existence. No celestial hierarchies here. Rather, both heaven and earth are subordinate to God. Heaven and earth differ from one another in respect to the activity of God. God has chosen earth as the place of His work. It is where He manifests Himself and where His plan—a plan that centers on humanity—unfolds. On earth, the eternal God enters history. This is the glory of earth. Heaven, by contrast, is the place from which the plan of God originates. God's activity begins in heaven and has earth as its destination. The distinction between heaven and earth is not a static quality or a hierarchy but a matter of where each fits in the plan of God. The superiority of heaven is not in itself but in that it is the place from which God rules and works and sends His Word.

Barth insisted that the biblical "hosts of the Lord" must include angels and not just the stars in heaven and the army of Israel on earth. He further contended that the plurality of the "hosts" who attend the Lord implies multiplicity, individuality, and order among the ranks of heaven. While he asserted that we cannot know angels in and of themselves, but only as agents of God's saving work as they perform various functions, he still could say quite a bit about them. For example, it "is their existence and nature to observe the will of God and stand at His disposal."[23]

Barth everywhere saw the work of the angels as subordinate to and glorifying the work of God in Christ. Examining Revelation 4, he observed that two classes of angels appear. The "four living creatures" represent the earthly realm, whereas the "twenty-four elders" represent the heavenly realm. He noticed that the twenty-four elders prostrate themselves before the throne after the four creatures (vv. 8–11). This is not because one group outranks the other in some kind of heavenly hierarchy. Rather, it is because the action of God on earth is the real occasion for the heavenly praise. The saving work of the Lamb prompts the angelic adulation of the Lord. In Revelation 5, all the angels join in praising Christ, the Lamb, for redeeming humanity with His blood. All of heaven focuses on this event.[24]

Angels are therefore ministers of God in His work of bringing salvation from heaven to earth. They are servants in the Christ-event. This means that any desire for an encounter with angels is folly. They are real, but they have no purpose of themselves to communicate to us. A faith that does not focus exclusively on God in Christ is demonic, even if it claims to experience angels. An angel that tarries among humans is no angel.

Similarly, a human cannot respond to the work of God by turning his back on humanity in order to join the ranks of the angels in mystical bliss. The angels have their sphere of praise and service, and we have ours. We must be ministers of the work of God on earth as they are creatures of heaven. Anything else is Gnostic.[25]

This does not mean for a moment that Christianity could do just as well without the angels. To the contrary, angels are pure witnesses of God to earth. They bring heaven to earth. When they speak it is God who speaks, and when they act it is God who acts. Since they are manifestations of heaven on earth, they stand against all idolatry as an attempt to comprehend heaven in earthly terms. If we do not acknowledge the angels, then we do not understand the mission of God in Christ. Barth went so far as to say, "To deny the angels is to deny God himself."[26]

Angels stand above humanity in that they directly witness the work of God, Barth contended, but they are below humanity in that God's work is directed toward people and not them. As pure servants and witnesses, they do not cooperate with God as fellow-laborers but simply move in complete accordance with His will. They do not in any way govern, plan, or originate the movement of grace from heaven to earth, but they are a part of that movement. They fill the atmosphere of heaven, and when they touch earth, it is heaven come in contact with this world. If the angels did not come here, then heaven would have no place here either. It is impossible that the great work of God, the bringing of heaven down to earth in Christ, could happen without the angels being present.[27]

Angels appear at the decisive moments of God's movement of grace between heaven and earth. Angels announced the conception and birth of Jesus (Luke 1 and 2), they gave the news that He had risen from the dead (Matt. 28:5–6), and were present at His ascension into heaven (Acts 1:10–11). In all this they serve as witnesses of the heavenly glory come down to earth and as manifestations of the presence of the kingdom of heaven. Still, they do not themselves accomplish anything—the work of salvation is all a work of God in Christ. They are notable for their absence during the earthly ministry of Jesus. They neither remain among humans nor empower them, since this would exceed the limits of the ministry of the heavenly witnesses.[28] We might also note that the angels accompany Christ in His return.

In short, the angels were for Barth a necessary annex to Christology.[29] They bring heavenly glory and mystery to earth, but they never do it in any context but that of the history of God's saving work in the Son as it develops from the beginning of Genesis to the end of the age. In them we see evidence that heaven has come down to earth. An angelology that focuses on anything other than Christ cannot be called a biblical angelology. The spirits of the occult, theosophy, and other religions cannot even rightly be called angels ("messengers") since the very term subordinates them to the gospel of Jesus Christ.[30]

Barth's determination to avoid abstract metaphysical speculation on the angels is both commendable and impossible to maintain. On the one hand, we must constantly remind ourselves how little we really know about the nature of the angels, even as we search the Scriptures that only describe their work. On the other hand, we cannot avoid saying something, however tentative, about who and what they are. Even Barth could not escape this.

When he claimed that the angels never "cooperate" with God, but that they simply carry out His will in the same way that a blade of grass bends in the direction that the wind pushes it,[31] what is this but a description of angelic nature? Philosophical reflection on angels does not necessarily corrupt biblical faith, just as theological constructs about the divine nature (for example, the doctrine of Trinity) do not necessarily demean a biblical understanding of God. We do, however, need to exercise great caution and remember the examples of excess and mythology that have bedeviled the angelology of Judaism and Christianity.

In his introduction to the study of angels, Barth gave a great deal of attention to the issue of whether faith needs to be supplemented by understanding. He rejected the idea that philosophical analysis can buttress our faith in the biblical doctrine of angels, and he even considered it harmful.[32] On the whole, I agree.

But is there not something else to say here? Even if we reject philosophy as a guide to or defense of the notion of angels, we can still use reason to enunciate what we believe. By "enunciate," I mean only that we ought to be able to clarify what we mean when we say, "I believe in angels." Christians do this very thing, for example, when they enunciate what they mean when they say, "I believe that Jesus is the Son of God." We may never understand fully either the incarnation or the angels, but we ought to have some notion of what we mean when we use the words.

Geddes MacGregor

Our last stop in the history of angelology is a theory that could have only originated in the last half of this century—that the angels are really a superevolved race of extraterrestrials. This is not the opinion of some New Age quack but of a respected philosopher of religion, albeit one who comes from southern California. Geddes MacGregor is Emeritus Distinguished Professor of Philosophy from the University of Southern California. His book, *Angels: Ministers of Grace*, reflects a lifetime of learning, and he makes his case with admirable lucidity.

Simply stated, his argument goes like this: First, humanity has long believed in angels. Second, we know that we got here by evolution. Third, because of the incomprehensible immensity of the universe and the countless star systems it contains, we can reasonably assume that life evolved on other planets. Fourth, we are still evolving ourselves, and we can likewise assume that some planets are ahead of us and some are behind us in the evolutionary trek. Fifth, therefore, we can assume that some life forms are as far ahead of us as we are ahead of "Lucy," the three-million-year-old remains of *Australopithecus afarensis*. Finally, sixth, these beings may be the spirits that communicate with us on a preconscious level as angels.[33]

The notion that the gods of the ancient world were really aliens is not new. The idea appears in many science fiction works and in some quasi-serious popular works. In the motion picture *Stargate*, the Egyptian god Ra was really an alien posing as a god.

MacGregor's case fails for two reasons. First, his scientific underpinnings are not as strong as he thinks. While this is not the place to go into it, the "fact" of evolution, on which he builds his case, is not established. Notwithstanding the antiquity of the universe and the fossil record, the case for evolution has many shortcomings.[34] Even if evolution or some form of it is granted, we cannot say that a long evolutionary road stretches out ahead of us. Some evolutionists believe that we are at the end of that road. Also, we cannot be sure that life exists on other planets. In reality, the number of conditions required for life to exist is immense, and some scientists have cogently argued that the odds against there being another life-bearing planet in the universe are enormous.[35]

More to the point, however, is the fact that if what we call angels are really superevolved aliens, then they are not angels at all but are aliens pretending to be angels. An angel is not simply more powerful or more advanced than us but is altogether a different category of being. An angel, by definition, is noncorporeal. We will get into this later in this book. For now we only need to recognize that an angel either has no body at all or has a body that is not composed of the stuff of this universe or of our physics.

Life on earth has always been by nature corporeal and, even if one grants the reality of evolution, it still is. Comments about how amazingly far advanced we are over "Lucy" miss the point entirely. We are no less creatures of flesh and blood than she was. We may be far advanced over jellyfish and snails, but we need oxygen and water and food, and we are still weighed down by gravity's hold on our bodies. Any life that evolved on other worlds would be the same since it, too, would be part of this universe, would be governed by the laws of physics, and would be of material substance. It is not reasonable to think that any species could evolve out of its essential, basic physics. A superevolved being that called itself an angel would be, like *Stargate's* Ra, a charlatan using high-tech smoke and mirrors.

⊛

It is not known precisely where angels dwell—
whether in the air, the void, or the planets.
It has not been God's pleasure that we should be informed of their abode.
VOLTAIRE

Precisely Where Angels Dwell

Major Questions about the Angels

THE TIME HAS COME FOR US TO FACE UP TO A FEW BASIC
questions about angels. Do they exist? What are they like? Do we have
guardian angels? I do not think I can tell you precisely where angels dwell.
(The answer "heaven" probably does not meet many people's standards
for precision.)

Still, our knowledge of them is not so sparse that we must shut our
mouths and say absolutely nothing. We can at least find out something
about the limits of our knowledge and learn how to think about angels.
That alone is worth the effort we invest.

Climbing the Chain of Being: Do Angels Exist?

This may seem an odd question to pose this late in the book; up until
now I have simply assumed with you that angels do exist. But it is time
to spell out what until now I have only implied.

You may reject the existence of angels for three different reasons, or you may believe in angels for three different reasons. Against the existence of angels, you may argue that spirits—minds without bodies—cannot exist, and therefore that angels do not exist. Or you may claim that belief in angels survives only as a relic of primitive religion. From this perspective, you could argue that angels are merely the church's way of baptizing a primitive, superstitious belief in good and bad spirits as are found in voodoo and the like. Anyone who continues to believe in such beings merely does so out of a desire that it be so, perhaps out of a Freudian neurosis. Or you can assert that angels and demons merely personify the works of God or the actions of nature, as well as qualities such as health, virtue, evil, or disasters. In this way of thinking, angels are not actual persons but a poetic way of thinking of the laws of physics or of God's activity in the world. In the terms of Jung's psychology, angels are part of the intricate religious symbolism of the human mind. Satan, too, in this mode of thinking, does not really exist but only gives a face and a name to the idea of evil.

On the other hand, you may believe in angels on the basis of the authority of the Bible (or, perhaps, on the basis of the Koran or the Book of Mormon). Or you may accept angels as real because you have seen one yourself or because you believe the accounts of people who say that they have had experiences with angels. Or you may be one of those rare individuals who has considered the philosophical argument for the existence of angels and has come to believe that they really exist.

The notion that angels are mere metaphors does not have a metaphorical leg to stand on. Of course, in poetry and even ordinary language we all speak of angels in nonliteral ways (for example, a child who is a "little angel"), but our real concern here is with the Bible. That is where the issue really comes out.

Some people prefer to take all biblical references to angels as metaphoric descriptions of the work of God or as personifications of His power, but this will not do. The Bible contains far too many references to angels that can only mean that they are actual, spiritual persons (1 Pet. 1:12, for example). To read the Bible with another sense would be to give it a meaning that would not have occurred to the original readers and was almost certainly not in the minds of the original authors. In the same way, when Matthew 4 describes a conversation between Jesus and Satan, it is unreasonable to take it other than as a real conversation between two real persons.

The opinion that belief in angels is a mere hangover from primitive religion is guilt by association rather than logical argumentation. It goes something like this: "Primitive peoples believed in all kinds of spirits, and we all know that they were wrong, don't we? Angels are spirits. So people who believe in angels are wrong." Aside from the patently illogical progression of this argument, it also presupposes some points while ignoring crucial questions.

It presumes that polytheistic spirit worship is the most backward form of religion and that religion has since evolved through monotheism and is now attaining pantheism in which "everything is God." Against this, some have pointed out that a pantheistic kind of religion, far from being the most evolved form of spirituality, may be the most primitive. As C. S. Lewis has observed, "Pantheism is congenial to our minds not because it is the final stage in a slow process of enlightenment, but because it is almost as old as we are. It may even be the most primitive of all religions."[1] Even so, do we really know that "primitive" peoples who contact spirits are altogether wrong? While I believe that followers of shamanistic and voodoo-like religion are misguided and that much of their religion is myth, it is another thing to say that the spirits they fear have no existence.

While it is possible to argue that many of the *functions* that people wrongly ascribe to angels may reflect a pagan background, that does not mean that angels *as such* do not exist. We should always keep in mind the thoroughly nonmythological presentation of angels in the Bible (in which angels do not drive the machinery of heaven, rarely have personal names, are not controlled by rituals and magic potions, and so forth). This begs the question of whether the Bible's presentation of angels has anything to do with pagan antecedents.

Psychological analyses of belief in angels tell us nothing about whether angels really exist. On this point, Geddes MacGregor has correctly stated that psychological critiques of religion "are no more studies of religion than studies in the psychology of bird-watching are studies of bird-watching."[2]

Do "eyewitness accounts" prove that angels exist? Not really. Of course, if you believe that you have encountered an angel, far be it from me to tell you that you are mistaken. For the rest of us, such anecdotes may encourage faith in angels but do not qualify as proof. Despite the explosion of angel-encounter stories in recent books and television specials, the fact remains that the vast majority of people, be they religious or not, have never encountered an angel. As objective evidence for their existence, angel sightings are only slightly more significant than the equally common (and to detractors, equally weird) UFO sightings. But we will say more about this later.

We still must deal with the thorny issue of whether we can accept the very idea of an angel—an intelligence without a body—as a real possibility or must reject it as a palpable absurdity. In one corner stand the materialists, who say that everything in existence, including minds and the process of thinking, is a function of matter and can be reduced to material processes. In other words, our thoughts are no more than the result of chemical functions in the brain, and therefore there can be no thoughts where there is no physical brain; hence the absurdity of the idea of a mind without a body. In the other corner stand all who affirm the possibility of a spiritual reality that is separate from the physical world.

Consider the notion of a round square. Now a round square is not just something that does not exist; it is something that cannot exist. It is by definition impossible and is actually inconceivable. Is a "mind without a body" like that? No. While some may find the idea hard to swallow, it contains no self-contradiction and is conceivable. Someone may claim that a mind without a body does not exist, but no one can say that it is a self-evident impossibility. We can imagine that angels are spiritual beings who do not partake of any of the properties of physicality that exist in this universe. The materialist can argue that angels are conceivable but do not exist (like unicorns) but has no right to say that angels are inconceivable and cannot exist (like round squares).

Now consider a human mind. Two things stand out here. The first is that the mind is able both to perceive and to think. Perceiving is something we share with the animals. Thinking, in the sense of working on a mathematical problem or considering the issue of whether angels exist, is something only humans do. Recognizing the reality of human thought saves us already from one materialist error, the error that only things that we can perceive are real. This error forces the materialist to affirm the existence of brains but deny the existence of minds (except perhaps in a purely functional sense). I doubt that many of us can accept the notion that minds are not real.

The second thing about the human *mind* is that it is liable to get out of kilter when something is wrong with the *brain* (Alzheimer's disease, intoxication, weariness, or being hit with a baseball bat). Now the materialist may feel he has proof that *thought* is only a function of the brain, but this is not so. Recall the difference between perception (an animal function) and thinking (a strictly human function). The difference implies that perception is a material function but that thought is a nonmaterial function, since otherwise animals ought to be able to think. This further implies that the brain is a *necessary* but not a *sufficient* cause for *human* thought. In other words, human thought cannot take place where there is no brain, but the brain alone is not an adequate cause for thought (hence, animals can suffer, enjoy, have feelings, and even something analogous to human emotions and personality, but they do not cogitate).

Before I go any further, I should hasten to point out that I do not mean the human mind is trapped in a body like a ghost in a machine or an angel in the prison of a human body. If that were the case, then injuries to the brain should have no effect on thought. Actually, it is hard to imagine how there could be any interaction at all between the mind and the body if the mind were simply spirit bouncing around inside a body of flesh. Instead, the mind is a melding of the incorporeal and the corporeal. The two are one in such a way that while they can be conceptually distinguished, they cannot be actually separated. This understanding of mind excludes the idea of transmigration of souls in reincarnation (since mind is linked to body), is fully compatible with the Christian doctrine of afterlife (which links eternal life to the resurrection of the body), and is analogous to the idea of God and man in Christ (since His humanity and divinity can be distinguished in discussion but in reality are eternally united in one person).

All of which brings us back to the angels. This understanding of human mind at least opens the door for believing in a nonhuman mind that has no body. Since we have animals (creatures with bodies and brains but no thought) and humans (creatures with both bodies and thought), can we not have angels (creatures with thought but no bodies)? The animals have perceptions, feelings, responses, and the like, but people have all of these with the addition of cognitive, rational thought. Is it not possible that there could be creatures with rational thought but no feelings or perceptions (at least none that are like what we experience)? If so, then we can at least affirm that angels are possible beings.

But can we go beyond saying that angels are possible and affirm on philosophical grounds (that is, without recourse to citing the Bible or personal anecdotes) that they actually do exist? Aquinas tried to do just this. He claimed that the "chain of being" requires that angels exist lest God's creation have an obvious imperfection.

If at the bottom of the chain are rocks, water, and dirt (simple matter that is not alive), and above these are the plants (alive but without perception), and above these are the animals (alive and perceiving but not thinking), and yet above these are the humans (living minds yet still material, from the dust of the earth), is there not a great gap if the next step takes us all the way to the immaterial, infinite, omniscient God? Surely there ought to be creatures in between who are immaterial minds but not infinite or omniscient! This place, it turns out, is held by the angels.[3] Aquinas therefore could contend that angels must exist.[4]

I do not know how you feel about the argument from the chain of being, but it almost persuades me. It makes a lot of sense. But in the final analysis, it is not enough. After all, it is always possible that God, for whatever reason, left a big gap in the chain of being. Ultimately, the only thing that persuades me that angels really exist is the word of a religious authority. In other words, I believe that angels are real because the Bible says so.

This leads us to the question of whether the Bible is a sufficient and reliable authority or whether other Scriptures, such as the Koran or the Book of Mormon (which both affirm the reality of angels), can serve that function equally well. Explaining why I am a Christian and not a Muslim or Mormon is more than I can do here. For brevity's sake, I will simply confess to you that for me the Bible has final authority and the Koran and the Book of Mormon have none whatsoever.

In summation, I believe that angels do exist and that no argument against their existence bears weight. Reports of personal encounters and the philosophical defense of the existence of angels serve as aids to faith, but not as its basis. Thus, I do not trust either logic or personal anecdotes to give me sufficient proof of the reality of angels. The only reason we can be sure that angels exist is that God has revealed it to us in the Bible.

Analyzing Donald and Mickey: What Are Angels Like?

What are angels like? Everybody knows the answer to this one, right? They have wings, haloes, and sometimes look like women, sometimes like men, sometimes like babies, and sometimes like a mixture of all three. Obviously, when we imagine angels we draw on images of angels from our culture—classical European paintings of angels and the like—and these images may or may not have anything to do with what angels look like. If anything, the androgynous images of angels in western art have turned people away from interest in angels. We need to abandon such imagery if we want to think seriously about angels. By the same token, we have no reason to think that they live on clouds, wear white nightshirts, or play harps. To be sure, some people emphatically claim that angels really do have halos or wings, but I think that most of us are willing to leave this momentous question unanswered.

Of more importance is the question of what an angel actually is. By this, I do not mean what an angel does (serves as a messenger for God, sings in the heavenly choir, and so forth), but more precisely, What is the essence of angel? When we get down to basics, we can give two alternative answers to this question.

One is that an angel is essentially like a very powerful and supernatural human. That is, an angel has some kind of clearly defined "body"—although the body is not made of the physical stuff of this world—that essentially functions the same way humans do. The main behavioral difference between humans and angels is that, unlike the little girl with a little curl in the center of her forehead, some angels are always very, very good and others are always horrid. This is the human-like version of the angels.

The other opinion is that an angel is more like a thought than a person. This is what we may call the Scholastic angel. In this approach, we can hardly say that an angel has a body at all. Perhaps the easiest way to explain this notion of angels is to contrast it with the human-like version of the angels. For shorthand, we will call the human-like angel "Donald" and the Scholastic angel "Mickey."

Donald has an identifiable body and face and plainly looks human, although his body is not of the mortal, physical stuff of our bodies. Some even think of Donald angels as coming in races and colors just like humans. Mickey, on the other hand, might assume a human form or any other form, but he actually has nothing like a body at all. If pressed, we can only imagine Mickey as something like a glowing light, but even that is nothing but our poor, fleshly imaginations at work.

Donald speaks to the other angels in a specific angel language, a language that some humans have been heard to use on occasions. Donald has a magnificent command of linguistics and of course can speak to people in their own language. But with other angels he carries on conversations, asks questions, and learns the latest scuttlebutt around heaven in the same way we do on the job.

Mickey never needs to talk at all, except on those occasions when he has a message to deliver to a human. He has no angel language because he has no need of language at all. We cannot even say that Mickey communicates with the other angels telepathically, because even telepathic communication might require words. We would do better to say that ideas without words simply move about instantaneously among Mickey and his kin. Mickey angels are in something like an electronic network, in which the spirits constantly exchange angelic bits and bytes of data at an astonishingly high rate of speed.

Donald is one smart guy, and he is always learning. Of course he is not omniscient like God, but he is always listening to other angels and observing the universe and in particular the world, and he wants to know as much as he can. He has a fantastic memory, but he learns basically the same way we do—by conversation, experience, and observation.

You might say that Mickey learns things but not as we do. If he were to write a book on the subject, it would be called *Everything I Really Needed to Know I Already Knew at the Moment of My Creation.* At the moment God created the angels, He gave each one all the knowledge that he needed. That knowledge distinguished each Mickey angel from the others. They never needed to ask or learn any of it, because it was all innate. Since then, what "learning" they have done has been by way of the angel network. In particular, they grow in knowledge when angels who began life with more innate ideas disseminate their knowledge.

Like anyone else, Donald has ideas and opinions of his own. Of course, he loves and submits to the one God, but this does not mean that he has stopped thinking. He sometimes shares his opinions with other angels or even with God Himself. Some sects of Judaism taught that God never does anything without first having a brainstorming session with His heavenly council of angels. Once they reach a decision, all the angels cooperate with God to see that His plan is carried out.

We can hardly say the same of Mickey. His mind is so thoroughly in tune with the will of God and so governed by God's thoughts that we can hardly speak of him as having opinions in any sense meaningful to us. It goes without saying that he never offers God advice or agrees to cooperate with God's plans. He simply does the will of God because of what he is—a pure servant.

The matter of Donald's sexuality is uncertain. Some say that all Donald angels are male, some that there are both male and female angels (Daisy?), and some that Donald is androgynous. Those who hold to the latter view say that this is a mark of a superior being, in which the principles of Yin and Yang are united. But Mickey no more has sexuality than a rock does. "He" is strictly neuter, although capable of appearing to a human as either a man or a woman. More on this subject later.

Donald occasionally has to pull out his great sword and do battle with the Donald devils. Some of the other angels are bigger and stronger than he is, and others are weaker, and the same is true of the devils. When Donald fights one of the devils, it is truly combat. They swing their swords, throw punches, and even toss hills and mountains at one another. From this, they can suffer weakness, injury, and exhaustion, although their injuries heal remarkably quickly. Some even say that they can in some sense "kill" one another.

Mickey never has any need to engage in combat. The fallen angels are simply excluded from God and His presence and as such are out of the network and cannot get back in. People who believe that angels are of the Mickey type rarely bother themselves with the question of whether Mickey can interact with devils at all.

Donald has tremendous strength, but he can get tired and need a break just as much as the next guy. As mentioned above, fighting demons is especially likely to wear him out, and you might see him stretched out under a heavenly tree trying to get some much needed R and R after a military campaign. Rest is hardly an issue for Mickey. He simply never suffers fatigue, boredom, or injury. He never rests or feels any need for rest.

It is just possible—in the thinking of some people—that Donald actually once was a human being who got promoted after death. That is why he is so human-like. Mickey, on the other hand, has no humanity in his background. He is pure angel from the moment of his creation. We will say more on this question too.

Donald fits in a hierarchy of angels who have either greater or less authority than he has. Donald's hierarchy resembles a military chain of command. Just as an army has generals, colonels, captains, sergeants, and privates, so Donald angels are organized into companies and divisions under archangels, thrones, cherubim, and the like. Higher ranking angels not only have authority over lesser angels, they are also bigger and have greater strength. Mickey angels also live in a hierarchy, but it has nothing to do with physical size or power or authority. Rather, where Mickey fits in the hierarchy of angels is a matter of how much innate knowledge he has. The angels closest to God are those with the most innate knowledge, and they in turn "communicate" knowledge with lesser angels. We will revisit this question too.

Donald is one of several species of angels. For example, if Donald is an archangel, then he is of the same species as all the other archangels although not exactly like any one of them, much as humans are all one species but with variation and individuality among them. The angels below him are of a similar but different species.

Every Mickey, on the other hand, is the only one of his kind. In the Mickey understanding of angels, every individual angel is a species unto himself. In the great chain of being, from the lowest Mickey angel to the one highest and nearest to God, thousands upon thousands of species of angels exist, and each species has an everlasting population of one. For those who believe that angels are of the Mickey type, the fact that they are incorporeal makes it impossible for them to have many members of one species in the way that animals can. Each angel is a species unto itself.

Some people, whose angels are of the Donald type, believe that these angels can still fall. After all, after so many billions of years just being good, even an angel can get bored. This is out of the question for Mickey angels. Having once turned to the grace of God and the blessed vision of His glory, they could never want, imagine, or be tempted to turn away. More on the fall of the devils later.

Donald moves very rapidly when he wants to and can easily make warp nine. But he still has to travel through physical space. His "body" moves from one place to the next in much the same way people do, by moving through and briefly occupying all the space in between.

Mickey can do that, but he does not have to. Actually, he regularly travels by taking quantum leaps. That is, he suddenly disappears from one place and immediately appears in another place that is perhaps light-years away without passing through the space in between. This does not mean that he zoomed through the intervening space very rapidly, the way Donald did, but that he never was in the intervening space at all. Physicists have only in the twentieth century discovered that such a thing can happen on the quantum scale. Within an atom, an electron can "jump" from one shell to another without really passing through the space between the two. How surprising the medieval theologians discovered a similar idea centuries ago![5]

Donald, like us, can only be in one place at one time. He is either in God's heaven or he is on earth or he is visiting Alpha Centauri or some such place. Mickey also can only be active at one place at a time. In one sense, however, he is always in the presence of God in that even as he works on earth, he still beholds the glory of God in heaven.

Donald is a wonderful person, and he has a great life. He flies up and down through the universe and looks down on people and just loves the little darlings even though they are not quite what they ought to be. He smiles and laughs and loves to feel the stardust blowing through his hair as he crosses a light-year of space in a couple of minutes. Donald can get emotional. While we can say that Mickey loves—he certainly loves God—he does not possess anything similar to the emotional life we know. Our love is only an analogy for his love, since our highly emotional kind of love is influenced by things like family ties, hormonal changes, Prozac, and so forth. Mickey has nothing like our feelings and emotions.

Where do you find Donald and Mickey angels? You can find Donald in many of the legends and works of fiction we have observed, in the mythology of many religions, as well as in much of the Pseudepigrapha and in the works of Emanuel Swedenborg. Milton's angels and devils, as described in *Paradise Lost*, could hardly be more human-like and still be angels. They suffer physical pain, get emotional, fight very physical battles, get tired, and can be heroic or ignoble. Metatron (of *3 Enoch*) was once a human being. Jewish legends are full of angels and devils that are almost comical in their humanness. New Age angels are often ascended humans. Modern Christian fiction has angels and devils whose emotional lives sometimes seem a little neurotic.

You can find Mickey in philosophical analyses of angels. The angels of Pseudo-Dionysius are certainly of the Mickey type, but in orthodox Christianity, Thomas Aquinas also espoused a Mickey version of angels. Karl Barth's angels are actually Mickeys too.

We should hasten to point out that few presentations of angels are exclusively one or the other. Angel literature is nothing if not eclectic and inconsistent. Many writers pick a little from here and a little from there and do not bother with whether or not it all holds together. Like much modern science fiction writing, these books do not allow facts and congruity to stand in the way of a good story. At the same time, it probably is not a bad thing that presentations of angels are not wholly one way or the other since we really do not understand the angel world. What may seem logical and consistent to us may in reality be wrong.

The danger of the human-like angel is that he is ultimately a creature of mythology. Just as the gods of Greece and Rome were immortal but quasi-physical, had emotional swings, ruled over different areas of nature, and functioned in a hierarchy modeled on ancient civic government, so the Donald-type angels do much the same except that they have higher moral standards than the pagan gods. Milton's *Paradise Lost* follows more than just the poetic form of the ancient pagan epics (*Gilgamesh, The Iliad,* and so forth); it commits the offense of turning biblical teaching on angels into a myth. This is not to say that real angels have no human-like qualities, but we should be suspicious anytime we read about angels who are noticeably like us.

The problem with Mickey is that he seems hardly like a person at all. All that instantaneous, nonverbal communication, coupled with a mind that has no emotion as we know it, does not learn as we understand it, and has nothing like a body as we know it—this makes it hard for us to feel that we are dealing with a self-conscious being. Even to speak of them as robots would seem to say too much. To go back to my earlier analogy, they seem more like bytes of data in some great computer program than anything else. It all seems too sterile, and it can lead to the kind of pantheistic and monistic view of God and the universe we find in Pseudo-Dionysius. We finally wonder if there is much difference between a Mickey-type angel and no angel at all. In other words, is Mickey just a manifestation of an invisible, impersonal "power" behind the universe?

So which is it: is an angel a Donald or a Mickey? The quick and dirty solution is just to say that an angel is a little bit of both, and I think that there is truth in that. But we all too easily pick and choose among possible angel traits to construct the kind of angel palatable to us—and we may get it all wrong. The New Age movement in particular has managed to glean the worst from both worlds in constructing its bizarre angelology. On the one hand, it moves toward a monism and an annihilation of all personality, but on the other, it has very human-like familiar spirits who may be described as anything from pompous and boorish to silly and giddy.

We should not write off Mickey as an impossible angel. The real problem here is that we cannot understand how spiritual realities are analogous to their earthly counterparts. We cannot imagine a being whose thoughts are so perfectly in tune with God that he in effect has no opinions of his own, and thus we say that such a being has no personhood at all. This may be more of a problem with us than with them.

We say that we have love and that the angels have love but that angel love is not the same as ours because it does not include emotion. For us, love without emotion is no love at all, and thus we feel that angels have no real love and thus no personalities. In reality, we face the same dilemma when we speak of God's love or His anger or jealousy or sadness. The Bible, in one way or another, attributes all of these to God, but at the same time affirms that God is above all human passions, that He knows in advance how everything will turn out, and that He never changes.

How can that be? God's love is not the same as ours; it is analogous. This does not mean that it is less real or that God is less of a person. To the contrary, His love is far more substantial than our hormone-driven whims. The same is undoubtedly true of angel "emotions" and "bodies."

In the same way, angels may have something we could call a language, but it might be so far removed from our ideas of language that we could with equal accuracy say that they do not use any language at all. The notion that an angel can behold the face of God and at the same time be off somewhere on a job is hard for us to grasp, but it is also wonderful.

In the final analysis, I believe that Mickey comes much closer to the real angels than Donald, who is ultimately a creature of mythology rather than biblical faith. I want to add that I do not accept the angels of Pseudo-Dionysius and Neoplatonism at all. I am more comfortable with

Aquinas (but with some reservations). Although angels are incorporeal and above the passions of the flesh, I believe that they are real persons with real personalities just as God, for all His omniscience and omnipresence, is a real person and not a diffused, pantheistic energy.

The biblical presentation of angels, after all, does have elements of Donald. They shouted for joy at creation (Job 38:7), observed the work of the apostles (1 Cor. 4:9), and from the church learn about the mystery of God's plan for humanity (Eph. 3:10; 1 Pet. 1:12). All of our efforts to construct an angelology that fully conforms to biblical teaching are at best an approximation. This is, in a strange way, comforting. If angels are heavenly creatures, then they must be to some extent beyond our understanding. Any angelology that is familiar and easy is probably wrong.

Hey, That's No Lady, That's My Angel! Do Angels Have Gender?

We have already seen that Jesus seems to imply that angels have no gender when He told us that they do not marry (Matt. 22:30). Our analysis of Donald and Mickey also reveals that it is very difficult to think of angels having gender unless we are prepared to believe in a very physical, human-like version of an angel.

Still, some people want to ascribe sexuality to angels. Some authors believe that all angels are male since they always appear in the Bible as male.[6] This notion is not new; the ancient Jewish book of *Jubilees* (15:27) goes so far as to claim that they are circumcised! We must question this for several reasons. First of all, angels do not always appear in the Bible as males. In Zechariah 5:9, two female angels with wings like storks carry away "Wickedness," who is also a woman. It will do no good to argue that this is merely a symbolic vision and thus that these women are not real angels or that storks are unclean and therefore creatures with stork wings cannot be angels.[7] Many angelic visions are highly symbolic, such as the visions of the seraphim in Isaiah 6, of the cherubim in Ezekiel 1, and of the giant angel in Revelation 10. The stork wings do not make the women of Zechariah 5:9 unclean and therefore not angels since the verse merely describes the appearance of the wings. The Bible elsewhere portrays angels as having the appearance of unclean animals (the cherubim of Ezekiel 1 had the faces of lions and eagles).

Even if all the angels did appear as males, that would not make the case that they actually were all males. A Polynesian of a few centuries ago, visited for the first time by a group of European sailors, would be unwise to conclude that all Europeans were male. More to the point, what we see in the Bible is how angels are for us and not necessarily how they are of themselves. When an angel takes on a certain shape, whether it be an armed warrior (Josh. 5:13–15) or a strange creature with multiple wings and eyes (Ezek. 1), it is for our sake and to communicate to us; it does not tell us what they are "really" like. By analogy, when Christ appears in Revelation 5:6 as a slain lamb with seven horns and seven eyes, it does not mean He literally looks like that.

In the ancient world, strength and authority resided with men and thus it is hardly surprising that the biblical angels, who were sometimes warriors and frequently issued commands, appeared as males. Even the fact that Genesis 6 speaks of the sons of God taking human women does not prove that they are males in their own realm; it only implies that they can (or perhaps could) transform themselves into males. As for angels in and of themselves, to speak of incorporeal beings who never reproduce with one another as "male" seems rather pointless.

Eileen Freeman opines that angels are both male and female on the grounds that gender pervades the universe in the biological world, in many human languages, and in the Eastern notion of Yin and Yang.[8] This proves little if anything about angels. Asexual reproduction does exist (in protozoa and lower invertebrates), and many languages get along very nicely without gender. As for Yin and Yang, I cannot say whether the idea has any truth at all, much less whether it applies to angels. Since gender is not even universal for this world, I do not see the need to ascribe it to the next.

The fact remains that we know nothing about angel gender. Speculation can seriously mislead us here. Belief that angels are both male and female can lead to the bizarre notions of angelic reproduction and emanations that we have seen in Gnosticism and paganism, and it is the doorway to angelic mythology.

On the other hand, belief that angels are androgynous beings is also unsatisfactory. It leads to the kind of art that portrays angels as effeminate males. As humans, we can only react with revulsion to such a being. We relate to visual images and ascribe value to them within our own earthly, human frame of reference. We might see strength, courage, and justice in a virile man or grace and compassion in a beautiful woman. But we see only a monstrosity in a hermaphrodite.

Therefore, I think we would be better off to understand angels as neither male nor female nor androgynous but simply as sexless. They are beings for whom gender has no meaning.

Pride, Lust, or What? How Did Satan and the Devils Fall?

We have looked at what the Bible says (or rather does not say) about the fall of Satan, and we have looked at various images of devils in the history of angel lore. We now need to summarize the issue.

How you answer the question of how Satan fell depends on whether your version of an angel is Donald or Mickey. If Donald, then you can inject all kinds of emotion and combat into the story. If Mickey, then you will dispense with all that and tell a much shorter story.

If your Satan is a Donald, then you believe that he fell because of pride, greed, lust, and ambition as described in very human terms. You have several options.

The first option: Satan fell aeons before the creation of this physical universe when he for some reason decided that he no longer wanted to be a high-ranking archangel but rather to take over all of heaven for himself. Perhaps it was, as Milton states, the day that God declared that all angels should bow before the Son. Or perhaps, after millions of years as a mere angel, he just got bored with the job. Whatever the occasion, he suddenly declared that he was taking over and a large number of angels, who were apparently as unhappy with conditions in heaven as he was, joined in. We have already seen that biblical support for this version is at best doubtful.

The second option: Satan and the other angels were all completely happy with affairs in heaven until the dreadful day when God created humans and, horror upon horrors, demanded that angels serve these wretched creatures of dirt and fluids. Satan had his principles. He was not about to stoop before these ghastly half-breeds, and quite a few angels agreed. So began the angelic rebellion.

The third option: Satan and his angels really did not fall until well after the fall of humanity into sin. It came in the Genesis 6 episode, when angels came down and had sexual relations with women. It seems that Satan and many other angels were looking down on earth and watching how people had sexual relations, and they finally could not resist joining in on something that looked that good. If you hold to this view, then you need to find an alternative explanation for the snake in Genesis 2–3. On the other hand, you can hold to a different view of the fall of Satan and still believe that Genesis 6 involved angels and women.

If your devil is a Mickey, then the fall is a much cleaner and more rational affair. In this view, some angels became blessed and the others became devils in the first instance after their creation. That is, God created all the angelic beings with fantastic innate powers and knowledge and, in the first moment of their creation, the free will to determine whether to seek their fulfillment in God or in themselves. Their very first act was to decide about God one way or the other, and the decision stuck for all eternity. If that seems unfair, remember that at their creation they already knew more than we will ever know in this lifetime, so they had enough information on which to base a decision.

In this interpretation, the one thing that angels did not have at the moment of creation was the bliss of a direct vision of God in all His glory. They had innate knowledge of God, but not direct knowledge of God. They could attain direct knowledge of God only by His grace; once they had received it, they could never lose it or desire anything else. After the beatific vision, they could never fall into sin. Before that moment, however, they had to decide whether to seek blessedness in God's grace or in their own persons. Being angels, they did not need time to think about their decision. As Aquinas put it, "they were all of them good in the first instant, but in the second the good were set apart from the wicked."[9]

Of all the portrayals of the fall of the devils, I find that of Aquinas to be the most satisfying (although I disagree with him in some points that I have not outlined here). Most significantly, in this interpretation the evil disposition *follows* separation from God rather than precedes it. My greatest difficulty with mythological (Donald) type descriptions of the fall of Satan is that they have him chafing under the rule of God or feeling ambition for power or turning his nose up at Adam or lusting after women *before* his actual fall. This is surely wrong. The inclination to selfishness, perversity, and viciousness is a *result* of turning from God, not the *cause* of it. The fall of Satan was nothing more or less than a simple rejection of God; the demonic disposition came later. The same is true of humans too, I believe, but that is a different story.

In the final analysis, we cannot now and perhaps never will fully understand the mystery of evil. The important thing is that we recognize the reality of a personal evil that transcends our earthly confines, not that we let our imagination invent a tale of how it all happened.

An Angel (and a Devil) on My Shoulder: Do We Have Guardian Angels?

We have seen that the Bible nowhere asserts that each person has a guardian angel and that John Calvin was unwilling to declare in favor of this notion. Nevertheless, the idea of the personal guardian angel remains among the most persistent and appealing of all concepts about angels.

Before proceeding, we must be clear about what we mean. We are not questioning whether the Bible declares that angels protect people or whether people can rightly claim to have been saved from trouble by an angel. There is no doubt about either of those questions. The issue is whether each person has a private angel assigned to him or her from birth as a special helper.

The notion of a guardian angel occurs nowhere in the Old Testament except by the most strained interpretation. It probably entered Christianity from Roman religion, which taught that a *genius*, or guardian spirit, protected individuals, families, and institutions. Roman families honored the genius of the family as part of the worship of the household gods.

Many early Christian writers affirmed that each believer (that is, each Christian) has a guardian angel, but not necessarily that each person does. Basil the Great wrote, "Among the angels, some are in charge of nations, others are the companions of the faithful . . . . It is the teaching of Moses that every believer has an angel to guide him as a teacher and a shepherd."[10] He had in mind Genesis 48:16, which in fact does not imply that every believer has a private guardian angel—it only states that the angel of the Lord, who is here identified with God, has given Jacob special protection.

Many Christian theologians have actually taught that every person has a guardian angel assigned to him or her at birth, but that the angel could do little good as long as his human ward was not a Christian. Because humanity is sold under sin, they thought, and because many people actually devote their children to a false god or an idol, most people are more under the sway of a "guardian devil" than a guardian angel. As soon as a person receives baptism, the angel is able to work effectively for him. Before conversion, however, the guardian angel may help to lead the person to faith.

In this view, the guardian angel seeks to lead a person into good, and the guardian devil seeks to draw him or her into evil. Cartoonists have popularized this doctrine for us; Goofy is caught in a moral dilemma between the Goofy angel on one shoulder saying "Give the money back!" and the Goofy devil on the other saying, "Steal the money!" The notion that every person actually has one angel and one demon assigned to him arose very early. The Shepherd of Hermas, a Christian document written by around A.D. 150, says that each of us has an "angel of righteousness" and an "angel of iniquity."[11]

Gregory of Nyssa (330-95) put it like this: "After our nature had fallen in sin, we were not abandoned in our fall by God, but an angel, one of the beings who have an incorporeal nature, was set up to aid the life of each of us. The destroyer of our nature, in his turn, did just the same by sending us an evil, pernicious angel to the detriment of human nature. It now depends on man, who finds himself between two angels, each one seeking to lead him in a different way, to make one triumph over the other."[12]

Islam has a similar doctrine. Something like this occurs in ancient Greek religion, in which the doctrine was that everyone was followed by a good and an evil *daimon*, or spirit. Also, the *Manual of Discipline* 3:18–21 (in the Dead Sea Scrolls) states that God created two spirits, the spirit of truth and the spirit of falsehood, in which man walks. It further explains that all the "children of falsehood" are ruled by the "Angel of Darkness," but it stops short of assigning guardian devils and guardian angels to every person.

Among Christian thinkers, the two major exponents of the notion of the guardian angel are Origen and Thomas Aquinas. Origen supported the notion of the guardian angel in various texts. For example, he stated that our guardian angels direct, rebuke, and chastise us to lead us into penance.[13]

Aquinas dealt with the matter of whether everyone has a private angel in *Summa theologica* 13, article 2, "Whether each man is guarded by an angel." He began (as was his custom) by listing various objections to the notion of private guardian angels, but the objections he cited are obviously of straw and he has no difficulty in overthrowing them. For example, he gave the objection that one angel is strong enough to protect many people and therefore private guardian angels are unnecessary, and then he easily dispatches that argument. Actually, Aquinas cited no evidence that private guardian angels actually exist; he only showed that their existence is not irrational. It is one thing to say that private guardians are a logical possibility. It is another altogether to demonstrate that you really do have one. By analogy, just because it is logically possible that people like us live in another galaxy does not mean that they really exist.

The notion of private guardian angels has led Christians into three dangerous areas. First, it provided another reason for people to get their babies baptized as soon as possible. Concern about guardian angels and devils is a poor reason to hasten baptism.

Second, the private guardian angel can easily take on the functions of God in the minds of some people. I have mentioned, for example, how Origen ascribed to the guardian angel the role of guiding believers into penance. He says, "We are not chastised by the Father of the family Himself, but by the angels whom He has sent as masters over us with the office of chastising and correcting each one of us."[14] In reality, the Bible asserts that Christians do receive their discipline directly from God and that this gives the surest proof that they are legitimately God's children (Heb. 12:7–8). The Bible does speak of angels as carrying out God's judgment on people (as at Sodom), but it never presents them as "masters" who personally train and discipline believers. The Holy Spirit, not some angelic spirit, breaks the human heart.

Third, the notion of the private guardian angel easily leads to the practice of praying to that angel. This custom, along with invoking the saints, began to arise in the fourth century. Ambrose (339–97), for example, said, "The angels are to be entreated for us, who are given us for our guard; the martyrs are to be entreated, whose patronage we may in a manner claim by the pledge of their bodies."[15] Jesus, I think, is clear on this subject: "Whenever you pray . . . pray to your Father" (Matt. 6:6). We should never invoke an angel.

I cannot pretend to know that we do not have private guardian angels, and I have no desire to make such a claim. As far as I can tell, we do not have sufficient reason to believe that each of us does have such an angel. We should be aware of the inherent dangers in the idea.

Finally, however, we should recognize that what modern gurus are marketing as guardian angels bears little resemblance to the traditional Christian guardian angel. Modern guardian angels, as described by their advocates, are altogether indifferent to the matter of whether an individual is Christian. Some today believe that animals and trees have guardian angels, so you do not have to be human! These new guardians have little concern with moral issues, and they never discipline their wards. Inasmuch as many modern angelphiles reject the idea of devils, their guardians never concern themselves with a struggle for the soul of a man or woman. Instead, they give nothing but "unconditional love" and only want their charges to come to the point of self-realization. Those who embrace this kind of guardian angel should not delude themselves with the idea that they stand in agreement with the Christian church.

The Last Flight Out: The Angels and the Moment of Death

Do angels carry our souls away when we die? This, too, is a very common notion, and it does have some biblical support. In the parable of the rich man and Lazarus in Luke 16, Lazarus dies and the angels carry him to "Abraham's bosom" (v. 22). This seems to be a straightforward statement that angels do carry us to heaven when we die, but some readers wonder about the quasi-parabolic nature of the story. In other words, they are not sure that Jesus intended us to take this as a literal description of the afterlife. Along the same lines, they question whether Jesus really intended us to understand from the story that the souls in paradise and those in torments shout back and forth to one another (Luke 16:24–31). The main point of the story is not to instruct us in the finer points of angelology, but to warn us that we already have sufficient reason to repent and that God already has sufficient reason to condemn us (Luke 16:31).

The belief that the angels escort the dead to regions beyond has spawned questionable ideas among Christians. First, people began to attribute the task of evaluating the dead to the angels. Since angels take charge of the soul at death, they supposed, the angels must have a role in judging the soul as well. Origen actually attributed the work of weighing the soul for its worthiness or unworthiness to the devils, but he also taught that we will ascend among the "choir of angels" where we will be examined to see how much "treasure" we bring with us and thus how great will be our reward.[16] Some connected the angelic judgment to the notion of purgatory. They thought that if the soul was not entirely pure an angel would make it pass through "the river of fire" and keep it there until all sin had been purged.[17]

Second, these teachings gave people another reason to pray for the dead, since they wanted the angels to accompany the departed souls on their way to heaven as well as show favor to the dead when they judged them. The Apostolic Constitution puts it like this: "Forgive him if he has sinned and make the angels well disposed toward him."[18]

The notion that lesser spirits (rather than God Himself) carry out judgment on people is not new. An ancient Egyptian painting portrays the god Anubis (a jackal-headed god) weighing a human heart in a balance. He does this in order to determine if the person in question is worthy to enter the Egyptian version of heaven, the land of Osiris.

In reality, we have no reason to suppose that angels judge us. All judgment belongs to God, and He alone can give eternal life. At most, the angels carry out the decrees of God. Also, once an individual has died, he or she is in God's hands. We should not pray for the dead. The notion of a purgatorial "river of fire" is pure mythology.

The role of angels in taking the dead to their new home has gained new importance in the recent surge of "near death experience" literature. Many people claim to have experienced clinical death. They say they rose from their bodies and met an angel. They often allege that the angel allowed them to return to their bodies. Near death researchers try to accumulate testimony from such individuals as evidence for what the "other side" is like. This is a major issue of its own, one that we will not try to tackle in this book. Suffice it to say that the evidence is unclear and contradictory and that observers have proposed interpretations that range from the highly skeptical to the highly credulous.

The Bible does give us one significant death experience. As Stephen was dying, he shouted out that he saw "the heavens opened and the Son of Man standing at the right hand of God!" (Acts 7:56). If he saw any angels, he did not think it important enough at the time to tell us about it. His eyes were fixed on Jesus Christ.

I have no difficulty in believing that the angels escort us into the presence of Christ, and I can accept that this is the implication of Luke 16:22, but I think we have sufficient reason to avoid making too much of this issue. The One to whom we are escorted is more important than those who do the escorting.

Do We Become Angels when We Die?

We have already seen that in *3 Enoch* a person became an angel. Enoch was transformed into Metatron. Many people believe that we all, and not just a few supersaints, can become angels at death.

Some authorities explain that the idea that we become angels began sometime in the medieval church. When a baby or small child died (as was very common), people would console the parents by saying that the baby had become an angel. The *putti*, fat little angel babies with wings, perhaps became popular in Christian art for that reason. On the other hand, the idea also has roots in the Western version of the wheel of life and reincarnation. The idea is that the soul is reincarnated as a human or as some kind of animal until it finally achieves enlightenment. At that point, instead of being reincarnated as a human or a lizard, the soul is elevated to angel status and is free from reincarnation.

Neither idea has anything to support it. The Bible is clear that angels are created beings. In the resurrection, we become like the angels (Matt. 22:30) but do not become angels. We can appreciate how the idea that babies who die become angels appealed to people, but the love of God is in itself the only sure basis for comforting grieving parents. The notion of reincarnation, on the other hand, contradicts the entire message of the Bible.

Are Angels Arranged in a Heavenly Hierarchy?

Ever since Pseudo-Dionysius, certain Christian theologians have been on a quest to discover the organizational structure of the angels. Do "authorities" outrank "thrones"? Are "seraphim" above or below "arch–angels"? I can think of few questions that are less pressing, but as we shall see, even Billy Graham felt a need to develop a hierarchy of angels.

The various terms that supposedly fill out the heavenly hierarchy occur in scattered passages in the Bible. Isaiah 6 describes the seraphim. Colossians 1:16 says that in Christ "all things in heaven and on earth were created, things visible and invisible, whether thrones or dominions or rulers or powers." Daniel 10:13 and 12:1 call Michael the great "prince" of Israel, and Jude 9 calls him the "archangel." These titles seem to imply that some angels outrank others and thus indicate that heaven has a hierarchy of angels.

This may be the case, but the texts do not say it as plainly as some would like. Karl Barth observed that in these passages, and in the very title "archangel," the point is not so much how the angels relate to one another as to how they relate to the people of God. Michael is a "prince" and "archangel" by virtue of his place as a minister to Israel, not by virtue of outranking the other angels.[19] We do not necessarily have any special insight into the heavenly administrative flowchart, but we can rejoice that whatever angelic titles we hear of, it is all for us and for our salvation.

We have already seen that "seraphim" is probably a description of what Isaiah saw in Isaiah 6—angels who shined like burning fire—rather than a title or rank in the order of angels. "Cherub" describes a function of an angel as a guardian and not a rank in the angelic pecking order.

The various terms found in Paul's letters (powers, authorities, rulers, thrones, and so forth) call for special comment. First, Paul never set out a complete hierarchy of angels; he did not even state that such a thing exists. He used these terms unsystematically and sporadically. In fact, it appears that many of the terms are virtually interchangeable. In a given context, he could have just as easily said "thrones" or "powers" or "authorities" with no discernible difference in meaning. He never claimed that one group outranks the other or, if they do, which is higher or which is lower on the pecking order.

Second, Paul was not always or exclusively speaking of angels in these passages. We will leave aside for the time being the texts that concern demonic powers (for example, Eph. 6:12). In a number of texts, he obviously had human authorities in view. In Titus 3:1, he said Christians should submit to "rulers and authorities," and he plainly meant human governments. This should only make us more hesitant about attempting to use these terms as guides to the angelic hierarchy. "Powers" and "authorities" are deliberately ambiguous as descriptions of human government; they can describe anyone from the local tax collector all the way up to Caesar himself. We should not treat terms that only generally describe human government as precise designations of the ranks of angelic government.

Finally, we should ask ourselves what possible benefit could come of knowing the ranks of the celestial hierarchy. The answer is none at all—unless we plan to invoke the angels according to their ranks or use the hierarchy as a ladder of spiritual ascent. If that is our purpose, then we are not Christians at all but sorcerers or Gnostics.

Can We Know the Names of Angels?

In the literature we have surveyed and in hundreds of other books as well, we can learn thousands upon thousands of angel names. I hope that you have seen, however, that this literature is not trustworthy. In all my readings, I have seen no reason to think that Metatron, Uriel, Moroni, Lilith, Yaldabaoth, or any of the other thousands of supposed angel or devil names are anything else than the creations of overheated human imagination.

Theoretically it is of course possible that an angel could reveal his name to us, but I think that it is knowledge we do not need. The Bible has kept the names of the angels secret for a reason (with the exceptions of Michael and Gabriel). Besides idle curiosity, we could only want to know the names of angels for a single reason: in order to invoke them. Just as angelic hierarchies allow people to think that they can call upon high-ranking angels, so angel names open the door to magic and mysticism by allowing people to call upon angels individually. As we shall see, modern angelphilia has a great deal of this.

☙

CHAPTER EIGHT

To one kneeling down no word came,
Only the mind's song, saddening the lips
Of the grave saints, rigid in glass;
Or the dry whisper of unseen wings,
Bats not angels, in the high roof.
R. S. THOMAS, "IN A COUNTRY CHURCH"

Bats Not Angels

New Age Angels, Part 1

THE NEW AGE MOVEMENT DEFIES EASY EXPLANATION
or even a clear definition. As a grassroots movement, it has no central
leadership to set an agenda. While New Age followers profess no authoritative Scripture such as the Bible, the Koran, or the Book of Mormon,
they freely draw on all of these and many other religious texts as well.

Although the movement has a number of characteristic teachings or
ideals, New Agers confess no common creed and resist no specific heresy.
One may speak of followers or adherents but not of members because it
has no central organization that one may join or support. Channelers,
Eastern mystics, followers of the occult, witches, students of near death
experiences, UFO watchers, nudists, animal rights advocates, certain
religious feminists, and angelphiles might all describe themselves as New
Agers. On the other hand, many who advocate tenets fully in keeping
with New Age ideology evade the label in order to avoid being written
off as flakes.

A Brief Primer in the New Age

All that said, the New Age has both a history and a set of fairly specific premises by which we may view it as a coherent movement. It is not just a buzzword.

I Got Them Post-Modern Blues

The rise of the New Age movement coincides with the shift to a post-modern culture in Western society. "Post-modern" describes a generation now disillusioned with the promises of modern science and culture. In the aftermath of the holocaust, nuclear weaponry, the Vietnam war, and the AIDS epidemic, people no longer believe that science can bring ease, health, and happiness. Disillusioned with the impotence of modern medicine before the likes of cancer, people turn to alternative healing. Also, in the wake of the breakup of the traditional family in the industrial era and in the social upheaval of the sixties, they grieve for the loss of their roots. They find that the material benefits of the modern age do not satisfy, and they yearn for values and significance, even if those values arise from myth.

Above all, they desire a spiritual life. They find the humanism of the secular city to be a cold philosophy for a lonely night. Yet the post-modern generation has not rushed back to the Christian God of their fathers. This version of God is "dead"—He perished in the scientific, secular era from which they just emerged. They identify Him with patriarchal oppression and ecological ravaging and also with the unyielding morality that they summarize in the word "puritanical." They find the spirituality of the East, the occult, and the gods and goddesses of the ancient world to be more appealing. Exotic rituals, a fairly easy and self-centered morality, and the promise of initiation into the lost secrets of life make for a heady incentive to a change of worldview. In short, the post-modern society wants spirituality, significance, belonging, and consolation against the impersonal nature of modern life. It frankly does not care how outlandish or irrational the answer might be so long as it fills this need.

The Road Heavily Traveled

Enter the New Age movement. A number of gurus, including Maharishi Mahesh Yogi of Transcendental Meditation and the one-time spiritual boy-wonder, Guru Maharaj Ji, shined briefly as superstars during the early seventies. Although their appeal did not last, they opened the door for the wider acceptance of Eastern spirituality in the West. Books began to appear such as *The Teachings of Don Juan,* by Carlos Castaneda, the mysterious *A Course in Miracles,* the bizarre *Urantia Book,* M. Scott Peck's *The Road Less Traveled,* and Marilyn Ferguson's *The Aquarian Conspiracy.* These and similar titles, with their esoteric teachings allegedly derived from spiritual masters of this or some other world, quickly found massive audiences. A number of individuals claimed to have special powers to contact and "channel" spirits, who were only too happy to instruct seekers in the ways of the universe (for a substantial fee). The most famous of these, J. Z. Knight, channels a 35,000-year-old ascended master named Ramtha. The New Age hit mainstream when Shirley MacLaine's book, *Out on a Limb,* came to television as a miniseries.

Targeted toward middle- and upper middle-class consumers, New Age books and paraphernalia (flotation tanks, domes, pyramids, etc.) proved to be highly lucrative. Major publishers, recognizing this great commercial appeal, began to market their products aggressively. Pilgrimages to Peru, the Amazon, India, and other spiritual centers gave sufficiently well-heeled clients the chance to attain enlightenment at a reasonable cost. Seminars in meditation, yoga, holistic healing, and contacting the spirits indoctrinated a generation in the new path to self-fulfillment. Jewelers got a boost as the market expanded for the ever-present crystals. The upshot of all this is a movement that is decentralized, upscale, narcissistic, often infuriatingly irrational, and unclear in its tenets and goals, but which has broad appeal and recognizable characteristics.

Easy Karma

If nothing else, New Agers hold this in common: humanity stands on the brink of a major evolutionary leap forward of spiritual dimensions. This means that as people contact their essential divinity as well as the spiritual laws that govern the universe, they will become more wise and balanced and will usher in a utopian era. In addition, many hold to the philosophy of monism (the belief that all is one). This entails rejection of the Christian belief that God is distinct from His creation. Many New Agers are pantheists (pantheism equates the universe with God). They also tend to amalgamate teachings from various religions and quasi-religions such as astrology. Many profess faith in divination (such as tarot) and psychic phenomena (such as ESP).

They generally reject the notion of evil and insist that our problem is not sin but ignorance of our own divinity. Some seem to hold to the Eastern notion that the material world is an illusion, but many embrace radical environmentalism (a hollow issue if the material world is illusion). Most New Agers believe that the physical world is real but that a Universal Mind (or Mind At Large) is a higher reality.

It is significant that monism underlies almost all their thinking. This implies that (since all is one) all have an equal claim to deity. The God of the Bible is no more truly God than any one of us, and we only have to recognize this in order to be free of the illusions of circumstance and limitation. We have the capacity to create our own reality, and when enough people realize this (as they say is happening now), universal bliss will begin. Monism also implies that morality is illusory since, if all is indeed one, the distinction between a moral act and an immoral one vanishes. At cosmic consciousness, we are able to recognize and embrace this alternate reality.

None of this is coherent. If the self is able to control reality, then New Age gurus ought to be able to do something more significant than bend a few spoons. Perceiving oneself to be God and perceiving reality in a new way is far from actually being God or from verifying this new perception of the world. But in the strange world of the New Age, one does not need to *do* anything to show that the self is God and creates its own reality; only insist that it is so. This comes close to asserting that the world we perceive is illusory, although New Agers would resist that conclusion.

New Agers have various opinions of Jesus Christ, but again, all have a common basis. Some say that Jesus was an Essene, a type of religious extremist whose teachings we saw in the Dead Sea Scrolls. Many allege that the Gnostic writings give a much more accurate portrayal of the life and teachings of Jesus than the Bible. Some say that Jesus derived His teachings from spiritual masters in India or even that He survived the cross and journeyed to the East after the event. All agree that Jesus was not the only begotten Son of God of the Christian faith. He was no more God than you or I, but what He did do was attain the level of enlightenment known as "Christ consciousness." The task for us is to do what He did and become what He became.[1]

Many believe in reincarnation, albeit in a sanitized form. In the East, reincarnation is understood to be a curse. The goal is to escape the wheel of suffering and rebirth through enlightenment. New Agers do hold to the idea that reincarnation is part of the evolution of the human species, but for them, reincarnation is kind of a Disneyland ride.

When they explore their past lives, almost invariably it turns out that they were poets, pharaohs, magicians, and healers. Shirley MacLaine believes that she was once an elephant princess. Very few were miserable serfs or slaves hauling bricks up the side of a mountain. The New Age movement is highly self-indulgent, the consummate yuppie religion. New Age centers are invariably in beautiful, expensive, and exclusive locations, such as the desert valleys of Sedona, Arizona. This has created the highly commercialized religious subculture we see today.

It has also given rise to new artistic expressions, especially in the emergence of a droning kind of somnambulant music designed to enhance meditation. Seminars in meditation that openly propagate New Age ideas take place in schools and major corporations. It accords well with new theories in education, as in the emphasis on high self-esteem as the goal of education. Its vision of the supernatural world has achieved a fairly complete victory over traditional Christian teachings in movies and television.[2]

And it has now entered the realm of the angels.

Basic Beliefs of New Age Angelphiles

James Sire has written that "it may seem strange that Christian theism does not have a developed angelology." He then goes on to explain that angels and lesser spirits, if one were to give them too much attention, would distract us from the most high God.[3] If Christianity has left a void there, New Age angelphilia has filled it with abandon.

Books from the New Age angelphile perspective now dominate bookshelves in the religion sections of major bookstore chains. The two most well known of these are *Ask Your Angels* by Alma Daniel, Timothy Wyllie, and Andrew Ramer,[4] and *A Book of Angels* by Sophy Burnham.[5] Others that are quite popular and contribute a great deal to this new understanding of angels include *Guardians of Hope* by Terry Lynn Taylor,[6] *Angels of Mercy* by Rosemary Ellen Guiley,[7] and *The*

Angels Within Us by John Randolph Price.[8] Together, these books paint a fairly complete picture of what I am calling New Age angelphilia.

I should mention that none of these authors, to my knowledge, calls herself or himself a New Ager and that some try to disassociate themselves from the movement. By the time we have finished examining their teachings, however, I think it will be clear that such disavowals are hollow. Their worldview and agenda correspond precisely with what we can only describe as New Age.

New Age Angelology

All of these books contain some kind of discussion of the nature of angels. The books generally agree with one another, but there are differences as well. Probably the best study of angels from a New Age perspective is that done by Burnham.[9] These books are quite eclectic in the sources they use. They freely cite the Bible, the Pseudepigrapha, the Kabbalah, the Koran, the Book of Mormon, and other writings on angels, such as those of Pseudo-Dionysius and Emanuel Swedenborg.

They do not distinguish one source above another in regard to credibility. They happily refer to the Mormon angel Moroni as no less a real angel than the Old Testament's Gabriel. They make little or no effort to reconcile contradictions in how these diverse sources understood angels. Doctrinal inconsistency does not concern them. Rather, they want to build a case that angels are everywhere and talk to all kinds of people with all kinds of religious backgrounds. Their point is that it does not matter whether you are Jewish, Christian, Muslim, Mormon, Hindu, or a believer in native American religion, you can still get into angelphilia and feel good about it. They want us to believe that awareness of and interaction with the angels is ancient and universal.

Some New Age angelphiles also look to the Gnostics for angel wisdom (this is not surprising; New Agers generally have a high regard for the Gnostics). Guiley offers a misleading summary of Gnostic teaching and mentions with apparent approval a Gnostic rite in which an initiate mystically marries his or her guardian angel.[10]

Most of these books will give you a list of the important angels and alleged angels (Gabriel, Michael, Raphael, Moroni, and so forth) together with a description of who these angels are and what they supposedly do. Also, they lay out charts of angel hierarchy and titles (archangels, powers, dominions, cherubim, and so on), just as was done by Pseudo-Dionysius.

They also link angels to ecology. Guiley, for example, says that totems "are roughly equivalent to the Judeo-Christian concept of angels,"[11] and *Ask Your Angels* says we need to learn about "nature spirits" and the "noble intelligence" of trees.[12] Some differentiate the angels and the "devic kingdom," composed of nature spirits. The latter "has duties of or relating to natural events, and all those things that are necessary to put the earth to rights."[13]

They also assert that angels channel messages through certain people. One angel showed up in a channeling session and declared, "My name is John, and I have come to teach about self-love."[14] Many angelphile books contain volumes of what angels allegedly dictated through their channelers. It is drivel, but we will come to that in the next chapter. Some claim that angels can choose to enter the human race and be born into human families—a kind of angelic incarnation.[15]

For a bizarre angelology, nothing surpasses the tedious book by Price, *The Angels Within Us.* He claims that within us are "twenty-two Causal Powers, or angels," that govern our lives. He gets the number twenty-two from the twenty-two major trumps of tarot cards, and he associates each angel with a card of the tarot. He also links his twenty-two angels to pagan gods and goddesses and to astrological signs. His angels include the angel of unconditional love and freedom (no surprise, given the New Age emphasis on unconditional love), the angel of illusion and reality, the angel of creative wisdom, the angel of order and harmony, and so forth. He associates the angel of creative wisdom, for example, with the Egyptian goddess Isis, with the tarot card of the high priestess, and astrologically with the moon. Each angel helps you become more true to "your holy self." With the assistance of the angel of creative wisdom, for example, Price decided to move his foundation to the Texas hill country.[16]

A Big Raw L

Angelphiles want to know the names of the angels with whom they are in contact. Many ancients believed that if you knew the name of a spirit, you had some kind of control over it, but that is not the point here. I think that New Agers do it because having a name for an angel makes it seem more authentic and personal. It helps them to convince themselves (and others) that the angel is real.

Angelphiles differ among themselves over whether the names are the actual appellations of their angels or just temporary monikers the angels adopt when dealing with mortals. Almost all, however, treat learning the name of one's guardian angel as highly significant. The authors of *Ask Your Angels* allege that much of the teaching of their book comes from the angel Abigrael (I do not know whether this is pronounced "Abby grail" or "A big raw L"). They call another angel-guide "LNO," which is pronounced something like "Eleanor." At any rate, they attach tremendous significance to the disclosure of these names. Alma Daniel marks her entrance into angelphilia with the discovery of the name of her angel, LNO.[17]

When you read angel books, you encounter more angels with funny names than could dance on the head of a really large pin. Most sound made-up and many are pseudo-Hebrew names built on the analogies of "Gabriel" and "seraphim." Thus, *Ask Your Angels* gives us pseudo-Hebrew in names like Abigrael and describes another angel as "supernaphim." Coming up with a good angel name seems to be a rite of passage for many angelphiles. Guiley calls it a "password" to "higher realms."[18]

Glowing Chakras

New Age angelphiles astound us not just with new revelations about the angels but also about ourselves. They blend Eastern mystical thinking and a popularized version of Western psychology into a unique, if sometimes incoherent, notion of human nature.

On the psychological side, they believe that nothing is so destructive to human potential as guilt and fear. Their books all sing the same refrain: the only thing keeping you back from peace, joy, love, and complete self-actualization is the guilt and fear of your own ego. If you can escape these negatives, you will overcome the anger, frustration, and lack of purpose that confounds your every day. The quest for a healthy self-image ranks high on their agenda.

This kind of thinking more or less dominates psychology in both the religious and secular world, and it is not surprising to find it here as well. Most of us can agree with some of this, moreover, although we would want to add that the question is not *whether* we should deal with negative emotions but *how* we should deal with them. We should also recognize that this is something that the New Age angelphiles have added to angel lore; traditional teachings about angels did not bother with how they can help you to self-actualize.

The mystical psychology of this movement indicates more clearly the direction they are headed. According to *Ask Your Angels*, the human body contains eight "chakras" (most of the New Age angelphile books speak of chakras at some point or other). These are "centers in the energy body that help to integrate it with our physical vehicle, and with our mind and our emotions."[19] They borrow this concept from Kundalini Yoga, which recognizes seven chakras (the *Ask Your Angels* authors have discovered an eighth). The eight chakras are called "root" (located at the base of the spine), "sexual" (lower abdomen), "solar plexus," "heart," "thymus" (this is the new one—it is in the upper chest), "throat," "third eye" (in the middle of the forehead), and "crown" (the top of the head). Each chakra functions as the center of an area of human activity. The "root" chakra governs survival and security, whereas the "third eye" provides intuition. According to *Ask Your Angels*, some people can see their chakras light up or feel them vibrate during meditation.

Ask Your Angels treats chakra awareness as fundamental to meditation and thus to connecting with the angels. By focusing on the chakras, we can remove any obstacles to meeting an angel. Also, knowing our chakras helps us to resolve all kinds of personal problems, they say. For example, we should maintain awareness of the "third eye" while preparing for an academic exam, and it is important to connect with the "root" chakra in order to resolve financial problems (because of the security aspect).[20]

Now, I cannot prove that the notion that we have eight chakras is just so much baloney (as I believe it to be). For that matter, no one can prove or even coherently argue that we have seven, eight, or fifty-seven varieties of chakras. The idea has no rational basis; it is something you can choose to believe if you want to. You should, however, recognize this as what it is—a notion out of an Eastern sect that has nothing to do with the angels. It is simply another variety of New Age mysticism.

Terry Lynn Taylor also combines mysticism with psychology and claims that we each have a "higher," "middle," and "lower" self. The higher self is wisdom, connection with angels, and intuition. The middle self deals with everyday life. The lower self is where we put things we do not want to handle. It seems to be the same as the psychological idea of repressed memories and feelings.[21] Taylor also defines the higher self as the "inner angel child" and "the pure and unadulterated essence of *you.*"[22] The goal of her book is to teach us how to reconnect with the inner child and rediscover joy. She wants us to "let go of this ridiculous notion of being an adult"[23] and be free of all the ego problems that strangle the higher self.

The idea that we can resuscitate the child within is attractive, and to some extent it is true. We can (and should) recover the joy of simplicity and wonder, as well as the faith of a childlike dependence on God (Matt. 18:2–5). But it is dangerously misleading to suppose that there is some wonderful, intuitive child within that we lost years ago whom the angels can reawaken. For that matter, we were not that well-connected with the mythical inner child when we were children. A few minutes at any schoolroom or playground should convince you that children are not always wonderfully child*like*; they have a stubborn habit of being child*ish*. Maturity is not such a bad thing: "When I was a child, I spoke like a child, I thought like a child, I reasoned like a child; when I became an adult, I put an end to childish ways" (1 Cor. 13:11).

John Randolph Price propagates a similar but even simpler doctrine. For him, there are two aspects to being human. One is the "ego," which he never defines but always describes as something that is bad. It only gives us illusions and is the source of all fear, doubt, hesitation, duplicity, and unhappiness. It is not the real you. The other is the true, divine, inner self, to which he gives a variety of names (the "I AM," "Christ consciousness," the "God within," and so forth). His clearest succinct statement on this inner self is that it is "your smiling, loving, joyous, all-knowing cosmic Self."[24] This higher self is always happy and good. It is the real you, but it is also God. The true self is also the true God, and it is one with all the other true selves in the great cosmic unity.

Just Be Yourself

From what we have seen of the New Age angelphile conception of human nature, it should come as no surprise that their primary moral teaching is very simple: love yourself. They relentlessly beat the drum for a mirror-kissing ideology in which the slogan "love yourself *unconditionally*" has become a mantra repeated *ad nauseum*. Since they contend that every manner of addiction (abuse of alcohol, drugs, relationships, food, and so forth) comes from lack of self-esteem, they make inner worth the foremost virtue of life. In a remarkable revision of Matthew 22:36–38, Price states that the first and greatest commandment is to "love your Lord Self" and then love others.[25]

Their testimonials describe shy people who suddenly become assertive through the angelic meditative techniques. To be sure, these testimonials are rather odd; one woman described herself as feeling like a rock, a tree, and an eagle. The angel LNO psychoanalyzes a young writer suffering from writer's block and compulsive eating as follows: "He fears that he is not loved, and that without love he will die. . . . He has not yet been willing to come to terms with his own lack of self-love, his own self-repudiation."[26] They describe this ethic in various ways; in native American religious terms, for example, we should "be true to our medicine."[27] Taylor is explicit about the goal of angelphilia: "The theme of this practice is to become authentic; the joke is that there is no special trick or key to becoming authentic."[28] We have already seen how the angel "John" came to a channeler for the express purpose of teaching "self-love."

The implications here are not immediately obvious. Most of us would agree that a poor self-image leads to self-destructive behavior and that a state of self-loathing is unhealthy. On the other hand, we must assert that moral standards exist independently of how we feel about ourselves and that some people feel terrific about themselves and are downright proud while engaged in all manner of evil. Also, the causal relationship goes both ways. We hate ourselves because we are doing wrong (we do not do wrong because we have a poor self-image), and we will not begin to like ourselves or be happy until we rectify the evil. When Taylor says, "In contrast, when the angels teach about purification, they just mean 'becoming purely you,' free of negative habits and negative perceptions,"[29] we need to ask whether there is more to purity than just being ourselves. After all, we may not be all that pure.

There Is a New Age Coming

If New Age angelphiles hold one thing in common, it is the belief that we are indeed entering a "new age." Like the "age of Aquarius" as rhapsodized in the musical *Hair*, it is to be a time of harmony, understanding, sharing, and happiness—and you will be glad to know that it is very near.

Their confidence in a coming world harmony arises from their belief that more and more people are becoming aware of the angels and that people who know their angels can do no wrong. As the angel "Sargolais" explains, "a species that is angel-aware cannot pollute, enslave, destroy, or kill."[30] Therefore, in the words of Mentoria the angel, "What is in this is the decline of all forms of violence, and an ascendance of all forms of loving and understanding, of compassionate outreach, of sharing, spiritual, material, and mental."[31]

All of this is because we are nearing the end of the cosmic evolution of human consciousness. Guiley explains this in terms of the teaching of Pierre Teilhard de Chardin. Although a Jesuit priest (his given name was astoundingly Catholic: Marie-Joseph-Pierre), Teilhard's evolutionary speculation was hardly orthodox. He believed that evolution had occurred in four stages—galactic, earth, life, and human. We are currently progressing toward the "Omega point," a state of Christ consciousness where complete harmony is achieved. Although Teilhard thought that this final stage of evolution was still in the distant future, Guiley believes it is upon us now.

Rosemary Guiley also endorses the theories of Gerald Hawkins, who believes that humanity has progressed in a series of "mindsteps," which are a kind of intellectual great leaps forward. Mindstep zero was the age of chaos, in which humanity saw the world but could not comprehend it. It began around 35,000 B.C. At Mindstep 1, the age of myth and legend, people explained the cosmos with mythical stories. It began in 3000 B.C. Mindstep 2, the age of order, began in A.D. 150 with the work of the astronomer Ptolemy, who explained the motions of the stars and planets with a highly complex set of mathematical equations (the earth was at the center of the universe). Mindstep 3, the age of revolution, began with the Copernican revolution in 1543. Mindstep 4, beginning in 1926, is the age of space. The time between mindsteps is getting shorter and shorter. Hawkins calculates that mindsteps 5, 6, and 7 will come in 2021, 2045, and 2051. What's next? We may contact extraterrestrials, learn to time travel, and get to the Omega point.[32]

Ask Your Angels similarly informs us that Abigrael says we are in the "third wave" of angel activity. The first wave was in biblical times, when angels appeared only to a few prophets and patriarchs, such as Jacob, Daniel, and Joseph. The second was in the medieval period, when they appeared to saints and seers, such as Mohammed, Saint Francis, and the Jewish mystics of the Kabbalah. Now, in the third wave, angels are revealing themselves to ordinary people. Songs like "Johnny Angel" and movies such as *It's a Wonderful Life* show that angels have broken into our day-to-day thinking, they say. All kinds of people are having angel encounters. The emergence of the thymus chakra was a major step toward the New Age.[33] It cannot be far away now!

Some angelphiles associate the New Age with the second coming of Christ, albeit in highly unusual terms. One opinion says that Christ will return as a woman but that it will not be a bodily return. Rather, the "feminine principle" will return to earth. Until now, patriarchy has dominated the earth, but with the "feminine principle," the qualities of compassion and (of course) unconditional love will reappear.[34]

Angelphile exuberance over the New Age knows no bounds. According to *Ask Your Angels*, the angel Eularia (who is the guardian angel for the United Nations) has "the blueprint for a harmonious and unified earth."[35] As people tune into the angels, they will discover at last solutions to age-old problems. Doctors will gain new insight on healing. Scientists will be able to put aside their particle accelerators and learn about physics from the angels who run the universe. Politicians, with the help of the angels, will actually solve some problems.[36] People will make discoveries and attain powers in a way unknown since Atlantis (!), says Price.[37]

Even this is only small potatoes. In the near future, selfishness will disappear! *Ask Your Angels* asserts: "One hundred years from now [the angels say] egoless cooperation will be commonplace—in families, business, and in government."[38] The norm will be leaderless collaboration with everyone freely creating and expressing himself or herself. The utopian and millennial frenzy here is hard to miss.

Dying to Become an Angel

For the most part, these books say little about the afterlife; one exception is *A Book of Angels*, but it is none too clear. The author, Sophy Burnham, describes an experience in which a friend guided her through visions of past and future lives (an account made somewhat bewildering by her comment that she does not believe in reincarnation).

At any rate, she lay on a couch, and her friend (a man) talked her into a meditative mood and guided her on her voyage (he asked questions and gave directions through her whole vision). He told her to follow a prick of light when she saw it—which she did—and to describe what she saw. She then walked through her dream of past lives, in which she was of a different sex or social class.

Next, she went to a future life and found herself as an angel (she does not use the term, but it seems fairly clear that this is what she means). She did not have a body, but she was able to choose to have one (with or without wings) at will. As a young angel, she soared and flipped in flight and was thoroughly amused and full of giggles. She noticed humans and was immediately fond of them. When asked (by her guide) if she was God, she had difficulty answering. She finally said no, she was not God, in that she was not the Source. But she could have easily said yes, in that she was full of Godness, as he was also. He asked if she would die someday, and she saw that in aeons to come she would drift away into a perfect void and make room for others. The guide then told her to come back, and she woke up on the couch.[39]

This vision amalgamates several religious ideas. The first (notwithstanding her assertion that she does not believe in reincarnation) is the notion that we progress through a series of incarnations toward spiritual perfection. This idea occurs in various Eastern religions but also appears in the West, as in the philosophy of Plato. In her vision, becoming an angel seems to be the crown of spiritual attainment. The final descent into the void sounds like the Eastern notion of Nirvana, the ultimate nothingness that signifies emancipation. From New Age thinking, she includes the idea that we are all in some sense God. Other angelphiles profess similar beliefs: "I think angels are human souls who have evolved and evolved, probably through lots of lifetimes, to get to the stage of being an angel."[40]

I would only make one observation. After devoting many pages and much reflection to the nature of angels, pages in which she frequently cites the words of the Bible and of Christian teachers, Burnham climaxes her book with a vision that in every respect contradicts biblical and Christian teaching. One should not be misled. Despite the appearance of a soft, personal form of Christianity, these books offer an altogether different gospel. The flutter you hear is of the wings of bats, not angels.

> GLENDOWER: *I can call spirits from the vasty deep.*
> HOTSPUR: *Why, so can I, or so can any man;*
> *But will they come when you do call for them?*
> WILLIAM SHAKESPEARE, HENRY IV, PART 1, 3, 1

Spirits from the Vasty Deep

New Age Angels, Part 2

NEW AGE ANGELPHILIA, AS WE HAVE SEEN, GROWS OUT
of and reflects the post-modernism of the larger New Age movement. It
remains for us to see how the angelphilia practically expresses itself as a
new religion.

Contacting Angels

The distinctive emphasis on New Age angelphilia is not its doctrine but
its assertion that anyone can initiate communication with the angels. It
is not just a matter of believing in angels or appreciating a few nice
stories. New Age angelphilia has the stated purpose of getting people to
make contact with their angels.[1] The methods of contacting angels vary
in complexity and ritual but all follow the same basic principles.

Holy Be My Name

John Randolph Price advocates a four-step approach to accessing
angels. First, we scan our consciousness for anything negative or

shameful from the past and cast it all on the "Love of God" within ourselves. Second, we look for negative traits such as jealousy, resentment, and anger within ourselves. Third, we make a surrender of mind, emotions, and body to the "Spirit within." Fourth, we meditate. Having done all this, we can be sure that an angel encounter is near: "At a certain point you will see a light up ahead, and you will know that you are approaching the angel." As the angel takes on physical form, we can look into its eyes and make whatever request we choose.[2]

Price, you will recall, describes twenty-two angels that supposedly aid us in our discovery of the higher self. He also provides written meditations on each of these angels to enable his readers to contact them. The meditations reflect the cult of self-love that New Agers advocate. One meditation says, "I am Divine Consciousness. I am Spirit, Soul, and a Body of Light, and within me are all the powers of the universe, for I am God individualized, the Trinity of God in radiant expression."[3] In another, Price says that at the end of his spiritual journey, "I will emerge as the one who says, 'He who sees me sees the Father.'"[4]

These extraordinary devotionals reveal not only the spiritual narcissism of New Age angelphilia but also show, ironically, that angels as living, real beings are irrelevant in its scheme. For example, the "angel of illusion and reality" can be "blocked by ego projections." In this situation, this angel becomes "the master manipulator and works closely with the ego to deceive, mislead, and defraud." However, when one is "more centered in the Presence," the angel will "illumine individual consciousness and spread the light of reality."[5] In short, the angel of illusion and reality has no independent existence or personality apart from what the (human) self makes it become. This does not say much for the significance or reality of angels, but it harmonizes well with New Age thinking. It also says something about how New Age angelphiles understand the concept of faith, but we will return to this later.

Eee Nu Rah Zay

Ask Your Angels has a whole pack of methods and exercises for making angel contact, but all revolve around what is called the GRACE process[6] (New Age angelphiles tend to use much Christian terminology, perhaps because it sets readers' minds at ease). GRACE stands for Grounding, Releasing, Aligning, Conversing, and Enjoying the contact (LNO herself contributed the last element, "Enjoying").

"Grounding" means centering one's mental and emotional energies. It is a relaxation technique that involves going to a quiet place, lighting candles, sitting in a comfortable position, and focusing on controlled breathing and the calmness in one's body. One may also focus on a picture of an angel or imagine roots growing out of one's feet. It is impossible to ground effectively without chakra awareness.

The technique of "releasing" expels negative feelings that may interfere with angel contact. These include fear, a sense of unworthiness, apathy, and the like. We are supposed to explore these feelings and then release them. The rationale behind this is quite odd: because we are earthbound and subject to gravity, our "vibration" is "denser" than angel vibration, and "releasing" discharges energies that have been blocked off and raises our vibrations to a higher level. The authors say that humming up and down the musical scale is helpful.

People can "align" when they become more aware of the world around them, *Ask Your Angels* tells us. When correctly aligned, one experiences fully the pleasures of the sights, sounds, and smells of everyday life. The book offers several exercises for aligning. For example, we can chant, "*Eee Nu Rah Zay.*" *Eee* means, "all that I am that is not physical, my mind and my emotions." *Nu* refers to the physical body, *Rah* refers to the soul, and *Zay* means "in the company of the angels." This chant ostensibly came from the angels in the key of C-sharp. The book does not tell us what language this is, but it is remarkably succinct.

"Conversing" refers to conversation with the angels. While conversing, it is important to have a notebook to write down the angels' responses. The book does not pretend that angels will actually manifest themselves visibly to someone who goes through the GRACE process; rather, the whole conversation takes place in one's own head. This raises serious questions, to which we shall return. The important thing is that the angel "contact" is actually an imagined, mental conversation. The individual asks questions and then waits for "answers" to pop into his or her head. These thoughts constitute a conversation with an angel.

Under the title "enjoying," *Ask Your Angels* introduces a method for divination. It tells how to make "angel oracle cards," which are shuffled, dealt, and interpreted according to rules that the book describes. These come in three categories: the names of the archangels (such as Gabriel), categories of angels (companion angels, connecting angels, technology angels, etc.), and specific instructions ("spend time with someone you love," "visit a healer," "open a book at random," etc.). By picking one card from each category, the devotee has fun with his or her angel.

Ask Your Angels also mentions other methods of divination and angel contact. For example, it encourages us to interpret our dreams as messages from the angels. If the inner harmonies are just not there, we can use the "angel vacuum cleaner" meditation technique. In this exercise, we imagine an angel standing before us with a vacuum cleaner, which the angel uses to "clean up bent energy" inside of us.[7]

Angel Brain Waves

Terry Lynn Taylor advocates that by meditating on angels we enter an "angel alpha state" (meditation allegedly floods our brains with alpha waves). She encourages the use of a mantra, such as "angel," to enter this state. She invites her readers to relax, take deep breaths, and avoid mental concentration. She also advocates visualization (for example, imagining yourself to be bathed in light). She, too, wants her readers to deal with negative feelings and memories: "when something pops into your mind that you want to eliminate, visualize angel window cleaners spraying the spot or clump with a cleaning solution and watch it vanish out into the universe to be transmuted."[8] As with all the New Age angelphiles, imagination plays a big role in her alleged contacts with angels. For example, she advises her readers to go into the angel alpha state, imagine that they are being carried through the skies by angels, and picture forests and lakes down below.[9]

Many of the angelphiles advocate the use of a mantra in order to invoke the presence of an angel. Again, they make their advice more palatable to hesitant North Americans by giving the practice a Christian façade. Guiley relates a story of how a woman saw a whole church full of angels while chanting the name "Jesus."[10]

An obvious problem one may have with this whole procedure is that opening one's self to the spirit world is dangerous; after all, who knows what may come in? The New Agers, although not unaware of the peril of encountering evil spirits, offer protection that is to say the least, thin. "Declare that only the presence of the kingdom of God, only the Christ consciousness, is welcome," Taylor advises. In other words, just tell the bad ones to stay away, and they will. This gives little reassurance, particularly after Taylor has said that we should ask the angels to take "free reign" in our minds.[11]

Simply stated, these books advocate that we contact angels by working through our negative emotions, entering a meditative state, opening our minds to an angel encounter, and then engaging in an imaginary meeting in which we hold a conversation with an angel in our own thoughts. To make the experience a little more concrete and memorable, we should write down what we think we hear the angels saying.

Crossed Wires

The obvious question here is this: What if we think the angels are telling us something, and it turns out not to be so? *Ask Your Angels* has a simple answer. If your angel gives you a wrong answer, then your own desires are in the way and the angel cannot get through.[12]

Christian pastors know well the experience of a distraught parishioner who cannot understand how the message he was sure he received from God turned out to be wrong. Christianity, however, has always discouraged private revelations and subjected them to public scrutiny (1 John 4:1: "Beloved, do not believe every spirit, but test the spirits to see whether they are from God; for many false prophets have gone out into the world"). The Old Testament was even more severe; anyone who claimed to have a message from God was liable to be put to death if his words proved false (Deut. 18:20–22). The biblical writers gave no support to the idea that contact with the supernatural world required no more than a simple technique or was for everyone.

New Age angelphilia, by contrast, encourages people in the strongest possible way to think that they can invoke messages from the angels. It also entraps people in a "heads-I-win, tails-you-lose" mind game. If the devotee "hears" something from an angel that turns out to be true or helpful, then the angel has spoken and it is proof that angel contact is real. If the message or advice turns out to be disastrous, then your own desires got in the way, and it was not the angel's fault.

The Angel as Shrink

When we contact angels, the books tell us, they can help us with psychological therapy. They recommend a number of techniques that are ostensibly the angels' way to self-discovery and personal growth. In reality, they are at best little more than common strategies from psychology with a few remarks thrown in to give the appearance of being angelic. At worst, they open us to moral and spiritual peril.

They tell us to use art therapy for dealing with the "monsters" we have within. The monster represents our inner anger and is supposed to help us release and understand these feelings. Some advocate that we make a list of our own weaknesses and imperfections, write down what we believe to be the sources of these negative traits, and fantasize about ways to eliminate those traits while asking the angels for help.[13]

Now there is nothing wrong with taking stock of one's weaknesses and flaws for the purpose of self-improvement. Centuries ago, Puritan devotional theology taught that we should each keep a spiritual journal and use it as a tool for sanctification. At the same time, I doubt that fantasizing is the best way to confront negative traits, and I wonder why anyone would ask for an angel's help rather than God's.

Many religious or semireligious books contain something about positive thinking and achieving your goals, and *Ask Your Angels* is no exception. In a five-step program, we make a deliberate choice about what we want, commit to getting it, visualize the goal, give thanks to the "Source of All," and release the goal "to the Universe, so it can then take over and deliver what you've ordered."[14]

Angelphiles especially like the "twelve-step-program" as a means of personal growth. This should not surprise us; the program has an ambiguous religious orientation and therefore fits easily into their agenda. It tells us to seek the aid of a higher spiritual power, but that power need not be the God of the Bible.

On one level, the angelphile presentations of the twelve steps add nothing to the program besides the repeated assertion that an angel can help you with this or that step. On another level, their presentations of the twelve steps shows us a great deal about the strange world of angelphilia. Step seven, for example, says that we are humbly to ask God to remove our shortcomings, and the angelphile interpretations try to bring the angels into the process. Taylor says we should meditate on the word "humble" with the aid of the angels.[15] *Ask Your Angels*, however, says we should call upon a "transformation angel" to help in our personality overhaul.[16] The point is not that the two books have different approaches—that is to be expected—but that the "angelic help" seems both a superfluous addition to the program and a wacky concept as well (transformation angels?). I am not going to venture an opinion on the merits or dangers of the twelve-step program; my point is that the angelphile approach at best adds nothing to it and at worst distorts it with such bizarre notions as "transformation angels" (as well as "attunement angels," "information angels," and the like). One more illustration will clarify how New Age angelphilia perverts the program.

The tenth step states that we should continue to take personal inventory and admit wrong in ourselves when it is there. This implies a fairly clear understanding of the difference between right and wrong and a determination to struggle against the wrong. Such concepts make New Age angelphiles uncomfortable, however, so a little reinterpretation is in order. Taylor comments: "No more black-and-white thinking; think only in angel colors. . . . To think in the colors of the angels, we have to get rid of the notions of good and bad. Everything exists as a separate and distinct event, encompassing many aspects."[17] In short, you do not need to feel guilty about anything because the arcane notion that some things are just wrong represents a throwback to subangelic reasoning. But this touches on the peculiar attitudes that New Age angels have to morality, a subject to which we shall return.

New Age angelphiles skillfully use psychology to coax neophytes to take the plunge. They say that ego often interferes with making contact with our angels. We need a strategy for coping with the "negative voice" that scolds us and tells us that we are not good enough for an angelic encounter. The negative voice manifests itself in "Unworthiness," "Pride," "Anger," "Apathy," "Fear of disappointment," and so forth. We deal with these attitudes by a releasing technique that involves "inhaling tolerance" and "exhaling judgment," and by tuning into whatever may be preventing us from contacting our angels.[18]

Everyone struggles to some degree with anger, guilt, depression, and the other negative feelings. The present age in Western culture, for better or for worse, emphasizes these and other aspects of "self-image." In listing these "negative voices" and offering a technique to deal with them, angelphiles no doubt touch many people who identify with the list and hope that angels will be their deliverance. That hope, I believe, is as vain as the angel exercises are silly. They will not free you from fear or guilt or lust. They are not without a deeper purpose, however. They induce people to lower their walls and allow alien spiritual powers to enter.

If you are entering the purported world of angels, as described in these books, and hear an inner voice say no, my advice is that you not write it off as a "negative voice" that needs to be assuaged and finally silenced. Listen to it. The only "spirit" you should open yourself to is the Spirit of God.

Fantasy Friendships

When angelphilia moves beyond ordinary psychology and attempts to show how the angels can really make a difference in your life, the teaching becomes even more strange. For example, angel contacts can help us resolve relationship problems, so we are told. First, we go into an "angel alpha state." Then we fantasize freely about people we know and ask the angels to give insights. We follow our stream of consciousness and ask what our role is with this or that person. We also visualize meetings between our guardian angels and the angels of other people. We should not be so crude as to ask, "Does Bertha love me?," but we can ask for insights on the nature of the relationship and ask what lessons we should learn from it.[19]

I find this teaching troubling. If you want to explore the meaning of your relationship with someone, you need to do it with that person and not sitting alone in a free fall of fantasy. Such a practice is almost sure to lead people astray. Even in Christianity, which discourages people from seeking specific messages from God and which looks with skepticism on an individual who claims that "God told me to do this," we have more than enough examples of people who say that "God told me to marry you" (or divorce you or spend more time with you or share your inheritance). How much more often will this happen when people are encouraged both to fantasize and to believe that the thoughts that pop into their minds are from the angels?

I suspect, moreover, that as people begin to delve into this activity, more direct attempts to manipulate other people through the aid of spirits will soon follow. I hardly need to add, I hope, that nothing good is likely to come from fantasizing about a meeting between your angel and your friend's angel.

Finally, these books include other techniques for building relationships that sound as if they came out of a "Saturday Night Live" routine, but which are apparently meant to be taken seriously. Price says you should learn to love by finding a rock and "for the next several days loving that rock as you have never loved anyone or anything on earth. Develop compassion and tenderness toward the rock; stroke it, speak to it, and tell it of its divine origin."[20]

What is wrong with this picture? Here's a hint: learning to love involves learning to deal with people who do things you do not like. This is not an issue with rocks.

Angel Light

One other aspect of contacting angels at least deserves a mention. New Agers frequently invoke angel light and the manipulation of angel light as one of the benefits of angelic communication. This probably comes from the familiar association of the angels with bright, shining light in the Bible and in art, as well as in stories people have told of angel encounters.

These books, however, take the concept to new lengths. Terry Lynn Taylor tells us that we can use angel light for healing. If we have a pain somewhere, we can take a beam of angel light and "focus it on the cells surrounding the area of pain or sickness." We can imagine it "entering the cells and permeating the tissue," and we can even send beams to others who are suffering. We visualize it as a "laser beam of white healing light." It also alleviates depression and is great fun to "play with."[21] Since we ostensibly can invoke the angels at will, I suppose it is no big deal to be able to manipulate the light in which they dwell.

Angel Wisdom

No religion that I know is absolutely devoid of wisdom, but sooner or later the errors of that religion will show through. This is true of ancient paganism, Islam, Mormonism, and New Age angelphilia.

On the positive side, for example, Taylor observes that impatient people often behave rudely, and she encourages her readers to find something that forces them to slow down, whether it be a hobby, chopping wood, or whatever.[22] She wants us to stop taking life so seriously and to foster a compassionate disposition.[23] *Ask Your Angels* aptly describes the psychological importance of forgiveness and opposes the use of drugs to achieve transcendence.[24]

On the other hand, much of the wisdom these books offer is of the hackneyed, fortune cookie variety. Taylor gives us such gems as "To attract, be attractive" and "No one is a failure who has friends."[25] Some of the advice they offer reads like old clippings from newspaper astrology columns: "You're doing the best you can. Be satisfied at any given moment, your consciousness is as high as you are capable."[26] Some of their sayings have an air of profundity but on close inspection say nothing at all. This is my favorite: "Beauty is truth, truth beauty. That is all ye know and all ye need know."[27]

I Am NOT Making This Up

One way to describe much of what you read from angelphiles is "weird"; another way is "really weird." Many New Age angelphiles had established their credentials as those who live on the fringe of reality before they got into angels. Flotation tanks, crop circles, and the like were already high on their lists. Crystals, a perennial favorite among those with alternative lifestyles, show up too. Guiley tells us that crystal "is light made visible and represents the balance point between two worlds, the seen and the unseen, the material and the spiritual."[28] I do not know what she means by saying that crystal is "light made visible" (light within the visible spectrum is already visible). I also find it hard to believe that a mineral is the link to the spiritual world. But this is probably just more spiritual double-talk, in which rationality is not an issue. On the other hand, *Ask Your Angels* assures us that through its exercises we can become friends with the animal, vegetable, and mineral kingdoms, as well as make contacts with the archangels.[29] In between sessions with Gabriel, you can converse with a dandelion or get to know a slab of gypsum.

Angels and Extraterrestrials

The angels work with the civilizations on other planets, we are told. Angels are "inter-galactic social workers" who help their clients improve the karmas of both humans and aliens. The angel Sargolais informs us that Andrew Ramer is only one of his 119 clients and that each client lives in a different galaxy. The dullard humans tend to ignore their angel guardians, but this is not true for the people on other planets or even for all earthlings. No, sir! The dolphins and whales stay in close contact with their angel friends. The angels cannot break through to us poor members of species *Homo sapiens* because they cannot enter our domain unless we let them in.[30] It seems that the Federation of Planets is not the only organization that follows the "Prime Directive."

Speaking of Star Trek and life on other planets, it turns out that we can learn about extraterrestrial civilization without bothering with warp drive. Our angels can tell us all about these matters. Ramer says that under the tutelage of his angels, he "studied Ice Age culture, and learned about life on other planets."[31] (I thought I had better cite him here, or you would think that I was just being silly and made this up.)

Lift those Wings! One, Two!

Personal contact with angels conveys other advantages as well. When you are especially feeling down, your angel can give you a "heart-to-heart transfusion of golden liquid light,"[32] which is apparently a real pepper-upper. Not only that, *Ask Your Angels* even includes an exercise that will help you grow wings! You close your eyes, connect with your chakras, and vertebra by vertebra you feel "golden seed pods" unfurl and spread out until you have wings. These are your "antenna to the angelic realm." Of course you cannot see these wings, but you can run them through a series of calisthenics: "Raise your left wing toward the ceiling and lower your right wing toward the floor. Reverse. Point them all the way back behind you. Bring them all the way around in front of you, tip to tip, and riffle them up and down."[33] I sometimes wonder if the authors of *Ask Your Angels* are playing a big joke on their readers.

The Reincarnated Spirit Guide Dog

Price tells how, during a time of severe business upheaval, the angel/goddess Athena gave him a dog. This dog "brought balance" back to his life "through joy and gratitude" and returned him to a "more harmonious state." This, I suppose, enabled him to get his financial house in order. Ten years later the dog "made her transition" (died) but "quickly returned" (was reincarnated) as another dog. This was during another period of major change in Price's life, and the dog has remained with him as a "beacon of calm."[34] Many people could tell a similar story while managing to avoid Athena and reincarnation: "I got a dog during a time of stress and she helped take my mind off my problems. When she died I got another dog, and I like her too." No doubt about it, pets can be therapeutic.

How I Saved President Bush

Much of this pales in comparison to some of the stories of spiritual adventure we get from angelphiles. My favorite is as follows. It seems that in late 1983 a Frenchman heard from his dead mother that the nuclear reactor at Cape de la Hague was going to have a meltdown on January 16 or 17 of 1984. He told a woman who had links to the "spiritual community," and the message reached such a group in Glastonbury, England (which happens to be on the same energy line as Cape de la Hague). The angelphiles developed a "plan of action" and put down crystals along the energy line. On the appointed day, they meditated and with the help of the angels transformed the atomic energy into "positive healing emanations." The result: there was no nuclear meltdown![35] Never mind that no one else had an inkling that there was any danger of one; the day had been saved!

Of course, angelphiles also take credit for rescuing the situation at the Three Mile Island incident. It seems that when the news hit about the problem there they floated out of their bodies and formed two enormous spheres around the reactor, so that it did not explode[36] (actually, the problem was a leak; it never was in danger of exploding).

If you start taking credit for preventing disasters that never happened, your spiritual heroics can be limitless. I might just as well claim that on April 1, 1990, I felt a special need to ask the angel Bambuz-El to protect President Bush. And sure enough, on April 1, 1990, he was not assassinated. Coincidence? *I think not.*

Angels Do Everything

It seems that once you get into angelphilia, you cannot get enough of them. You believe that angels are everywhere, that they do everything, and that there is an angel for every purpose. Taylor tells us, "If you are feeling joy, you are feeling the angels."[37] She further tells us that there are "angels for every occasion," including "healers," "worry extinguishers," and "prosperity brokers." If you cannot find the kind of angel you want on the list—no need to worry—there are "designer angels, who can help with almost any task you assign."[38] It goes without saying that there are special angels for events such as birth and death and recovery from illness.[39] Some angels specialize in education. When you suddenly have a good idea, I hope you are not so vain as to suppose that you actually thought of it yourself. Not at all! An angel gave it to you.[40] If you have an injury, you probably need a "wiring angel" to come in and redo your circuitry[41] (with apologies to columnist Dave Barry: I am not making this up).

Pagan religions assign little gods to every thing and event. Fairies live in trees and flowers, river sprites and nymphs govern bodies of water, animal spirits live in the beasts, while other spirits specialize in luck, war, joy, disease, good crops, protection on sea voyages, and so on and so forth. When angelphiles invent a different angel for every occasion, they are not doing anything new. It goes with the territory.

Dangers of the Land of Spirits

From all that has gone before, you may have the impression that I consider New Age angelphilia deleterious for the soul. That is true. As I conclude this chapter, I would like to outline what I regard to be the salient dangers of the movement.

Something New

First, New Age angelphiles promote nothing less than a new religion. The popular books cited above claim to promote teachings that anyone of any religion can incorporate into his or her beliefs. In reality, the angelphiles offer an alternative religion.

They offer a new source of revelation. All of them, as we have seen, advocate imaginary angel encounters as a source of personal revelation. But many of these books go beyond that. *Ask Your Angels*, for example, calls itself "a primer for learning how to talk to celestials" and adds that one's own personal angel notebook will become "a textbook for your life."[42] Many books contain detailed instructions and teachings from alleged angels. Price describes how the angel of creative wisdom (a.k.a. Isis) revealed how the relationship between humans and angels works.[43] *Ask Your Angels* gives the revelations of the angels Sargolais and Abigrael, among others. For example, Sargolais makes the remarkable claim that angel bodies can be in several places at once.[44]

The angels give proverbs, such as "Stop judging yourself," "Let go," and "Remember who you Are [sic]."[45] They declare something analogous to a doctrine of sin and redemption, although they reject traditional notions of sin. Abigrael alleges that on "more regular planets" where the flow of love has not been stifled, the angels "aren't hidden" and the "mortal and angelic worlds have a full and cooperative aspect."[46] This is the condition to which *Ask Your Angels* wants us to return.

As we have seen, they offer prophecy, such as the prediction that we are soon to enter the age of egoless cooperation. The angel "Shandron" declares that there has been "a turning of a dispensation for your world" and that angels like himself "carry forward the vision" of where humanity is going.[47] If one takes these revelations seriously, then one must conclude that Isis, Sargolais, Shandron, and others have done no less than give the world new insights into truth. In short, their words are the scripture of a new religion.

Something Old

This new religion, however, does little more than repackage and combine aspects of old paganism. They advocate, in everything but name, a return to household gods. In many pagan societies, such as the Canaanite civilization that Israel confronted, private homes had small shrines with images of the gods that protected the household. People believed that they could not possibly matter to the high gods; these private gods gave them reassurance of having their own personal, caring deities. While the rituals and ceremonial devices may differ, the essential ideas are the same.

The angelphiles advocate that you create a "sacred place" in your home, decorate it with whatever sets you in the proper mood, light a candle or incense, and go through the routine of contacting your angel. Guiley asserts that "unlike the Judeo-Christian God, who is abstract and has no form or face, angels are personable."[48] They are nice, near, little gods.

As in classical paganism, moreover, you can go beyond your own personal angel and contact the greater, specialized angels. *Ask Your Angels* recommends that you contact Gabriel if you are having problems in a love relationship, Uriel if you face financial problems, and Michael to advance global peace.[49] We have already seen how Price identifies the angels with the gods and goddesses of classical paganism such as Isis, Athena, and Hermes. Taylor states, "You can think of archangels as major angel archetypes, similar to the gods and goddesses of Greek and Roman mythology." She also revives the muses, goddesses to whom the ancient Greeks attributed artistic inspiration, as angels "of creative inspiration."[50]

Ask Your Angels embraces the "Gaia Hypothesis," a notion of radical ecology that asserts that the earth is a living intelligence. Gaia is the ancient Greek mother goddess, and *Ask Your Angels* identifies Gaia as "the Earth Angel"[51] (not to be confused with the rock and roll golden oldie of the same name). Guiley describes an angel called the "Silver Lady" who turns out to be none other than the moon goddess of Wicca.[52]

We have already seen that angelphiles endorse methods of divination, especially with various kinds of cards.[53] Interpretation of omens, whether by looking at the entrails of a sheep, following the path of an eagle in the sky, or manipulating sacred objects is common in paganism and the occult.

The angelphiles embrace other ancient teachings that are inimical to Christianity as well. The angel LNO, as quoted in *Ask Your Angels*, endorses an analysis of the human condition that resounds with the Gnostic theory of emanations: "Within each human is the divine spark, the God That Is. Through the soul's descent into physical matter, that spark becomes covered over, hidden, yet it remains within each human individual—and indeed within each living thing. Our function is to ignite the spark within, to fill you not with 'our' thoughts, but to connect you with the knowingness that you already possess. You forget. Humans forget because the descent into matter lowers consciousness and brings about forgetfulness."[54]

We have already seen that New Age angelphiles promote the doctrine of reincarnation. Examples in their literature abound. In a diagnosis sure to puzzle the average back specialist, LNO asserts that a certain young woman named Melody experienced back pain because in another life she was burned at the stake for being a heretic.[55] Also, the angel Sargolais tells Andrew Ramer that among other things he has been a midwife and mother[56] (in prior lifetimes, not via an operation). Reincarnation lingo derived from Eastern religion, such as "karmic growth,"[57] is bandied about with abandon.

The Unrecognizable Bible

New Age angelphiles often distort traditional Christian concepts and terminology. For example, Taylor reinvents the notion of grace: "Simply put, grace is a moment when we allow ourselves to be loved unconditionally by God. The moment may last for a split second or it can last for days or years; it all depends on how often we make ourselves available to grace."[58] Such an understanding of "unconditional love" jettisons the need for both repentance and atonement and turns grace—a work of God—into a mere attitude adjustment on our part.

No one more thoroughly distorts the biblical message than Price in *The Angels Within Us*. He cites the Bible constantly but, with uncanny consistency, he manages to get the interpretation completely wrong on every occasion. When he alludes to Jesus' saying about the camel and the eye of a needle (Matt. 19:24), he says it means we should rid ourselves of fear, guilt, judgment, and pride. Actually, Jesus was speaking of the deceitfulness of wealth. Also, quoting Jesus to the effect that the "Lord is one," Price says that Jesus means "the divine consciousness, the Master Self, is the one Self of every individual on this plane and beyond." Actually, Jesus' saying has nothing to do with Price's monism. Take a look at the context (Mark 12:28–30). The meaning is that the Lord alone (and no one else, including the self) is God, and that the greatest command is to love God with all your heart. But for Price, Jesus' claim "I and the Father are one" (John 10:30) applies equally well to the rest of us.[59]

Many New Agers present their worldview vis-à-vis Christianity more honestly. They frankly confess that their beliefs directly contradict Christian and biblical teaching. Angelphiles, however, dress their teachings in sheep's clothing. Frequently citing the Bible and in particular Jesus, they try to portray themselves as either friendly to Christianity or as giving the deeper, hidden meanings behind the sayings of Jesus. In reality, they distort the Christian perspective in every detail.

The Moral Life of the Holy Self

The New Age angelphiles also revise morality. In a word, old-fashioned categories of right and wrong are illusory and entrap us in feelings of guilt, low self-esteem, and a judgmental spirit. *Ask Your Angels* states simply, "Slowly, surely, we are collectively emerging from this illusion of evil" through recognition that God is the "One Ultimate Life Principle, from which all else emanates."[60] Price constantly speaks of the dangers of "ego" (which sounds strange from a man who wants us to adore our "Holy Self"), but by this he does not have the traditional notion of pride in mind. For him, "ego" simply describes the illusions of evil and want, which are dispelled when we recognize our ultimate divinity. The flip side of this is the idea that the angels come to us with unconditional love and that they never rebuke.[61]

This angelic indifference to morality manifests itself in various ways, particularly in sexual relationships. It seems that angelphiles have difficulty making marriages or "relationships" last. Now I want to be careful here, for you may think that I am just being mean-spirited and want to score a few easy points by gloating over personal problems some of them have had. After all, no segment of society (including the church) is immune in this regard. But, reading their anecdotes, I have been genuinely surprised at how frequently those who are in tune with their angels experience divorces and broken relationships.

Guiley tells the story of a certain Roseann who, thanks to the angels, came to feel that the trees, mountains, and all people were part of her. Oddly enough, her family found this concept difficult to follow. By this time, she was channeling a whole pack of angels, and one of her familiar spirits told her that it was time for her to become a "universal spirit." He went on, "You have many to reach, and being with [your husband] is not where your life's path is anymore. You love him and he loves you, but it is time to separate." They got a divorce.[62]

Two of the authors of *Ask Your Angels*, Alma Daniel and Timothy Wyllie, once had a "partnership," and when it ended LNO counseled Ms. Daniel with an interesting bit of homespun wisdom: "When you have cooked an egg, you cannot cook it again . . . . When something is done, it is over."[63] The point was that she should have no regrets about a failed relationship and move on.

It is strange that the sanctity of marriage means so little to the angels, that their only concern is that people not feel guilty. Yet Guiley gleefully tells the story of two "lovebirds" named Ray and Kathleen. Ray had a failed marriage and a series of "relationships." Kathleen reportedly had a domineering husband. While struggling over her marriage, she met Ray at a conference. They began a long distance affair, and Kathleen, after discovering that sex with Ray was the best she had ever had, concluded that she deserved to be happy. Certain that the angels were rejoicing with her, she left her husband. From Guiley's account, it appears that Ray and Kathleen still live apart but that they meet as often as possible to make love, and when they do, the angels surround them with an aura.[64] I do not want to prolong this, but it seems to me that we have significant adultery here. But I suppose that if you are one with the universe and you have discovered that life's purpose comes from your own inner light to self-fulfillment, concepts like adultery mean very little.

Believing and Making Believe

Do New Age angelphiles really believe in angels, or do they merely pretend that angels exist? It may seem absurd to wonder whether they believe in angels—their books spew out an endless stream of messages from the angels, encounters with angels, and angel lore. But a curious tendency in their writings gives us pause.

The English language distinguishes between "believing" and "making believe." To believe something is to be sure that it is true or really exists. Belief may involve imagination, but it actually functions independently of the imagination. I believe photons exist even though I cannot come up with a meaningful imaginary picture of one. On the other hand, I do not believe that unicorns exist, but I can imagine one very vividly. Belief does not involve any control over the object of belief. I believe that the city of Paris is real, but my mind has no control over Paris.

Making believe (or "pretending") depends entirely on imagination. The object of making believe is unreal or perhaps real but not present. A child can pretend to be fighting a dragon (unreal) or flying an airplane (real but not present). The one who makes believe controls the object of his pretending. The child who fights an imaginary dragon can kill it, befriend it, or be killed by it. "And, as imagination bodies forth / The forms of things unknown, the poet's pen / Turns them to shapes, and gives to airy nothing / A local habitation and a name" (Shakespeare, *A Midsummer Night's Dream* 5.1).

Angelphiles are adept at giving the objects of their imagination a local habitation and a name, and they want us to do the same. Taylor forthrightly describes an angel encounter in the terms of an exercise of imagination. "To use our sense of taste to know angels, we must imagine something pure and sweet, with no aftertaste or trace of bitterness, like a cloud of cotton candy spun with the sugar of heavenly fruit."[65] Apart from the fact that this sounds like an advertiser's description of a new ice cream flavor, it has nothing to do with the reality of angels or what they may really be like. It is an act of make-believe. Elsewhere, she tells us to imagine that angels are window cleaners who wash the windows of our souls, and she encourages us to plant a "mind garden" and imagine the angels as the gardeners. Like a little child with no playmates, we all need imaginary friends. "Basically, I'm suggesting that you become best friends with your guardian angel! Pretend you have an invisible friend who witnesses everything you experience and with whom you can share insights."[66]

Although more bubbly about it than her fellow travelers, Taylor is not alone in this. Price states that contacting angels "begins in your imagination."[67] According to Guiley, accessing the angels is a work of "creative imagination."[68] *Ask Your Angels* endorses the angel-as-invisible-friend idea; it suggests that when you are sick, you should pretend that your angel is pouring healing light into the medicine you take.[69]

To be fair, these books insist that angels are real and not just imaginary. In this sense, I suppose we could answer our initial question by saying that yes, they do believe that angels are real. We must remember, however, that they regard the higher self as God and as able to create its own reality. The very act of imagining and naming the angels makes them real.

In Guiley's words, "the guides that come out of the unconscious are the same as the spirit powers."[70] All of this leaves me a little uncertain about whether the guides I conjure up have any existence apart from my imagination. I do not know if angelphiles distinguish between that which I imagine and therefore is real [because I am "God"] and that which I imagine but is not real. I do not see how they could consistently make such a distinction.

The Bible calls us to faith in God (and in the angels), but it actually discourages imagination about these things by prohibiting the use of idols. Also, Christian models of prayer do not call for exercise of the imagination. Notwithstanding the fact that Christians sometimes feel a strong presence or a sense of direction during prayer, Christian devotion does not involve making believe that a two-way conversation is going on. To the contrary, we believe that some of the greatest praying may take place during the "dry seasons," when God's presence is not felt at all. Above all else, the praying Christian confesses that God exists apart from the mind of the believer.

Special Friends

We finally come to the last, and perhaps ultimate, question of New Age angelology: the person of the devil. Given their advocacy of total openness to supernatural powers, what do they make of the danger of embracing a demon in the guise of an angel of light? In a word, they are rather dismissive. Beyond that, their books are not all in agreement.

Burnham believes in evil "as a palpable force in its own right"[71] and has a good understanding of the traditional notion of the demonic. Taylor also says that there "may well be fallen angels," but she thinks that they will stay away if we do not pay any attention to them and maintain a good sense of humor. "So why give attention to believing in and concerning yourself with demons and fallen angels?" she asks.[72] To put it simply, some of them believe that devils may be real but that we can easily avoid them.

Frequently, however, New Age angelphiles view Satan as just a good angel with a lousy job. He does try to tempt people, but that is merely to steel their characters and make them better persons. He works as a metaphysical drill sergeant. In one supposed vision, Satan opened his cloak to show a bright light shining beneath, thus revealing his true, good nature. The devil said that he "longed for the time when, having done his work, he could resume his former role among the white angels."[73]

Ask Your Angels likewise tells us that according to their "angelic informants" old Beelzebub came to earth with "loving intentions" to strengthen our spiritual resolve through temptation. Christ and the devil "are on the same side."[74] For Price, Satan is one of the twenty-two angels that guide us. He functions as the angel of "materiality and temptation" by reminding us of the "falsehood and delusion of the ego and the bondage to outward appearances." You can "call forth this angel and communicate with him as you would with a special friend."[75]

I cannot but wonder if New Age angelphiles have made too many special friends of this kind.

CHAPTER TEN

We will proceed no further in this business:
He hath honored me of late; and I have bought
Golden opinions from all sorts of people.
WILLIAM SHAKESPEARE, *MACBETH* 1, 7

Golden Opinions from All Sorts of People

Jews, Roman Catholics, Protestants, and the Angels

WHAT DO PEOPLE TODAY THINK OF ANGELS? WE HAVE heard what the New Age advocates say, but what about the Judeo-Christian religions? What are modern Jews, Roman Catholics, and Protestants saying about the spirits beyond us?

Not surprisingly, you can find a variety of opinions within each of the three major Western religions, from Roman Catholics who no longer believe in angels to Jews who are hard-core angelphiles. Neither of those examples, however, would be the norm. Each of the three groups has its own orientation to angels and a common opinion among most followers. We do well to consider what they are saying.

Jews

Angels play a major role in the Jewish faith, but it is a rather strange role. They appear everywhere in rabbinical stories and Jewish legends but, for most modern Jews, they are not real. We have seen the excessive angelphilia of the Qumran period and of books such as *1 Enoch*. We also have seen a movement away from angels and a studied ambiguity in the Talmud and especially in the writings of Moses Maimonides. In the modern period, however, angels are demoted to the level of being no more than fictional characters in parables.

The *Encyclopedia Judaica* asserts that belief in angels has all but disappeared among Jews.[1] A recent interpreter of Jewish angelology, Rabbi Morris B. Margolies, concurs. He writes that "angels are better understood as symbols of forces that operate within every one of us" and that "angels are metaphors for the most basic human drives and emotions."[2] Thus he can say that "the angels with whom we occasionally commune come from within ourselves."[3] This is not to say that angelphilia does not exist at all among Jews, but such attitudes would be in the minority.

Margolies regularly interprets angels as moral object lessons. For example, discussing Genesis 28:10–17, in which Jacob sees angels going up and down a stairway to heaven, he construes this image to mean that "life is two-directional. Its valleys are as normal as its peaks, its defeats as frequent as its triumphs."[4] A pleasant moral lesson that, but I hardly think that it is the point of the vision. Jacob himself interprets it to mean that he is in a holy place, a spot where earth and heaven meet (v. 17).

Margolies follows a long tradition among the rabbis, who felt that it was necessary to depreciate the importance of angels lest the common people fall into angel-mania. He cites the Talmud: "Every single day God creates a new host of angels who, having sung His praises, vanish from the scene."[5] Creatures that endure only a single day can hardly be of great consequence.

The rationale for the abandonment of angels is that Israel can only serve one God and thus any other spiritual beings might threaten the purity of Jewish monotheism. We can understand the fear of angelphilia and the implicit danger of polytheism, but the outright abandonment of angels is misguided.

Of themselves, angels are no threat to the uniqueness of God. If the existence of other spiritual minds in heaven somehow makes God less special, cannot the same be said of human minds on earth? Monotheism is not enhanced by having God absolutely alone in heaven. He would not be a greater being if there were no other persons in the universe. Also, we should not reject angels out of fear that people will worship them any more than we should burn Bibles out of fear that people will misinterpret them. In addition, the rabbinical move to radical unitarianism, in which the heavens contain nothing but a single, monolithic deity, is in part a reaction against the Trinitarian and incarnational theology of Christians.

They are thus left with a lone deity whose angels are mere metaphors and whose humans will perish with the dust, leaving nothing eternal in the universe but the one God. If God is the only enduring being, one could fairly say that ultimately God is the only being that exists. Ironically, this kind of Judaism finally comes round to a kind of monism such as exists (in radically different forms) in paganism and the New Age movement. Christianity rejects monism in all its configurations, be it pantheism or radical unitarianism. God is unique but not alone. Human and angelic minds, though created, are real and abiding and will neither vanish nor merge into "the One."

Rejection of angels repudiates historic Judaism. Dismissing the angels as metaphors and personifications contradicts the natural meaning of the Hebrew Scriptures and many segments of early Judaism, and it also ignores the daily religion of the biblical Israelites. While we cannot claim complete understanding of their beliefs and practices, it is indisputable that their spiritual world had more occupants than just God alone. Our survey of the Old Testament and pseudepigraphal writings on angels makes at least that much certain.[6]

The basic creed of Israel is "Hear, O Israel, the LORD, the LORD is our one God" (Deut. 6:4). English Bibles traditionally render this as, "Hear O Israel, the LORD is our God, the LORD is One." This sounds as if it could be a unitarian monotheism, but even this does not assert that no other spiritual beings exist. The New Revised Standard Version has it: "Hear, O Israel: The LORD is our God, the LORD alone," which is much better than the traditional translation. In any case, the main point of the text is that Israel should have no other god (such as Marduk or Baal or Amun-Ra), but only the Lord. The text does not teach anything about the nature of God Himself (whether He is a unitarian or a Trinitarian God), and it certainly does not teach that no other spiritual beings exist. Finally, as Karl Barth says, the very title "LORD of Hosts," used so frequently in the Old Testament, "excludes any idea of a lonely God sitting on His heavenly throne in an empty or formless heaven."[7]

Roman Catholics

Roman Catholics have always been more open to angels than have Protestants. Pope Pius XI prayed every day, morning and evening, to his guardian angel. "We have always seen ourselves as wonderfully helped by our guardian angel. Very often, we feel that he is here, close by, ready to help us," he said.[8] Pope John XXIII similarly described his own attention to the angels when he addressed a group of priests: "We particularly ask our guardian angel to deign to help us in our daily recitation of the holy Office, to help us say it worthily, attentively, devoutly, and in that way please God and do good to ourselves and to the souls of others."[9]

Roman Catholic liturgy also refers frequently to angels. For example, the prayer for the dedication of a bridge includes the line, "Deign to send your good angel from heaven to guard and protect this bridge."[10] Even when blessing a field, the priest prays for the expulsion of the devils and asks that God send the angels.[11]

The Roman Catholic world contains many shrines to angels, the most famous being Mont Saint-Michel in France, a center of devotion to the archangel Michael. A number of Catholic monks and scholars, including Bernard of Clairvaux (1090–1153), the Jesuit Francis Borgia (1510–72), and Cardinal Bérulle (1575–1629) encouraged devotion to the angels.[12]

The recent *Catechism of the Catholic Church*, on the other hand, gives an unremarkable presentation of angels. It is, as one would expect, orthodox and traditional, but it is unencumbered with strange legends, traditions, or excess. It avoids the term "guardian angel," for example, and describes the notion in rather muted tones: "From infancy to death human life is surrounded by their watchful care and intercession. 'Beside each believer stands an angel as protector and shepherd leading him to life.' Already here on earth the Christian life shares by faith in the blessed company of angels and men united in God."[13]

But Catholic tradition is rich with stories about holy men who saw angels and battled devils. The following example is fairly typical:

In the lives of the Fathers it is told how one day St. Isodore the hermit went up on to the roof of his hut in the company of Abbot Moses whom the devil of impurity had been tempting for some time. "Look towards the West," Isodore told his visitor. The abbot saw a noisy host of devils as if preparing for battle. Then the hermit said, "Look East," and Abbot Moses saw a countless multitude of holy angels—the heavenly host, more resplendent than the sun. "Those whom you saw in the West," said the hermit, "are who attack the saints; those you have seen in the East are they whom God has sent to succour the saints. You must see that we have numbers and strength on our side." The holy Abbot Moses returned to his cell comforted.[14]

For these reasons the Roman Catholic Church maintains a long tradition of invoking angels by name. One cardinal of the church asserted that angels would show themselves to those who love them and call on them. Some priests therefore exhort the faithful to treat their guardian angels as lifelong friends.[15]

The Angel Watcher

Eileen Elias Freeman is the most well-known Roman Catholic interpreter of angels in North America. She has been featured in magazines and on television, and she has published an account of her experiences with angels entitled *Touched by Angels.*[16] She has a master's degree in theology from the University of Notre Dame. She also publishes a newsletter for angelphiles, the *AngelWatch™ Journal.*

Freeman herself has encountered angels, she says. As a child, she was terrified by the thought of death, and this terror became all the more real after the loss of her grandmother, with whom she was very close. Her fear vanished when she was visited one night by an angel who announced that he was her guardian angel and she had no reason to be afraid.[17] Years later, she had another angel encounter in New York City. An invisible hand pulled at her shoulder and prevented her from entering a building where, unknown to her at that moment, a murderer was about to go on a rampage.[18]

Then, beginning in 1979, she began to hear the voices of angels with names like Enniss, Asendar, Kennisha, and Talithia. She went out to the desert (she was living in Arizona) and prayed to Jesus for understanding about what all this meant. She began to have flashes of spiritual insight that she felt came from the angels, and for three years she kept a journal of her thoughts. She called this twelve-hundred-page journal *The Guardians of the Earth.* In it, she describes the new relationship that is developing between angels and humans ("The Pilot Program") and tells how angels can heal our lives of evil. She describes how angels and humans are drawing closer "as this present age winds down" and envisions a transformation of society through human-angelic cooperation.[19]

She believes that about 250 years ago angels began a new way of working with people on earth. She thinks that the angels have entered into a closer relationship with their wards and that these angel-human partnerships work for the spiritual transformation of the world. For her, this is simply "another means by which God bestows grace upon us."[20] She believes that in every moment of her life, her angel Enniss communicates with her in a relationship more intimate than marriage.[21]

From all I can tell from Freeman's book and from conversation with her, she is a devoted Roman Catholic Christian. Notwithstanding the peculiarities of the "Pilot Program" (about which I shall have more to say), she holds to a basically orthodox angelology. Whenever she goes beyond ordinary, Catholic teaching on angels, she makes it clear that she is only giving her opinion (for example, she believes that angels have gender[22]). She is a devoted fan of C. S. Lewis. Both publicly and privately, she argues that it is more important to worship God and God's Son than it is to know the angels. She criticizes Roman Catholic angel groups that have lost that perspective.[23] *"If we are not committed to seeking God,"* she emphasizes, *"we will never be able to establish a fruitful relationship with our angels."*[24]

All in all, however, I find Freeman a study in contradiction. She at times reflects New Age thinking in her language and concepts, while at other times she exhibits Christian concerns and beliefs. Like most Christians, she worries that openness to the spirit world without discernment is an invitation to the devil. She says that we do not need a medium in order to contact an angel and that we should run from anyone who promises a method to attract an angel into putting in an appearance.

Freeman also describes various "points of discernment" whereby we can know whether we have really experienced an angel encounter. She believes that a true angel encounter will not leave us feeling confused or afraid and that a real angel will not force anything on us but will point us to God. She also suggests that an angel encounter will leave a person better than he or she was before and that we should examine what the angel says by what we know to be right. She also says, no doubt correctly, that any being you can summon at will through various rituals is probably no angel. Unlike some New Age angelphiles, she says it is not enough just to tell the demons that they are not welcome.[25] She concludes, "I can't emphasize this enough: We must *always* test any kind of spiritual encounter."[26]

On the other hand, much of what she advocates bears an uncomfortable resemblance to the New Age teachings that she eschews. To begin with, these messages from Enniss, and in particular *The Guardians of the Earth*, are troubling. Notwithstanding that Catholics do not hold a *sola Scriptura* ("Bible alone") view of revelation, is it not the case that Jesus is the final and supreme revelation of God? Is revelation given by angels not only decidedly inferior but even obsolete? Remember Hebrews 1! If so, what would a Christian need or want in the twelve hundred pages of the teachings of Enniss?

Although I have not seen the book (I do not believe that she has published it), her own description of *The Guardians of the Earth* should trouble the thoughtful Christian. For a believer in Christ, it is Jesus who has done the final work of redeeming humanity and He alone who brings in the new creation. What is this angelic plan that has supposedly been going on for 250 years? Does God have a Plan B? Freeman's account of how the angels are now working with people in order to transform the world echoes New Age teaching.

Also, notwithstanding her concern over discernment and her warnings that there is no sure way to initiate an angel encounter, I am troubled by her advocacy of seeking angel contacts and the intimate relationship she describes between herself and Enniss. Like the New Age books we have examined, *Touched by Angels* describes grounding techniques we can use to prepare for an encounter. We are to sit alone in a room, say a prayer, and then reflect on the question, "Who am I?" In a second exercise, we ask, "Who are you, God?" and reflect on our beliefs about God. She also urges that we reflect on our motives, relax, and become more angel-aware. There is nothing here as zany as flapping your make-believe angel wings, but the parallels to New Age angelphilia are unmistakable. Also, like her New Age counterparts, she makes much of how angels are pure love and that they teach us to love ourselves. Her close relationship with Enniss reminds me of Abigrael, LNO, and that crowd.

Finally, and for me most disturbing of all, Freeman seems willing to play down her Christianity in order to encourage angel watching. She asserts that "angels have no religion" and that "An angel's creed is Love."[27] If the Bible is accurate in what it says about how the angels sang at the birth of Jesus, how the demons reacted when He encountered them in His ministry, and how the angels adore and praise Him in heaven, then I think we can say that angels have a highly specific creed. It is centered on Jesus. Even the devils believe and tremble (James 2:19).

In fairness to Freeman, she might contend that this is only the starting point and that as someone gets to know his or her angel, that person will gain a more accurate understanding of God. She may see this as a form of gradual evangelism. But as she advocates using any religious tradition (Jewish, Christian, Moslem, or whatever) for prayer,[28] we have to raise questions. I do not understand why a Christian would advocate anything other than prayer to the Father through Jesus Christ.

Also, her statements about her faith in Christ sometimes have a this-is-just-my-personal-opinion air about them. She says that her prayer "is always addressed to Jesus, because I see him as God in human form." Then she continues, "You should make your prayer to the highest source outside yourself."[29] By comparison, her advocacy of the reality of angels is much more aggressive and, we might say, evangelistic. She goes out of her way to convince the reader that angels are real and worthy of our attention.

This could hardly contrast more strongly with the evangelism of Paul. He had no interest in spreading the gospel of the angels. Instead, he was determined to know nothing but Christ and Him crucified among the people to whom he preached (1 Cor. 2:2). In short, Freeman's approach makes me worry that angel watching can become for a Christian a serious distraction away from Christ.

Face Off with the Papacy: The Strange Case of the *Opus Sanctorum Angelorum*

Religious movements in Europe tend to be about twenty years ahead of what is happening in North America, and this rule has held true for angelphilia. Well before the current craze of interest in angels on this side of the Atlantic, the Catholic Church in Europe already had a flourishing angel movement that went under the name of the *Opus Sanctorum Angelorum* ("Work of the Holy Angels") or, in German, *Engelwerk.*

The Story of Gabriele Bitterlich. The Engelwerk story, which you may accept, reject, or interpret however you wish, goes like this.[30] A German woman named Gabriele Bitterlich began the movement. Born around the turn of the century and married in 1918, she at that time began to recognize her powers as a seer. She had already had quite a few extraordinary experiences. When she was four years of age, her brother closed her in a barn, but she was not tall enough to unlatch the door and open it. An angel, whom she took to be her guardian angel, opened the door. She ran and announced to her mother, "I have seen my guardian angel!" She reported other visitations as well, but she soon learned to keep quiet about this matter—her mother slapped her in the face whenever she claimed to have seen her angel.

The birth of her son Hansjörg (May 4, 1923), who would eventually become a priest and lead the *Engelwerk*, was especially traumatic. It was a tubal pregnancy, and on the night before his birth, she had a vision in which she saw her as yet unborn son as a child with a great book in his hand (Hansjörg would eventually prepare the handbook that guides the *Opus Sanctorum Angelorum*). She also saw the angels and Jesus on a cross, who came down and spoke to her.

The following years, during which Germany went from total economic collapse to domination by the Third Reich and finally to defeat in World War II, were extremely difficult for Bitterlich. Still, she held her family together and cared for other children as well. She entertained the children through these years with a remarkable ability to create fairy tales about gnomes who lived in the forests. In November of 1946, she fell deathly ill and received the last rites. Suddenly, she heard the Lord tell her that her work was just beginning; she was healed of all her diseases.

She began to write down her revelations. Night after night, she either had blissful visions of angels and heaven or harrowing encounters with devils and hell. Her principle guide was an angel who called himself the "Eye of God." Satan, too, came to her in various forms, but she could always recognize him by his cold, hateful eyes. Her visions attracted a great deal of attention. In 1961 Bishop Paulus Rusch approved the beginning of an organization dedicated to the angels. The organization soon took up residence in a castle of St. Petersburg, Germany, and became the *Engelwerk*. She moved there and made it her home until her death in 1974. She became increasingly bizarre in her old age. One day, all the priests associated with St. Petersburg had to march around the castle performing an exorcism. Frau Bitterlich had claimed that there was a demon behind every tree.[31]

Growth and Controversy. The message of the *Opus Sanctorum Angelorum* (hereinafter OSA) quickly found fertile ground in central Europe, Portugal, and Brazil. As of 1990, the movement claimed that seven cardinals and fifty bishops were among their number.[32] They also profess to having a following among Protestants, Jews, and Muslims. They conduct retreats and have a tape ministry in North America.

Concern and alarm about this movement grew along with the movement itself. When German Catholic theologians had a chance to examine their teachings, many began to charge that it was a rebirth of Gnosticism and Kabbalah within the German Catholic Church. Others became alarmed over the difficulty of gaining access to the secretive group's teachings. The OSA from the beginning shared its doctrines only with the inner circle of the fully committed.

As the controversy grew, *The Munich Catholic Newspaper* (*Münchener Katholischen Kirchenzeitung*) began to investigate. The matter came to a head when the paper published an article on August 14, 1988, under the heading, "And Lucifer gleefully rubs his hands together." The article detailed particulars of the heretofore secret handbook of the OSA. Like a sorcerer's guide or the *Testament of Solomon*, the handbook gave the names of both demons who had the power to harm people and angels who could thwart them.

In addition, the book endorsed some astonishing superstitions. For example, it claimed that spotted black cats, spotted black chickens, pigs, shiny-haired dogs, and other animals were especially open to demonic influence and should be avoided. On the other hand, animals such as sheep, donkeys, and hares were good omens. After encountering one of these, a person could feel safe against demonic powers. The OSA also made much of a mystical numerology that focused on the numbers 1, 3, 4, 7, and 12.[33]

The OSA claimed secret knowledge of the names and functions of many angels. Among these are Jebusiel (angel of fugitives), Ariguel (helper of all the forsaken), and Malchidiel (angel of tranquillity and security during struggles and persecution).[34] Like the Essenes of Qumran and many subsequent apocalyptic cults, the OSA taught that humans are caught in the middle of a titanic struggle between angels and demons and that the end of history was rushing upon us.[35] The OSA, of course, claimed to be the one group that understood what was happening and in which salvation was assured.

The OSA showed other cultlike characteristics, including mind-control over its members and rigid demands for secrecy. One ex-member, a theology student named Walter Herholz, came forward to describe life on the inside of the organization. According to Herholz, the OSA suppresses all independent thinking among its members. The group demands unquestioning submission to their teachings, which it regards as the definitive guide during these end-times.[36]

In the OSA promise of secrecy, the initiate vows before God and Mary to remain silent about the "treasures of the Work of the Holy Angels" and asks the angels for help in keeping this vow.[37] Herholz alleged that they keep fearful members in check by threatening to hand them over to Satan.[38] The notion of a guardian angel was itself a powerful weapon for controlling the minds of the members, since a leader could always say, "Your guardian angel told me that you are supposed to do this."[39]

Bishop Graf Soden-Frauhofen emerged as a principal opponent of the OSA. He exposed many of the abuses detailed here and made what must be considered the telling criticism of this and all angelphile groups: "What kind of role is left for Jesus Christ, who in the Christian understanding is the only mediator between God and humanity? In the soteriology of the Work of the Angels, all of our life in Christ would be replaced by the work of the angels and especially their queen, Mary."[40]

We can hardly overstate the importance of the Bishop's charge. Many angelphiles readily acknowledge that Jesus is the Son of God and that He died for the sins of the world. In this, their Christianity is disarmingly orthodox. But angels, not Christ, stand as mediators between heaven and earth. In the practical work of sanctification it is the guardian angel, not the Holy Spirit, who leads and teaches the believer.

In paganism, the high gods often received official acknowledgment but in the daily lives of the people played no real role. That function—protecting and guiding the individual—was taken up by lesser deities and household gods. In the OSA, as in much Christian angelphilia, Christ has become something of a high god and an official part of the creed to whom each believer gives the perfunctory bow before moving on to his or her daily walk of faith with that special companion, the guardian angel. Nothing expresses this quite so clearly as one of the prayers of the OSA:

> We kneel before your majesty and thank you, O God, that you have sent to each of us a close heavenly companion who leads us according to your will to lead us to your glory and to reveal your love.
>
> We promise here, before your eyes, to love our companion as a brother and to listen to him, when he speaks to us in the voice of conscience. May he lead us safe to heaven!
>
> Lord Jesus Christ, Our Redeemer, take my hand and lay it in the hand of my angel and mark the sign of salvation over it as your blessing for our salvation.[41]

Especially troubling for Catholics, the OSA also incorporated its theology into the Mass and Eucharist. They mystically linked their celebrations of the Mass to the struggle between angels and demons and to the work of the OSA.[42]

Roma locuta, Causa finita? Understandably, the Roman Catholic Church grew increasingly uncomfortable with the excesses of the OSA. In a letter sent to Rome on December 1, 1977, Cardinal Joseph Höffner, Archbishop of Cologne and President of the Conference of German Bishops, formally requested an examination of the organization and their teachings and of the private revelations to Frau Bitterlich as well. On September 24, 1983, the Roman Congregation for the Doctrines of the Faith (*Congregatio pro Doctrina Fidei*) communicated the decision that the OSA should conform to church teaching: "In particular, it should not spread among its members and among the faithful a type of veneration of the angels that consults them by 'name' on the basis of alleged private revelation (attributed to Mrs. Gabriele Bitterlich). Nor will it be permitted for anyone to make use of these names in any proclamations whatever produced by the community."[43]

The Vatican also forbade the use of the so-called "promise of silence" and demanded that the OSA conform to the normal Catholic liturgy. Following this, in a development that left me wondering if Roman

Catholics are really all that different from Baptists, the decree of the theologians was more or less ignored. Rome spoke, but the case was hardly closed.

Still, the theologians continued their work and came away more convinced than ever that the teachings of the OSA constituted a serious break with the Scriptures and the teachings of the Roman Church. In June of 1992, therefore, they issued another statement that was even more explicit and direct. It includes, for example, the following decisions:

> Visions that come forth from the presumed revelations of Mrs. Gabriele Bitterlich concerning the world of the angels, concerning their personal names, companies, and functions, are not to be taught or propagated in any way, whether explicitly or implicitly, in the organization or structure of the Work of the Angels, whether for worship, preaching, spiritual formation, public or private spirituality, for ministry or mission. This arrangement applies to any other institution or association approved by the Church.
>
> Use and publication of books or other writings containing the aforementioned visions are prohibited both within and without the association.[44]

In addition, they forbade various forms of consecration to angels. The congregation also directed that delegates should be appointed to make sure that this time their decisions were taken seriously.

If you contact the OSA today, you will get a sanitized statement describing who they are (no mention of Gabriele Bitterlich or the revelations to her) and the nature of their work. They present themselves as a dutiful Roman Catholic organization that promotes spirituality through silent meditation with the aid of one's guardian angel. They profess allegiance to Christ and assert that the Work of the Holy Angels stands against moral decadence, Satanism, and the New Age. They say that they no longer use prayers of consecration to guardian angels, but they present this decision more as part of an ongoing discussion in the Catholic Church than as a direct rebuke to their work. At least in the material that I have seen, they make no mention of Jebusiel or any other supposed angels. Of course, they have a history of guarding their secret knowledge within an inner circle. Of one thing I am sure: Rome has not heard the last of the Work of the Holy Angels.

What is the significance of this work for those of us on the western side of the Atlantic? Apart from the fact that the OSA does have a North American work, the movement shows that devotion to angels can quickly take on all the characteristics of a cult. Strange visions, superstition, mind control, and maintaining closely guarded secrets are but a few examples of where angelphilia can lead.

Evangelical Protestants

Evangelical Protestants, for whatever reason, have been much more interested in the devils than the angels. Also, evangelicals tend to put their angelology into the form of fantasies and novels. We will consider both of these phenomena in more detail later. Even so, we do have some examples of evangelical angelphilia and a few books that describe the traditional Protestant view of the angels.

Billy Graham

I would not describe Billy Graham as an angelphile. If any man ever built a career preaching Christ alone, it is he. Still, Graham wrote a famous book on angels (*Angels: God's Secret Agents*),[45] and he provides a good window to the contemporary evangelical attitude toward angels. As we would expect, Graham is traditional and orthodox in his presentation of angels. At times, however, he speculates a good bit.

He lists ten orders of angels in his ranking of the heavenly powers; this is unusual since traditionally they have nine orders. He cites two texts in support of his hierarchy (Col. 1:16 and Rom. 8:38),[46] but some of the orders he lists are not in either text. In reality, these two passages do not set out to list the angelic hierarchies, nor do they match one another.

He thinks that Michael is the only archangel and is the "Prime Minister" of heaven on the grounds that no other angel is called an archangel in the Bible and that Jude 9 calls him "the" archangel.[47] Yet the Bible never claims to give an exhaustive account of the heavenly administration, and calling Michael "the" archangel does not mean that he is "the one and only" archangel. Also, Graham fails to see that when Daniel 10:21 calls Michael "your prince" it means that Michael is a special guardian over Israel. It does not mean that Michael is the highest ranking angel in heaven.

We could give many other such examples of speculation and questionable exegesis. Graham does not seem to have given the subject of angels a great deal of thought or research. Beyond these problems, Graham's book is warm and devotional and contains many stories of angelic activity from the Bible and recent history. He also does something many other books do not do—he describes how angels are agents of wrath.[48] Most important, he keeps the real focus of the book on Christ. That is, he uses the angels as pointers to guide people to Jesus. In this, he remains true to his calling.

Marilynn and William Webber

In contrast to Billy Graham, two evangelicals who could easily claim the title of angelphiles are Marilynn Carlson Webber and William D. Webber. Their book, *A Rustle of Angels*,[49] contains all the ingredients that are *de rigueur* for a good angelphile book. It has a brief angelology, many stories of encounters with angels, a discussion of whether one can meet an angel and, like Freeman's book, guidelines for discerning whether the spirit who just spoke to you was good or evil.

Marilynn Webber's background is remarkably similar to Freeman's. Her interest in angels began early and grew out of childhood fears, and as a young woman she, too, was saved from death by an angel. She was crossing some railroad tracks while lost in thought (a teacher of hers had been diagnosed with cancer), when suddenly she looked up to see a steam locomotive bearing down upon her. Too paralyzed to move, she stared into the face of the panicked engineer. Suddenly, somebody pushed her off the tracks, but there was no one there. She believes that this push, like the hand that held Freeman back from the scene of a murder, came from an angel.[50] Also, like many angelphiles, Marilynn Webber possesses a substantial collection of angel figurines.

More than anything else, the Webbers' book details the stories of people who have had angel experiences. When the Webbers attempt an angelology, they are rather modest in their ambitions. They briefly mention the teachings of Pseudo-Dionysius, Aquinas, and others, but they conclude that we really do not know much about angel organization. The only thing they are sure of is that *"there is no inefficiency, no needless duplication of effort, and no work left undone."*[51] I imagine that means that the angels are more efficient than the federal government. The Webbers also make use of the idea of the guardian angel, which, as we have seen, leads to some confusion.

In keeping with standard Christian teaching, they affirm that people do not become angels at death but that angels are a special order of creation.[52] They also hold to the common notion that Ezekiel 28 and Isaiah 14 describe the fall of Satan. This, as we have seen, is dubious. As do many others, they go beyond what is written in their attempt to fill the gaps in their demonology, and they completely misunderstand Revelation 12, a text we have already examined.[53]

On the subject of angel encounters, they stand apart from the rest of the angelphiles. They correctly affirm that the Bible says nothing about how to meet an angel, and they do not offer any prayer or meditation exercises. They assert that all prayers should be to God, and it is clear throughout that the only God that they affirm is the God of Jesus Christ. No mushy pluralism here!

Their "points of discernment" for distinguishing a true angel encounter from a demon encounter are similar to Freeman's, except that they more explicitly use the tenets of the Christian faith to judge an encounter. Their first guideline is that the angels "will never tell you anything that is contrary to what is found in the Bible."[54]

They do attempt to give guidelines for when an angel is likely to minister to us. These are when we are heartbroken, when we face temptation, when we are doing God's will, and at the time of death.[55] Even this is not exactly in line with what the Bible teaches. Some people encountered angels when they were opposing God's will (for example, Balaam on the way to curse Israel). And although it is true that the Bible describes angels ministering to Jesus after His temptation, His case is unique. Most often, angelic visitations in the Bible are altogether unexpected (for example, the annunciation to Mary and the dreams of Joseph). From the standpoint of the Bible, there is no way to predict when an angel might help someone, except that they sometimes come to a person who is in trouble.

The Webbers represent a kind of traditional, orthodox Christian angelphilia that appreciates and seeks to affirm the ministry of the angels. In this, they do a service to Christians and call us back to a fully developed belief in the supernatural. They avoid many of the pitfalls of other angelphiles. They do not claim to have secret revelations, and they maintain the central place of Christ. Still, they could have done a little more homework—and yet at times they say more about the angels (and devils) than they really should.

Graham and the Webbers are fairly typical of the North American evangelical version of popular angelology. *Angels, Angels, Angels* by Landrum Leavell, *Angels: Elect and Evil* by C. Fred Dickason, and *Angels Around Us* by Douglas Connelly are similar. While on the whole quite traditional, Connelly, for example, uses some peculiar exegesis to attempt to fix the time of Satan's fall and takes the unorthodox position that good angels can still fall from grace[56] (contrast St. Augustine: "Every Catholic Christian knows that no new Devil will ever come in the future from the ranks of the good angels, just as he knows that the Devil will never return to the fellowship of the good angels."[57])

To summarize the Protestant evangelical approach to angels: they tend correctly to believe that angels are real while they turn our attention on Jesus. Yet Protestants hold to a number of traditional interpretations and speculations while remaining blissfully ignorant of the background and implications of these traditions. At times, they feel free to develop peculiar ideas about angels based on unusual interpretations of the Bible.

CHAPTER ELEVEN

There are more things in heaven and earth, Horatio,
Than are dreamt of in your philosophy.
WILLIAM SHAKESPEARE, *HAMLET* 1, 5

More Things in Heaven
and Earth

Anecdotes about Angels

MICKI STELLA, A FORMER MISSIONARY COLLEAGUE OF
mine in Korea, once told me of her encounter with an angel. Her story
goes like this:

It happened several years ago on an evening in October.
Some twenty teams from the U.S. had come to Korea for Korean-
American evangelistic crusades in as many cities. I lived in Pusan,
where our Baptist Hospital was located, and every evening I
transported hospital personnel to evangelistic meetings outside
the city.

One night, five of us were returning to Pusan on a narrow
two-lane highway. The meeting in the second city had ended late,
and a flat tire made our arrival time in Pusan even later. We were
all concerned about that, because at that time Korea was under a
midnight curfew. We decided that the person who lived farthest
away would keep the car until she got home. She would drop the

178

rest of us off at locations along the way where we could get home easily. Since my apartment was more out of the way than the others, I offered to take a taxi home from my drop-off point.

The place I chose was a normally busy intersection about fifteen minutes' driving time to our apartment. It was a familiar location. I passed through it many times a week during the daylight hours. But I had never been there that late in the evening, and how different it was! For the first time I noticed that there were two small yellow canvas tents close to the corner. They were only small and insignificant diners during the day but, as I quickly realized from the noise inside, they were drinking houses at night (the Korean equivalent of a cheap bar). About the same time I became keenly aware that the intersection was all but deserted. Korean taxis, usually seen in such abundance, were conspicuous by their absence. Their drivers were anxious to get home before curfew.

Within a few minutes a group of five men emerged from one of the yellow drinking houses. They were stumbling-drunk and noisy. One of them broke away from the others and started to come toward me with his arms extended in front of him. In broken English he said, "Come with me for one minute." I began to walk to and fro in an attempt to find an escape. I was afraid of going farther down the very dark street, but his four friends blocked the sidewalk in the other direction. The six of us were the only people on that usually busy street. "No. I don't want to go with you," was all I could say. I was beginning to panic, for I could see that I was trapped.

Suddenly, a large Korean man appeared from the alley leading to the open-air market. He walked deliberately in our direction. What immediately struck me was that he was so different from any Korean man I had seen in my dozen years in Korea to that time. He was *big*—a really burly-looking man—whereas Korean men of that time were almost always short and slight of build. Immediately I just knew he had come to help me! My fear was replaced by a very strange sense of peace. He walked to a point between me and my would-be assailant and just stood there as solid as a rock.

The drunken man looked at him and came to the same conclusion—this man was my protector. He stopped in his tracks, then turned to go with his friends, who had already begun to walk away. I watched him just long enough to see that he was gone for good, then turned to thank my protector, who had not spoken a word. *No one was there. This is impossible,* I thought. I called to him. There was no answer. I even walked further down the dark street to the alley and called into that black hole which was normally a busy market, but heard no response.

Giving up on that, and realizing I was still in a very tight time constraint, I walked toward the intersection again to hail a taxi. Just as I got there, an empty taxi appeared! I yelled, with an intensity reserved for desperation, *"Taxi!"* It stopped! Through those dark and deserted streets we got home in record time. Praising the Lord, I paid him and got out! I soon realized that the Lord had sent His angel to protect me.[1]

Knowing Micki as I do, I have no doubt that her story is true and that she genuinely encountered an angel. Her story, like many others, inspire us and give us another reason to thank God. I know of other stories that I have either heard firsthand or have read, and many of them are convincing and appealing.

Stories of Faith and Inspiration

There are many other stories of angels and miracles to be found in Christian literature.

Former missionary and Wheaton College president V. Raymond Edman, while serving in Ecuador, experienced firsthand the point of Hebrews 13:2, which says that some have entertained angels without knowing it. He says that one day as he was eating his lunch at home he heard a knock at the gate and went out to find an old Indian woman.

Speaking a mixture of Spanish and Quichua, she asked, "Are you the people who have come to tell us about the living God?" Startled, because the Indians were hostile to strangers and none had ever spoken words like that, he finally answered, *"Mamita,* yes, we are."

She then prayed a beautiful prayer in which she invoked God's blessing on their home and asked that many would believe the gospel. She then said farewell and turned away. After a moment's hesitation Edman went outside the wall to speak to her, but she had vanished. He was stunned because now that he was outside the courtyard wall of his home he had a clear field of vision for fifty yards, and in the moment he had hesitated she could not have gone ten. He ran to the next corner but she was not there, and the neighbors on the street said that no Indian woman had come by. For days his heart was strangely moved.[2]

⊗

Joan Wester Anderson relates the story of a woman named Myra who worked in a Teen Challenge mission in Philadelphia. The mission frequently suffered from a gang who occasionally came to hurl threats and obscenities at the mission.

One night, although she was alone, Myra felt that she should tell them about Jesus. When they came, she prayed and went out to them. They threatened to throw her in a nearby river, but she finished what she had to say and went back inside. The next night they returned, and she once again went out alone to them. They began to hurl more abuses at her, but suddenly they became quiet, turned, and left.

A few days later they returned to the center, but this time were better behaved. When asked why they had turned away on the earlier night, they said that they had been frightened away by a man whom they had taken to be her boyfriend. He stood behind her, was seven feet tall, and had on a "classy white suit."[3] She had no boyfriend, and no such man was in the mission.

⊗

Anderson also tells the story of Kenneth Ware, an Assemblies of God minister in France during World War II. His wife Suzie was a Jewish believer in Jesus. As an American and the husband of a Jew, he was arrested and beaten but released. He and his wife finally found themselves penniless in Lausanne, Switzerland.

On a morning in 1944, Suzie prayed for "five pounds of potatoes, two pounds of pastry flour, apples, pears, a cauliflower, carrots, veal cutlets for Saturday and beef for Sunday." A few hours later, a large man with white-blond hair and a blue apron over his work clothes appeared at the door: "Mrs. Ware, I'm bringing what you asked for."

She said there was a mistake because she had not ordered anything. He ignored her protest and brought in the delivery—exactly what she had asked for. She was about to say that she had no money to pay him, but the reprimand in his eyes sealed her lips. The Wares looked out the window to see him leave by the only exit, but he never appeared.[4]

Other Stories

Other stories, however, are not convincing, are perplexing in their implications, or are both. What are we to make of the hundreds of angel stories now making the rounds in books, magazines, and television specials? In my studies, I have read or heard of angel stories that led people to embrace doctrines of reincarnation or other Eastern notions. I have read of miracles concerning people who make no claim to Christian faith either before or after their experience. Some of the stories are very strange (and dubious, in my opinion), but others are very similar to the stories about angels that Christians tell.

⊛

Rosemary Guiley tells of a group of angelphiles who had made the number 22 their "high sign" since 22 is "a master number, of high vibration." They came to realize that this was their "secret sign" through a series of "synchronicities" in which the number 22 frequently appeared. One day a member of the group wandered through a grocery store in a state of depression muttering, "I am weary unto death." When she went to make her purchases, the total came to $2.22, which was "a signal to her to snap out of her mood."[5]

⊛

Sophy Burnham, the same woman who told of an out-of-body experience when she floated around as an angel, tells of one experience when she saw an angel. She had gone skiing in Val d'Isère, France. One day she was skiing on hard-packed snow when she went off the *piste* (a track), fell, and careened down a steep slope. As she continued her fall, all her efforts to stop on the hard, steep, rocky surface failed. She gave up trying, and waited to bang into a tree or rock.

Suddenly she saw a flash of black go past her and she came to a stop. A skier dressed in black from head to toe had raced down from the *piste*, braked himself below her, and allowed her to fall into his leg to stop her descent. She looked into his eyes. "They, too, were black, but full of such light I could not move."

She thanked him, but he only turned and raced back up the hill to the *piste* using the maneuver that skiers call the herringbone. She hurried to try to catch him, but he was far too fast, and when he made it to the top he shot past her husband (who was standing on the *piste*) without a word. She soon arrived back at the top, from which she and her husband had a clear view of the valley below, but the black skier was nowhere in sight. They skied down via the *piste,* but they got a jolt when they looked up. Had the black skier not stopped her when he did, she would have fallen off a rocky cliff and most certainly died.[6]

Burnham also published the letter of a woman named Susan who says that she was at one time sad, searching, and bitterly angry at God. One night she went out and heard the song that declares "Broken dreams ... give them all to Jesus," and she only became more furious and bitter and went back home. Back inside, crying, she suddenly experienced "healing."

She heard a voice say, "I'm as gentle as a lamb, and I don't hurt." She realized that she had blamed God for everything. Then she had a vision. "I was shown that This Spirit, or This Immense, Creative Being was literally in everything."

She realized that it was larger than any priest or rabbi and that this "Spirit of Love knows absolutely No Bounds. It loves Buddhists, Taoists, Christians, Jews, Moslems, on and on and on with incredible Love." She saw how people who use drugs and abuse themselves need to know this kind of loving care. "It's a state of mind," she says, "and it costs nothing."[7]

I could give many other examples; hundreds of such stories have been published in books and reenacted for television. These three are sufficient examples of the types of stories you are likely to read, although there are many variations. The story of the $2.22 "synchronicity" is typical of the kind of coincidence-story that angelphiles love to tell. Sophy Burnham's ski adventure is very similar to many saved-by-an-angel stories. A person suddenly is in great danger. An angel appears in human form out of nowhere, does something extraordinary to help, and abruptly leaves. When the person tries to catch a glance of the mysterious helper as he walks (or skis) away, he is inexplicably gone.

Susan's vision is similar to other angelphile vision stories. A person is in deep depression, is perhaps suicidal, but then sees a vision of white light or a shining angel or heaven, and he or she is lifted out of despair. Frequently such a person goes on to abandon drugs or alcohol and then in some way tries to share the message he or she has received. Some paint angels for people. Some embrace a new theology, such as reincarnation or Susan's apparent pantheism and notion of universal love.

Evaluating Angel Stories

What are we to do with all these stories? How do we tell if they are true or not? How do we deal with their conflicting implications, since some seem to vindicate Christian doctrine but others go in the opposite direction?

Angels and Other Possibilities

If a person claims to have seen an angel, one might explain the event in several ways. First, the person may have really seen (or experienced) an angel. In many of the accounts I have read, I believe this to be the true explanation. Others are possible, however.

Someone may have been deceived either unintentionally or deliberately by another person. For example, someone may have received help from a stranger who abruptly "disappeared." The stranger may have been just a human, and he may have departed quietly and quickly and thus seemed to have disappeared. In this case, the one who received the help jumped to the conclusion that the person was an angel.

Another possibility is that the one who saw the angel hallucinated. This would seem to be more likely in cases that are visionary in nature, as when someone sees a bright, shining angel in his or her bedroom at night or when someone thinks he sees angels in or around a church. I hasten to add that sometimes people see visions of angels that we should take seriously. Elisha opened the eyes of his servant so that he could see the troop of angels that protected his home (2 Kings 6:17). Still, we must recognize that in some cases, the angels someone claims to see may be hallucinations, particularly if the person is unstable.

A person who claims to have seen an angel may be lying. We should be especially suspicious of anyone who claims to have seen angels and also has some religious message to give to us. Nothing enhances the authority of a spiritual teacher more than the idea that he or she has had visions of angels or devils, has spoken with angels, or is delivering a message that comes from an angel. We should be immediately suspicious of an alleged angelic encounter that comes from someone who tries to make something of it, who tries to establish his claims to religious authority by it, or who dwells too much on it.

Sometimes a person who claims to have seen an angel may be suffering from false memories. When I first heard of this my immediate reaction was to dismiss it as another "syndrome" invented by psychologists, but continued reading has convinced me that it is not only real but amazingly powerful. Researchers have demonstrated how easily people can have false memories. Lawyers and psychologists must now wrestle with false memories in criminal cases and in therapy. Some people have detailed memories of suffering sexual abuse as children even though it never occurred. Others have false memories of an even more outlandish nature; for example, some remember and fully believe that they have been abducted by aliens and taken away for a period of time in a spacecraft. False memories can be detailed, precise, and lengthy. Also, a therapist or authority figure can suggest false memories. Those who attend angel seminars in which a personal encounter with an angel authenticates the members and proves that they have true spirituality may be setting themselves up for false memories.

Somewhere between the lie and the false memory is the tendency to exaggerate. A person may have had an unusual experience but exaggerates the details either deliberately, out of a confused memory, or out of a desire to believe that more happened than really did. If someone deeply desires an encounter with an angel and has an experience that has certain unusual features, that person may intentionally or unintentionally embellish the story to make it seem more angelic than it actually was.

Then there is the possibility that the encounter was supernatural but not angelic; in other words, some people may be deceived by a devil in the guise of an angel of light. Sometimes Christians are too quick to attribute the alleged supernatural experiences of others to demonic influence. Still, we must recognize that it can happen.

Having said all of this, I do not think it is always possible to evaluate a story from afar and come to any meaningful conclusions about its truth. If I have only read a story from someone whom I have never met and if I have no idea whether the person is trustworthy or stable, it is very difficult for me to confirm or deny the story. Personally, I tend to give people the benefit of the doubt, although I have read quite a few angel stories that I do not consider credible.

As Christians, we cannot allow ourselves to fall into the kind of thinking that says that angel stories by Christians are true, but those told by others either are not true or are demonic. Such thinking has no evidence to support it; rather, it is a case of choosing to give credence to what we are most comfortable with. I doubt that we can attribute to demons stories about individuals being saved from danger. As far as I know, demons are not in the habit of saving people. Of course, many of the other possibilities we have mentioned may come into play (false memories, lying, and so forth). We should not be alarmed if a genuine miracle occurs in the life of someone who has no faith or false faith, nor should we feel a need to debunk every miracle story. There is a common grace of God, whereby He causes the sun to shine on the just and unjust alike. In some cases, the individual who experienced some kind of angel deliverance was not predisposed to look for supernatural intervention, was surprised when it happened, and did not try to prove anything by it or make too much of it. These stories, in my mind, are the most credible.

By contrast, the stories I find least credible are those that involve visions, voices, and the teaching of angels. These are much more likely to involve the "lying wonders" of devils or simply the lying lips or deluded minds of people. I give no credence to modern revelations from angels, regardless of whether the humans involved are Christian. It may not be impossible *in principle* that an angel could give a revelation to someone today; I just have never read an account, whether it came from New Agers, Roman Catholic angelphiles, or whomever, that I had found believable. The alleged revelations always move from the heretical (you are God!) and superstitious (beware of black cats—they have demons!) to the trite (just love yourself!) and silly (flap your angel wings!).

Uncertain Guides

As we have seen, many Christian books on angels give guidelines for evaluating an encounter with an angel. Typical ideas are that an angel never communicates things that contradict the Bible, that the encounter should leave us feeling ready to serve God, that the alleged encounter should not violate common sense, that we need to ask whether the "angel" may really have been a demon, and so forth. I frankly consider these checklists to be a waste of time.

First, I do not need to prove or disprove the authenticity of someone else's alleged encounter with an angel. If someone claims to have been saved by an angel from dying in a car accident, it is not necessary for me to determine all the facts in the case or definitively state whether that person actually encountered an angel. This is especially so when I do not know the person in question and am only reading about the experience in a book or magazine. In many of these cases, I can simply accept at face value that the individual believes that he or she was saved from a difficult situation by an angel. I leave it at that, unless for some special reason I need to know more.

On the other hand, if someone claims to have a *revelation* from an angel and tells me that I should follow this instruction because it comes from an angel, I will turn away regardless of whether the alleged revelation seems to agree with the Bible or not. There is no place for familiar spirits—angels who teach new doctrines or predict the future—in Christianity. In any case, I should not base my life and faith on someone else's supposed revelation from an angel.

Second, I doubt that these guidelines for discernment are necessary or accurate for my evaluation of my own experiences. Again, because of the importance of avoiding familiar spirits, I have no need for angels to come and give me doctrinal instruction. Any angel who claims to have new revelations should be sent packing. If I am somehow helped by an angel (by being pushed out of the way of a train or something like that), I do not think I will need guidelines to help me know if it was a real angel. In any case, the praise for the unexpected help goes to God.

Some of the guidelines are based more on intuition than anything else. For example, the often repeated notion that an angel encounter always leaves us encouraged, clearheaded, and ready to serve God has little in the Bible to support it. Lot and his daughters, after their angelic encounter, went downhill morally (Gen. 19). Balaam encountered the angel of the Lord and went on to attempt to curse Israel (Num. 22). Zechariah encountered an angel and ended up a mute (Luke 1)!

The real point is that one should never seek an angel encounter or base one's beliefs on another person's angel encounter. Supposed "guidelines" for evaluating angel encounters only encourage us to think that we have the key to discern whether or not an encounter is real. This in turn can have the dangerous effect of leading us to seek angels. If I had to make my own list of guidelines, it would be quite brief: First, never seek to meet an angel. If one should surprise you and minister to you somehow, praise God. Second, do not take candy from strangers, and do not take revelation from angels.

Anecdotal Evidence and Angelic Authorities

I have already pointed out that personal anecdotes about angel encounters are of limited value in proving anything. Anecdotal evidence is always the most suspicious. Nutritionists know that any diet, no matter how wacky ("eat nothing but bananas and lard for one month, then add liver") can "work" for some people.

Yes, there are many people who claim to have encountered an angel. There are many other people who claim to have seen spaceships piloted by aliens with big, purple heads and long, skinny limbs. There are people who have spoken with ghosts, people who claim to have met the abominable snowman, and people who claim to have spotted the Loch Ness monster.

On the spectrum of credibility, I believe in angels but do not believe every alleged encounter. On the other hand, I do not believe in alien spaceships at all. But we cannot go around having our whole worldview turned upside down every time we hear a new anecdote. Sometimes we simply have to let stories pass by with no more than a curious glance, even while we acknowledge that there may be things in heaven and earth that are unaccounted for in our philosophy.

Finally, we should recognize that the fact that a person has encountered an angel or devil does not make him or her an authority on anything, including angels. The black garbed skier who saved Sophy Burnham from her fall may have been a real angel, but this does not validate any of her opinions on angels, religion, or God. People who have encountered angels are not necessarily wiser, better, or more spiritual than other mortals. Again, anyone who seeks to make mileage or gain credibility out of an alleged meeting with an angel is immediately suspect.

The Apostle Paul considered "boasting" about encounters with the supernatural to be both folly and arrogance, and he only spoke of his own experiences indirectly and with much hesitation and embarrassment. He actually considered his *suffering* for Christ to be a much more certain and worthy validation of his message than any of his visions. As for the latter, he felt that there was little to be gained from talking about them (2 Cor. 11:30–12:6).[8]

If this were played upon a stage now,
I could condemn it as an improbable fiction.
WILLIAM SHAKESPEARE, *TWELFTH NIGHT* 3, 4

Improbable Fiction

Angels in Evangelical Novels

PERHAPS IT HAS NEVER OCCURRED TO YOU THAT SATAN sometimes gets embarrassed about his antisocial behavior. Or maybe you never thought of an angel carrying a faithful dog to his heavenly reward (unless you are an aficionado of *The Far Side*, in which dogs in heaven chase trucks made of Spam). I am sure that, until recently, I never worried that a lapse in prayerfulness on my part would lead to some poor angel getting beaten to a pulp by a gang of demon-thugs. Well, if you have never pondered these things, then you have never ventured into the world of Christian angel novels.

Angels have entered Christian fiction in a big way. New novels by evangelicals ostensibly take us into a world where spirits are the main characters. The books are popular, some are well written, and all are easy to understand. We cannot think of fiction simply as stories that are untrue and that need not be taken seriously, however. "Truth," or at least strong opinions about truth, does not confine itself to books of history,

---

theology, and philosophy (in other words, to nonfiction). In reality, nothing spreads ideas as effectively as good fiction. In the mid-nineteenth century, *Uncle Tom's Cabin* mobilized the American North against Southern slavery. Today, we may well wonder how many people believe that interstellar travel can happen (and that aliens are visiting us) because of *Star Trek* and *Close Encounters of the Third Kind.*

Fiction can mold religious beliefs too. Recent films, for example, portray the afterlife and the devil. Even people who do not walk away from motion pictures such as *Ghost* or *Rosemary's Baby* saying, "Yes, I believe it is exactly like that," may be influenced more than they know. When a story is told well, it takes a highly critical mind to resist being drawn into its belief structure. Good fiction is powerful precisely because it deadens the critical faculties while the audience enjoys the story.

Now that the "angel novel" has emerged in Christian writings, some readers will inevitably welcome ideas from these stories as genuine Christian doctrine. I would even venture to say that for many people Christian fiction constitutes their main source of information on angels and demons. Perhaps they feel that because a book is written by a "born-again Christian" and published by a recognized Christian publisher, they can trust it. This being the case, our study of this present confusion over angels would not be complete without a look at what these books are saying.

To do this, we will look at three books in detail. The first is the 1941 classic by C. S. Lewis, *The Screwtape Letters.* This is valuable to us because it provides something of a control—its main characters are demons, but it was written before the current craze of interest in this area. Along the way we may mention a few other of Lewis's fantasies as well. The second is the phenomenally successful novel *This Present Darkness* by Frank Peretti. We need to examine this venture into the angelic realm, if for no other reason, because so many Christians have read it. Our third book, *Stedfast,* by Roger Elwood, is important because it purports to give the angelic view of the world. Our task is to see whether and to what degree these books are accurate and edifying.

The Screwtape Letters

In *The Screwtape Letters,* Lewis used correspondence from a senior, experienced demon (Screwtape) to his nephew Wormwood, a young demon who is assigned to the task of keeping a particular young man from God. Screwtape encourages, rebukes, and instructs the apprentice tempter in the things that help to bring a Christian down.

Lewis's presentation of the demonic realm is obviously artificial. To begin with, no one can take seriously the notion that demons have nephews or that a senior demon might sit at his desk and write letters to inexperienced tempters out in the field. Screwtape has a title right out of the British government—his Abysmal Sublimity Under Secretary. In addition, Screwtape sometimes mentions the "college" (an academy where young demons learn the art of temptation), a "Philological Arm," and a demonic intelligence division.[1] The latter detail may reflect the fact that Lewis wrote the book during World War II. Demons who fail to bring down their charges face either being eaten by other demons or being sent to the "House of Correction for Incompetent Tempters."[2]

This quaint and familiar picture of demonic "life" makes the story entertaining and easy to follow but also dispels any pretense of giving an accurate picture of the spiritual world. It is not that Lewis does not believe that demons are real. He simply makes no claim of instructing us on what the spirits are really like and goes out of his way to be clear on that point. He wants us to focus on *our* spiritual conflicts, and he does not allow any conjectured demonology to get in the way.

We do not read of any dialogues between demons and angels, much less of any battles, probably because such a scene would cross the line between obvious fiction and what some would have taken to be an accurate portrayal of life among the spirits. It is also to Lewis's credit, I think, that he carefully avoids making God or Christ a character in his book. In fact, he will not even use the name of Christ but only refers to him as "Him" or the "Enemy" (remember that this is from Screwtape's perspective). As a literary scholar, Lewis knows that an author assumes control over his characters, and he is not about to do this with the Lord.

Through the instructions of Screwtape, Lewis skillfully shows us how authentic spirituality differs from the shams by which we deceive ourselves. Screwtape does not care if Wormwood's young man feels concern for distant, unseen people, but he becomes alarmed if the man starts to show kindness and patience toward the people he sees every day. He wants to keep the man in an artificial kind of spirituality that neglects the basic duties of prayer and charity. Screwtape wants the church to acquire "the defensive self-righteousness of a secret society or a clique."[3]

Screwtape tells Wormwood to make sure that his "patient" prays about his mother's sins but neglects to pray for her rheumatism. He adds, "I have had patients of my own so well in hand that they could be turned at a moment's notice from impassioned prayer for a wife's or son's 'soul' to beating or insulting the real wife or son without a qualm."[4]

Lewis also speaks of "positive pleasures"—things that are not strictly spiritual but which are good for the soul. These include a book that the young man reads "because he really enjoyed it and not in order to make clever remarks about it to his new friends"[5] as well as a walk down a country road. He wants us to see that God's goal for us is that in every respect we become healthy, happy, and caring people.

Lewis's insight into Christian sanctification never fails to amaze. He observes that unlike the demons, who merely consume people, God wants humans to become qualitatively like Himself. To do this, and to enable His people to become of strong character, God may withdraw from their conscious experience and so force them to walk more by faith. As Screwtape says, "Our cause is never more in danger than when a human, no longer desiring, but still intending, to do our Enemy's will, looks round upon a universe from which every trace of Him seems to have vanished, and asks why he has been forsaken, and still obeys."[6] His description of sin is equally discerning: "An ever increasing craving for an ever diminishing pleasure is the formula."[7] Throughout the book we encounter wisdom of this kind. We find what it is to give of ourselves and what it is to be peevish and selfish, and we discover what knowing God is all about.

In short, *The Screwtape Letters* is not actually about demons but about sanctification. If we learn anything about demons at all, we learn that they are thoroughly uninteresting in their evil. They are neither heroic nor tragic but might be best described as pure expressions of everything we do not like about ourselves. There is no danger of our being fascinated with the demons here. On the other hand, after reading this book, we cannot help but be more aware that they are real.

This Present Darkness

We are in a different realm altogether with *This Present Darkness*. The story is set in Ashton, U.S.A., a small college town that has become the center of a conflict between Christians and angels on one side, and New

Agers and demons on the other. The New Agers are taking over the town and its college to create a world center for their movement, "Universal Consciousness." Behind the earthly conflict, and for the most part unseen, angels and demons battle it out for control of this turf.

Peretti is a fine writer. The almost-four hundred pages of his novel move quickly, and he knows how to finish a chapter leaving the reader with a hunger to know what comes next. He manages to avoid the inanity that characterizes some recent Christian fiction and might be described as something of a Christian version of Stephen King. As King might do, he sets his tale in the closed community of ostensibly idyllic rural America, invades that community with an insidious evil, develops the characters of those who resist it, and brings the conflict to a climactic conclusion.

Peretti's angels and demons are remarkable characters. All of his spirits are male (although they can appear to a human as a woman), presumably because they are all warriors. The angels are a jaunty troop, with names like Tal and Guilo, and have huge muscles and gleaming eyes. They like nothing better than to get into a fight and throttle a few demons. They will do whatever it takes to thwart the demonic plots—including stealing one of the bad guys' trucks! The demons, on the other hand, are grotesque. They are like Klingons with talons and bat wings. Deformed and vicious, they snarl and fight even with one another and are kept in line only by raw power as the bigger demons whack and intimidate the smaller, weaker ones. A jealous demon may even betray another and hurt their cause. If Peretti's vision is right then maybe we can rest easy—Satan's house is divided (Mark 3:25–26)!

In all of this we should see that Peretti has taken a major step beyond Lewis. Whereas Lewis presented demons in a manner that was obviously unreal in order to focus his attention on the inner struggles of the Christian life, Peretti appears to be giving us a realistic picture of an angelic conflict that is waged around us. Notwithstanding the comic book qualities that his spirits possess, Peretti's book, unlike Lewis's, does not disavow any notion that it is a portrayal of the real world of angels and demons. While one might contend that Peretti's fiction is not meant to be taken in that way, he has blurred the distinction between fantasy and reality considerably. Unlike Lewis's *Perelandra*, for example, *This Present Darkness* takes place in the real world, and it describes in a lifelike manner the difficulties of life in a small town and its church. Since most of his evangelical readers already believe that angels and demons are real as well, should they not assume, perhaps unconsciously, that Peretti's portrayal of life among the spirits is fundamentally accurate? Considering Peretti's skill as a writer, this is a decided possibility, and it is already happening. Spiritual warfare advocate Steven Lawson states approvingly: "More and more people . . . . [are] applying as fact the same principles Peretti used to craft his novels." [8] That being the case, his presentation requires some scrutiny.

First and foremost, Peretti's spirits often engage in "physical" combat. Each one carries a sword, and when they fight, they can dismember or "kill" one another. If you cut them, they will bleed. If a demon is killed, he plunges into the abyss; it is not clear what happens to an angel if he gets killed. We have already seen that this notion misses the point of passages like Revelation 12.

The outcome of the battles among Peretti's spirits helps to determine, and is determined by, the outcome of battles between good and evil among humans. But it is not always evident which one is the real arena of combat: is it the angelic or human conflict? While the book presents angels as beings whose function is to assist believers, it sometimes appears that the real battle is among the spirits and that the humans are more of a prize to be won. Also, Christians at times seem to be auxiliaries—they provide "prayer cover" for the angels as they go forth into combat.

Several problems arise here. All of this combat among the spirits leads to a carnal view of our spiritual struggles. We can easily get excited over how great it would be to strike down some demon, but our real spiritual victories come simply in developing greater integrity, compassion, and knowledge of God. The notion that above our heads some angel is punching out some demon may be titillating, but I doubt that it is an incentive toward growth in grace. It is an appallingly fleshly vision of spiritual struggles. Genuine victories come when we persevere in faith despite hardship or disappointment, when we pray for our enemies, when we learn how to be compassionate and generous to those in need, and when we keep ourselves unspotted by the world. The desire to see a demon split open by an angelic sword, although it seems spiritual, is a return to the weapons of the flesh in our fantasies.

The conflict between Peretti's angels and demons is so comprehensive that human personality is at times altogether subordinated. One character, "Bobby," is a vicious criminal possessed by various demons of witchcraft, rape, and violence. Living in a kind of daze, he meets the evangelical pastor who in short order exorcises him of his demons. Bobby undergoes an immediate conversion, and at once becomes a wonderful young man. All of the evil in his life appears to have been a matter of being dominated by demons and not at all a function of his own actions.[9] The presentation of Bobby's conversion makes it seem that our real problem is not our rebellion against God; it is just that we have these demons ruining our lives. Every bad guy in the book is to some degree involved in demon worship. In the Bible, our fundamental problem is not demons but sin.

This vision of earth as an arena of warfare between angels and demons gives us an oddly dualistic version of Christianity. "Dualism," again, is a religious teaching that asserts that good and evil are two dominant and equal principles in the universe and that they are in constant conflict. In *This Present Darkness*, instead of a world in which God is active and sovereign, we have a world in which God is strangely distant and in which angels and demons, who are roughly equal in strength, vie for control. In the Bible, as we have already seen, there is no question of demonic powers being in any sense a real threat to God's work. To the contrary, we have seen that in the Old Testament the demons are wholly under the sovereignty of the Lord; and in the New Testament they are altogether defeated at the cross and the Resurrection.

Many evangelicals are willing to give Peretti praise for his emphasis on the need for constant prayer in this book. That, indeed, is a positive aspect. However, because of his idea that spiritual warfare involves combat among the spirits, there are problems. Christians have always understood the warfare of prayer to have two essential functions. First, we give God praise and thanksgiving and confess to Him our sins. Second, we offer requests for ourselves and other people. It is a "spiritual warfare" in that by prayer we glorify God and, in ways we do not understand, allow Him to work through us in the world. It is not, as far as the Bible is concerned, a matter of assisting angels in their fight with demons.

Perhaps the strangest moment in the whole book comes near the end when the angel Tal is in mortal combat with the demon lord Rafar, and Tal is having a bad time of it. The earthly struggle is by now over; the sinister New Age priestess is dead and all the other bad guys have been arrested. The Christians, in the midst of their celebrations, feel a sudden need to go back into intercessory prayer. They do not know it, but they need to save Tal's angelic skin. In some mystical way, a woman senses that the demon's name is something like Raphael, and Bobby, the ex-demoniac, recognizes it as Rafar. When the Christians rebuke Rafar, the demon's power is broken and Tal lives to fight another day.[10] This is, to me, the most troubling and illustrative moment in the book—Christians are interceding for an angel! Scripture never hints that such a thing is necessary or desirable. This perhaps indicates where one can go when one loves the angels too much.

Stedfast

If *This Present Darkness* is bold in its speculation about the angelic realm, the novel *Stedfast* truly charges into angel areas where theologians fear to tread. Its author, Roger Elwood, is gratified that "the Christian reading public is more than a little receptive to fiction that tackles subjects more serious than fluffy romances."[11] There is certainly no doubt that Elwood deals with difficult subjects—questions about which the Bible says little or nothing—but if Christian fiction is made significant only by letting our imaginations run free in areas where God is silent, then maybe a little fluff is not such a bad thing.

Stedfast is part of a trilogy that includes the books *Angelwalk* and *Fallen Angel.* In his books, Elwood not only shows us what the angels do but tells us their inner thoughts: *Stedfast* is written in first person as the narrative of an angel of the same name. Stedfast the angel is devoted to his human charges, is quite sentimental, but has an irritating habit of speaking in sentence fragments. He has had a remarkable "life." His best friend is another angel named (what else?) True. Stedfast and True were the guardian angels, respectively, of Adam and Eve. Since the fall of man, Stedfast has had various assignments guarding people through the ages, and in his book he tells us of some of his adventures (True was left behind to guard Eden).

Some of Stedfast's reminiscences are not theologically significant but just a little odd, if not offensive. For some reason, Stedfast defends Robert E. Lee's service for the Confederacy during the American Civil War and assures us that there are plantation owners in heaven: "Slaves were, to them, well-nigh members of their family, given similar privileges. Their slaves got such food, good clothes, and medical attention that were equal to that of any white person on the plantation"[12] (this is a good example of the jawbreaking prose we get from Stedfast). Stedfast even recalls one group of slaves who voluntarily defended the plantation against the invading Yankees, and he assures us that emancipation ruined what for these slaves had been a very fine life. You know, I never knew that.

Of more concern to us is the theological message of this book. In the blurb on the back cover, we read that Elwood "has been compared to C. S. Lewis for his allegorical writing style." Whatever one wishes to make of comparing Lewis to Elwood, one thing is clear: *Stedfast* is no allegory. A true allegory, such as Lewis's *The Chronicles of Narnia* (or Bunyan's *Pilgrim's Progress*) makes no pretense of representing the real world of angels or humans but instead, working in an artificial world, makes use of obvious symbolism to teach spiritual truths. When we read *The Lion, the Witch, and the Wardrobe,* we know that there is no Narnia, that animals do not talk, and that Aslan the lion, while a Christ-figure, is not a portrayal of the real Jesus Christ. We recognize that through all of these symbols Lewis is teaching us a great deal about God and ourselves, yet we are never in danger of confusing the reality of Christian beliefs with the fantasy world of Narnia.

Stedfast is altogether different. Elwood's world is not Narnia but Earth. His creatures are not talking mice and horses but humans, angels, and demons; and the setting for his human-angelic encounters include Eden, the American Civil War, abortion clinics, and the rooms of dying patients. As with Peretti, Elwood has obscured the line between genuine Christian beliefs and the fictional world of the author. Elwood has gone even further in that he does not create fictional situations such as "Ashton" and "Universal Consciousness," but he deals with circumstances that we either know to be historical or which are very close to home. He goes so far as to make the risen Christ a character in his book and to put words in His mouth.[13] In my view, this is an outrageous presumption and is highly irreverent.

As we follow Stedfast through his adventures, he speaks to us on all kinds of subjects. Hearing alleged truths from the mouth of an angel, the uncritical Christian reader will be confused. Where does Christian doctrine end and fiction begin? Elwood does not give his reader any guidelines. If there is any doubt that people are taking his musings on angels seriously, one need look no further than the endorsement by Joni

Eareckson Tada on the back of the book: "It's nice to be reminded how real, how solid, how ever-present the spiritual world in which the angels live . . . really is."

On close inspection, one finds many problems with Elwood's presentation. At times, he simply contradicts the Bible. For example, he tells us that at the creation Eden was crowded with angels since "they were to be caretakers of this new place."[14] The Bible tells us that Adam was to be the caretaker of Eden (Gen. 2:15), but one of the first rules of angelphiles is, "Angels do everything."

Some of what Stedfast tells us is highly sentimental if not, well, goofy. He has a soft spot in his heart for lobsters and tells us that before sin entered the world they were herbivores. Back then, they did not have a care in the world, but now that they have to hunt their prey, their lives are full of stress and fear.[15] I rather doubt that nervous tension is a significant problem for crustaceans.

More significantly, he tells us that dogs, or at least good dogs, go to heaven. When a boy's beloved dog is at the point of death, Stedfast appears to the boy, speaks to him for a moment, and then disappears. Just as he does with dying Christians, he takes the dog's spirit up to heaven (cat owners need not fear—a cat makes it into heaven, too, and he and the couple who were his earthly masters are reunited and are a family again).[16]

Now someone may want to respond that if Stedfast wants to tell us that dogs and cats go to heaven it may be an odd idea, but there is no real harm in it. It is nothing more than a quaint, sentimental hope and, after all, who knows that they do not go to heaven? True enough, we do not know that they do not go to heaven, and the notion that they do is perhaps appealing.

There is genuine danger here, however, of a hope for a carnal afterlife. By "carnal," I mean simply a hope for a continuation of what we like best on earth. In certain Islamic teachings, the afterlife is a sensual paradise. Mormons look for a reuniting of husbands and wives in heaven, where they can continue to procreate as they had on earth. The Bible, by contrast, tells us very little about the resurrection except that there will be no marriage (Matt. 22:3) and that we do not know exactly what we will become, except that we will be like Jesus (1 John 3:2). The important thing is that the focus of our hope be upon God. Knowing Him and being with Him should be the fulfillment of all our aspirations. The picture of a husband and wife in heaven running to each other's arms while Fido leaps about their feet wagging his tail may seem attractive, but the Bible implies nothing of this precisely because it is an allurement to the flesh and from our first love. What Elwood presents is the kind of confused theology that angelphilia encourages.

Elwood does not contradict the Bible but goes far beyond what is written when Stedfast visits the abortion clinic. Before I get into this, I would like to remark that I am opposed to abortion and consider its legalization to be an offense that is sure to bring God's judgment. In this, Elwood and I are agreed.

When Stedfast tells us what goes on in the spiritual realm at the abortion clinics, however, I begin to get concerned. He tells us that angels are in the womb with the fetus from conception until birth unless the process is interrupted by abortion. If a woman does abort the fetus, an angel takes the spirit of the fetus up to heaven where it matures and then lives eternally with God. In one scene, a Christian woman abortion protester dies in front of a clinic and goes to heaven where she sees the spirits of recently aborted babies being taken to God. One of the babies, we are told, would have been a great scientist, and another would have been president.[17] What are we to make of all this?

The notion that an angel is in the womb with a growing baby is eccentric but perhaps not especially significant. The Bible says nothing about this, but if anything, I would prefer to think that angels simply show special care over pregnant women. (As a man, I have to wonder if a woman can really be comfortable with the notion that an angel is also in there for nine months.) If nothing else, this idea exhibits the excessive sentimentality of this book.

Then there is the idea that this or that aborted fetus would have been a scientist or president. Aside from the fact that I do not think that there is any "would have been" in heaven, we have to wonder in all honesty why none of the angels point out that this or that child would have been a drug pusher or a pimp. I do not mean to sound cynical, but I think that the latter possibilities are at least as likely if not more so.

Most important of all is Stedfast's teaching that aborted fetuses all go to heaven and grow up with God. Now I should say at the outset that I do not know what becomes of aborted fetuses and you don't either; the Bible does not tell us. It is one of the secret things that belong to God, and when we speculate on this, we go way beyond what is written. Many people believe that all dead babies go to heaven because David, after the death of his infant son, said, "I shall go to him, but he will not return to me" (2 Sam. 12:23).

We must be careful, however, because even if David were speaking of heaven in that text, he was not talking about all babies going there but a baby who was a child of a believer and a son of the covenant people (a concept that was very important to David). More importantly, however, it is not clear that David had a special revelation about the question of what happens to dead babies. When he spoke of the child and him going to a common place, it is more likely that he simply meant *Sheol*, the Hebrew word for the grave or place of the dead. All David really said was, "Where he has gone, I shall go too," meaning that the child was dead and he would follow soon enough.

Ecclesiastes 6:3–5 speaks to the issue in far more bleak terms but is closer to the question of what happens to an aborted fetus. It says that a stillborn child "comes from vanity and goes into darkness" and that it has not known anything. This is certainly not a picture of aborted or miscarried fetuses going up to heaven. But just as 2 Samuel 12:23 does not really teach that babies go to heaven, so this text does not really teach that aborted or miscarried fetuses are annihilated. The "darkness" of which Ecclesiastes speaks simply means that they have never known the light of the sun, and they have not "known anything" in the sense that they never participated in this life. Once again, we are back to the point that the Bible simply does not tell us about the fate of aborted babies.

Why does the Bible not tell us what happens to them? Is Elwood's idea thus comforting and helpful? On this point, I believe that the Holy Spirit is wiser in keeping things from us than Elwood is in giving us speculation. I hope it has not escaped your notice that if we did know with certainty that aborted fetuses go to heaven and are raised by the angels in the presence of the Father, then we would have to say that being aborted is about the best thing that can happen to a fetus. They never get sick, they never suffer the loss of a loved one, they never get beaten up or raped, they never sin, and best of all, they are never in danger of going to hell. Trying to give us a powerful, heavenly argument against abortion, Elwood has given us the strongest (and strangest) argument for abortion.

Once again, I am in no position to say that aborted children do not experience some kind of salvation, but I am saying that we do not know and that speculation does more harm than good. The proper response to this and similar questions is not to look for a secret answer but to trust God. Our hope is not in some theological argument, however tightly reasoned or emotionally appealing it may be, but in the goodness, wisdom, and mercy of God. If we truly believe in God, we need no other answer. Our task, as the hymn tells us, is simply to trust and obey. We can oppose abortion and preach the gospel, but we must leave the things that are beyond us in God's hands.

Many aspects of *Stedfast* are oddly mythological or pagan. In the Greek myths, the gods are for all practical purposes just people with a lot of power. They are not spirits as we understand the term. Some are basically good and others are for the most part evil, but like people, the majority are a mixture of both.

The same is true of Elwood's spirits. He has two evil spirits in the book, Satan and another demon called Observer. He tries to make them seem horrible by disfiguring them, but all he succeeds in doing is make them pitiable. In fact, it is hard not to pity them when we read of the regret they express over what they do and what they have become. In one episode, Stedfast tries to stop Observer from snatching a soul to hell, a soul whom he had known to be a very pleasant fellow. In Stedfast's words, Observer "looked at me, quite sadly in fact, and said, 'You do not know everything, Stedfast.'"[18] It turns out that the man had been a Nazi war criminal.

My concern here is not with the war criminal but with the portrayal of Observer. Do demons really regret what they do? Are they capable of remorse and sadness? Should we feel sorry for them? No. The Bible tells us that they experience terror at the prospect of judgment (James 2:19), but never sadness over a lost soul, which is a moral response. In Elwood's world, even Satan experiences regret and shame over wanting to drag a boy down to hell and feast on him there.[19]

An immortal being cannot be a mixture of good and evil but must be either perfectly moral or wholly corrupt. Being immortal, they have no restraints on corruption once it has begun. We humans, by contrast, buffeted by the troubles of life and in the brevity of our earthly existence, can have both good and evil in part. It is for this reason that we are cut off from the "tree of life" (Gen 3:24). Were we immortal in this fallen condition, we too would experience unfettered corruption.

In describing Satan in this human way, Elwood does not give us the terrible demon of the Bible but a creature of mythology. We should add that the idea that demons drag the souls of the wicked off to hell and there consume them is also out of mythology.[20] In the Bible, Satan is not the king of hell. The Lake of Fire is a place of torment for him no less than for anyone else. And he does not eat people; he accuses them.

God, too, is presented in rather human terms. In explaining why a particularly fine young Christian athlete was struck down early in life, Stedfast states that "the Holy Spirit felt that this young man would be particularly sensitive to demonic oppression since he had been given so much in his life."[21] Apart from the fact that it is not clear why a handsome athlete should be especially sensitive to demonic oppression, it never occurred to me that God based decisions on how He "felt." A feeling is an intuition, a hunch based not on knowledge but intuitiveness. God does not suppose—He knows. This may seem to be a petty criticism, but it is not. When we begin to fantasize about angels, demons, and God, we inevitably begin to create them in our image. The artist who tries to paint God ends up painting a man (or perhaps a woman, these days). The result is not a portrayal of God, but an idol—which is where the road of angelphilia inevitably leads.

Elwood's presentation of what angels are is also unusual. When trying to explain to an old woman how it is that he can remember everyone he has ever known, Stedfast says, "We are children of God, Dottie. We are extensions of Him. We remember just as He remembers." What does it mean to say that angels are "extensions" of God?

Perhaps the single greatest indication of a pagan or decadent theology is the blending of spirituality and sexuality. It is found in ancient pagan religions, in Christian heresies of various kinds, and in the neopaganism of the present age. Here, too, Elwood comes very close to crossing a line. Speaking of the relationships that Stedfast and True had with Adam and Eve prior to the Fall, he writes, "What it was like for a man and a woman in the most ecstatic moments of their passion was very close to what True and I felt. We were 'married,' in a sense, to Adam and Eve. Indeed, we had the greatest possible intimacy."[22] This relationship was "communion, yes, but also connection, *angels and humans as almost a single entity, an interweaving of one with the other.*"[23] He especially speaks of the bond between True and Eve.[24]

Now I, for one, have no desire to be interwoven with an angel, but more to the point, the notion that Adam and Eve had some kind of intimate union with guardian angels not only goes beyond Scripture but contradicts it outright. Adam, before the creation of Eve, was alone; his wife and not an angel was to be the companion suitable for him (Gen. 2:18–24). A union of the flesh should be only with one's spouse; a union of spirit should be with Christ. Elwood's angels come close to taking over both functions. The peril here is perhaps greater than one might imagine. My reading leads me to believe that in some angelphiles, especially among women, the yearning for an angel encounter can be very strong. If loneliness and unfulfilled sexual desires are mixed in, the idea that one might be "married" with "the greatest possible intimacy" to an angel could be dangerously attractive, and the result would be thoroughly pagan if not demonic.

Stedfast is not healthy reading, but for our purposes it is a valuable case study. It shows where a longing to look into the realm of angels can lead. We will wander into areas we do not understand, try to fill the gaps in our knowledge with our own imagination, and finish with a pagan religion that has many little gods made in the image of man.

We have already seen that a fascination with angels and devils is fraught with danger. Out of their fantasies, people create a world that is a distortion of biblical teaching. The result is not a stronger, more supernatural faith but a degenerate version of what spiritual life ought to be. In this kind of decadent religion, the illusion that one has insight regarding the spirits replaces the struggle for growth in grace.

The great enemy of truth is very often not the lie—deliberate, contrived and dishonest—but the myth—persistent, persuasive and unrealistic.
JOHN F. KENNEDY

The Great Enemy of Truth

The Powers and Spiritual Warfare

I HAVE A FRIEND, A KIND AND GENTLE CHRISTIAN woman, who used to be demon-possessed. The story of her young life is tragic, horrifying, and finally inspirational. It grabs your attention and yanks you out of your comfortable, orthodox slumber. Many Christians have awakened to the fact that what we are about is not just professing a set of beliefs or even making our way along the pilgrimage of life, but that we have also entered a conflict involving powers beyond us.

More than any time in the past, Christians are naming, confronting, and doing war with spiritual powers. This is the Protestant angelphilia. Some Roman Catholic missionaries believe that on entering a new area they should seek the aid of the guardian angels of that place or people. Protestants, if anything, are more likely to bind the demons of the territory they enter! While we may not be able to say why Protestants have such a lively interest in demonic powers, we must recognize that this is our distinctive approach to focusing on the spirits. We must also determine how much of this is helpful and true to the gospel.

Two distinctive Protestant approaches to the "powers" have emerged. One is that of Walter Wink, whose writings form the theological undergirding for the political activism of liberal Protestantism. The other began in charismatic churches but now has gained wider acceptance among traditional, evangelical Protestants; it is the "spiritual warfare" movement.

Demonizing the Opposition—
The Powers of Walter Wink

Do you believe in a real, personal devil? Or do you think he is just a personification, only a symbol of evil, and even a child's bogeyman now grown up and taken too seriously? Or perhaps you would like a third alternative, one presented by New Testament scholar Walter Wink.

He dates his interest in the "powers" to a sabbatical in South America where he came face-to-face with the full force of evil. The oppression and institutional violence overwhelmed him, and he came to see that we must take seriously the reality of spiritual powers that rob people of their humanity. He turned to a study of the New Testament teaching on the "powers" and what emerged was a theological trilogy: *Naming the Powers, Unmasking the Powers, and Engaging the Powers.*[1]

He regards the powers neither as personal beings nor as mere personifications of evil. They have no identities apart from us; they do not swirl around in the sky above us. But neither are they projections of our fears or metaphors born of the imagination. Instead, spiritual powers are the internal, subjective side of the external works and institutions of human beings.

By "subjective," we do not mean "imaginary." The spirits Wink describes have real force, presence, and existence, but it is not the kind of personal, separate reality we normally imagine in the person of Satan. The power structures of Nazi Germany, for example, involved more than an external government, a military, or even a set of doctrines. The internal side of Nazism was a real spiritual entity that exercised control over both masters and victims in the German state. The phrase "Aryan spirit" was more than an expression; it was a reality. The same could be said for the "spirits" of capitalist conglomerates and communist dictatorships. In New Testament times, spiritual powers held sway, for example, in the imperial might of Rome.

Wink begins by recognizing the fluidity of terms in the New Testament, in which powers can be heavenly or earthly and can do good or evil. From this, he moves to the conclusion that spiritual powers are the inner dynamic of external, human power structures. Just as the demons in the New Testament craved a body to inhabit, so the spiritual powers do not exist except as the inner dimension to human power systems. The earthly and heavenly dimensions of power are bound together.

Thus, for Wink, the spirits can pop up in surprising places. Satan, for example, appears in the Bible both to accuse people of sin and to draw them into it. Wink observes that Satan is "not an independent operative, but rather *the inner and actual spirit of the* [Christian] *congregation itself when it falls into the accusatory mode*" as in the case of the incestuous man of 1 Corinthians 5. Because of the man's sin, Paul had no choice but to call on the church to condemn him and in so doing invoke the spirit of Satan, to whom the man was "handed over." Wink observes that the spirit of Satan here does a good work; the condem- nation has a salvific effect.[2]

Of course, Satan is also evil, and Wink can say with equal emphasis that "*Satan is the real interiority of a society that idolatrously pursues its own enhancement as the highest good.*"[3] In other words, Satan is also the spirit of greed and idolatry. You might say, therefore, that Satan is wherever we find him, but he always emerges from the *human* mentality of a judgmental spirit, hostility, or lust for power (to name but a few). We do not create him—remember that for Wink the spirit is "real"— but he emerges only within our minds and actions and has no existence apart from us.

Wink treats the demoniac as the individual who succumbs to both the external pressure of social oppression and the internal pressure of psychological pain. He actually develops two classes of demoniac. The first involves the "inner demon," in which some aspect of a personality has been wounded or alienated from the rest of the person. The wounded element may develop a personality all its own—a "demon." For Wink, to say that a person struggles with "inner demons" is to imply genuine psychological struggles, but not with a personal demon who can exist apart from the person involved. Outside the individual, the inner demon has no existence. Still, it is "real."

The other type of demoniac has an "outer" demon. Some people cannot withstand the pressures of a cold, vicious culture. This weakness Wink regards as sometimes a sensitivity to the enormity of society's guilt. The "madman" cannot cope with the evils that "sane" society easily endorses. Thus, he argues that the guilt-ridden navigator of the plane that dropped the atomic bomb on Hiroshima was judged insane by a society that refused to acknowledge its common guilt for mass murder. In that case, the "demoniac" has fallen into his sad condition primarily because of the external pressure of a depraved social order. Such a person, in his view, suffers from "outer" demons. The madness of society has been localized in the individual.[4]

Wink concludes that every challenge to evil, be it in society or in the individual, must include the spiritual dimension. In his view, Martin Luther King, Jr., was right to sing hymns while he marched for voter rights. To try to confront institutional evil without taking into account the spiritual side is merely to set up an alternative demon of power. By the same token, no form of Christian spirituality deserves the name if it does not challenge the external manifestations of evil in human society. A private pietism wrongly separates the human world from spiritual life.

In addition, we should not deal with the psychological maladies of the individual without taking into account the spiritual needs. Wink's studied rejection of the traditional notion of the demoniac by no means minimizes the spiritual dimension of cases of apparent demon-possession or a wounded psyche. A purely secular approach to psychological therapy overlooks the reality of the spirit within the individual.

What are we to make of this? An obvious but somewhat superficial criticism of Wink is that his view of the spirits does not conform to the Bible's. It is easy to point out many passages where the biblical writer self-evidently regards an angel as a personal being. Wink himself acknowledges as much. But he believes that the movement toward his interpretation of angels and devils already occurs in the Bible itself. It is more important to discern if his outlook contradicts biblical Christianity on a more fundamental level or whether it carries implications or tendencies we should reject.

We have to begin by saying that Wink's work has value. Although I do not think that we can or should avoid the Bible's teaching that there are personal spirits "out there," Wink's argument that a "spirit" is also the real, powerful, and internal force of a human institution has some validity. When Paul speaks of the "powers," the word includes the inner, spiritual dimension of, say, the Roman state with its devotion to the goddess Roma, its rituals in honor of Caesar, and its thrilled adoration of the war trophies of its legions. We should recognize that institutions carry with them something that is greater than any individual, law, or action of that institution. Families, corporations, associations, and states have both an outer and an inner dimension.

Wink's insights also serve as a check to the excesses of evangelical and neo-Pentecostal spiritual warfare. He correctly contends that people are often exorcised of demons that are really manifestations of their own personalities and traumas. Such people need love and guidance, but an exorcism will do little good and possibly great harm. It would be nice if we could free ourselves from anger, lust, unhappiness, and pride merely by exorcising the appropriate demons, but in many cases it is not possible.

Also, Wink forces us to ask ourselves if the institutions and ideologies we participate in are "demonic" in Wink's sense. If I can treat Satanic power as simply something "out there" in the person of Satan, then it is easy for me to accept beliefs and practices of my community and not ask questions about the "spirit" that governs it. Also, if I treat the "spirit" of my nation as purely a subjective and unreal notion, I fail to see that addressing the evils of society is a *spiritual* enterprise and not just a matter of changing a few policies.

Exorcising the Politicians

Problems with Wink's analysis include but go beyond his rejection of the biblical notion of personal angels and devils. One immediate problem is that it is hard to know if we should ascribe to the spirits (as Wink defines them) the kind of significance that Wink advocates. I suspect that there is a sense in which the spirits of institutions are real, but Wink has exaggerated their importance for the New Testament. An army may have *esprit de corps*, but this is not something I want to focus my theology on.

More importantly, Wink's approach makes it dangerously easy for him to demonize political viewpoints with which he disagrees. Throughout the books, he constantly champions leftist causes. Ecological activism, feminism, nuclear disarmament, promotion of gay rights, and so forth are for him all aspects of legitimate Christian work. By contrast, nuclear deterrence, the activity of the CIA, many aspects of capitalism, and apparently everything on the conservative political agenda are in his view not merely bad policy but *demonic.*

With consummate ease, he categorizes whatever he dislikes as a power that is fundamentally opposed to the gospel. Given his understanding of the meaning of "spirit," this is indeed an easy thing to do. He cannot see that those who advocate conservative approaches to social problems may be no less concerned than he over matters of peace and social justice. Those who advocate deterrence of aggression through military strength and deterrence of crime through appropriately severe punishment of wrongdoers operate from a desire for less violence in the world, not more (and they can cite Rom. 13:3–4 for support). In Wink's logic, such arguments are ruled out of order before they can even be voiced since they are *by definition* expressions of the demonic system of domination and militarism.

His notion of powers finally becomes highly pliable to the individual's political viewpoint. When he describes the supposed "spirit" of a given institution or ideology, I get the impression that he is really describing *how he feels* about that institution. Wink goes so far as to endorse the idea that the faithful should ritually exorcise conservative political leaders because they are "in the grip of evil."[5]

I have rarely seen conservative Christian political activists be so quick to classify opinions they do not share as demonic or to endorse such a bizarre approach to dealing with politicians they dislike. Wink is neither the first nor the last person to give a theological defense of his political ideals, and the results are no better in him than in anyone else.

This readiness to demonize the opposition naturally grows out of Wink's notion of the spirits. If I believe that a spirit is the inner dimension of an external human institution, and if I believe that some politician's administration of that institution and the ideology he applies to it are wrong, then that politician (or institution) is inevitably demonic. If, on the other hand, I believe that demons are separate beings, I had better have good reasons for calling a politician or any- one else demonic. The fact that I dislike his or her politics is not enough.

This tendency involves more than rhetoric or political ideology; it is a great spiritual danger. Nothing is so harmful to the soul as the notion that my thoughts are God's thoughts and that He is on my side. It precludes repentance and a broken heart before God. It replaces true contrition about one's own actions with a false repentance for the sins of others. If I advocate nuclear disarmament, it requires no great humility or work of the Spirit for me to cry out, "Oh, God, forgive us for the sin of the Hiroshima bomb!" Such pseudo-repentance would be more a basis of smug self-satisfaction than anything else. It would be much more momentous if people repented over sins that arise from political viewpoints that they share. Pro-life Christians should repent over those who gun down workers at abortion clinics, and pro-choice Christians should repent over the evil of the abortions themselves.

Wink's approach also makes it impossible to listen to one's political opponents since they are by definition duped by a demonic spirit. In a strange twist, his theological analysis makes dissent against *his* political viewpoint impossible. This is a foundation for the fanaticism of the ideologue. Ironically, such a person is the best example of Wink's notion of domination by a "spirit." Wink asserts that he developed his model to help us understand how we can oppose evil without becoming evil ourselves; in my view, he could hardly have failed more thoroughly.

The Original Gospel or a New Gospel?

Wink frequently modifies New Testament words to reflect more appropriately his understanding of the gospel. He retranslates the word *world*, for example, as "Domination System." "Do not love the world..." becomes "Do not love the Domination System...," as if 1 John 2:15–17 were an agenda of ecology, feminism, and other elements of the modern left-wing.[6] For Wink, the real point of the conflict between the world (a.k.a. "Domination System") and the kingdom of God (a.k.a. "New Reality") is *political*. Any religious teacher who advocates a new interpretation of Christianity on the basis of peculiar translations of biblical words is immediately suspect.

He also rejects the traditional understanding of the death of Christ on the cross. In fact, he believes that the apostle Paul was himself somewhat confused about the matter. This is not the place to examine his ideas on the atonement in detail, but I believe that it is fair to say that Wink's view implies that Jesus' crucifixion did little more than exemplify nonviolent resistance to the Domination System. In and of itself, the cross did not defeat the powers, and it certainly did not atone for sin.[7]

His interpretation of the cross grows naturally out of his understanding of the powers. If they are the internal dimension of human institutions, then it is difficult to imagine how the death of Christ fundamentally affected them except as an example to others of how to confront the powers with nonviolence.[8]

Praying for the Peas

The greatest problem with Wink's theology, however, goes beyond politics and retranslating some ideas. It is (and here we have to use a bit of jargon of the type that is dear to the theological *cognoscenti*) purely a theology of immanence.

When we say that God is immanent, we mean that God is present with His creation. When we speak of transcendence, we mean that God is self-sufficient and apart from His creation. A balanced, healthy doctrine of God maintains both His immanence and transcendence. In the modern era, however, theologians have overemphasized the immanence of God at the expense of His transcendence.[9]

Wink does not address the question of the nature of God Himself but concentrates on the powers and spirits. In this area, however, we see that his notion of spirit is purely immanent. Angels, demons, powers, and spirits may "really" exist, but they only exist as the interior dimension of human persons and institutions. Apart from us, they are nothing. We can speak of them as heavenly beings all we want, but our eyes never rise above the horizon. The biblical distinction between heaven, which is the realm of angels, and earth, which is the realm of humanity, disappears entirely; all is of the earth.

Much more is at stake than nostalgia for the good old days when angels were angels. The whole point to recognizing a transcendent God is that God's kingdom is not of this world (rather than not of this "Domination System"). The world is good and is a creation of God, but it is not spirit. God and the angels can be among us, but they are not of this order of existence.

The road Wink follows is the road to pantheism or paganism; already in his books we see a movement in that direction. It may come as a bit of a surprise that Wink contends that the pagan gods are also real. He asserts that the Bible is not monotheistic but henotheistic. Henotheism means that while we worship only one god we can affirm that other gods exist too. The Lord is not the only God; He is chief of the divine counsel and patron God of Israel.

Now for Wink, of course, the gods are real only in the sense that angels are real—they are part of the interior of humanity. They are the archetypes of the human psyche, and we must take them into account. If we suppress them, they will come back to haunt us in the underworld of society and our minds. We must reckon with the power of Aphrodite, for example, if we are to integrate sexuality into our lives.

From this line of reasoning, Wink defends the use of idols among pagans and concludes that we need to honor the gods in our lives. He says, "We must therefore have an altar. But what is the proper gift? The ego is desperately trying to hold its own, overmatched by a god—and we are told that ego must itself be sacrificed. That it must abandon control, so that the entire Gestalt of the self can absorb, digest, and integrate this new thing. . . . The 'altar' frees us to honor the gods without worshiping them, to keep our distance and yet relate to them."[10]

The notion that we should integrate the gods into our lives to achieve wholeness has roots in Jung's psychology. The weird idea that we should honor pagan gods but worship only the one God is a new twist on the Roman Catholic notion of reverence for Mary and the saints. But the whole thing is a return to the Colossian heresy: we need the aid of the powers in order to achieve spirituality and wholeness! Forget the teaching of Paul, who tells us that whoever does this has abandoned the head, who is Christ (Col. 2:19)! As in New Age angelphilia, Wink tells us to relinquish the ego to them. We are dismayed that he who had told us that we can disarm the powers leads us straight into their hands.

This is not the end of Wink's road, however. He argues that matter, too, is spiritual. He begins by observing that the physical elements of nature are suprahuman (but not personal beings) and that they are the conditions and boundaries of life. As such, we should have respect for them, and he regards making nuclear weapons as the ultimate defilement of the elements. He correctly states that materialistic science deifies matter even while it treats it as something to be controlled. He reminds us that God is above the elements; in this, he acknowledges the transcendence of God. Unfortunately, he describes the elements as "theophanies" or "revealers of God."[11]

A theologian of Wink's caliber knows that a theophany is not merely a revelation about God but an appearance of God Himself, such as when God appeared to Moses. Biblical Christianity teaches that nature reveals the glory of God (which is His divine power; Rom. 1:20), but not the person of God Himself. We see the results of God's power in the earthquake, the fire, or the wind, but God Himself is not in them. Rather, God reveals Himself in the Word (1 Kings 19:11–12). We do not see or know God in the elements. However much we may praise His handiwork in creation, we know Him only by the Word, Jesus Christ. Even as Wink exhorts us to honor the God who is *above* the elements, he invests too much spirituality *in* the elements. He has moved away from the gospel of the living Word to the gospel of nature.

Not only this, he wants us to return to the ancient religious notion that the earth is alive. He mistakenly believes that the scientific view of nature is the same as materialism. To be sure, some scientists are materialists, but viewing the world as inanimate is not necessarily materialism (which asserts that matter is the ultimate principle of the universe and that there is no spirit or God at all). There is a third way between the pagan view of the world as a living soul and the atheist's materialism: God is maker of heaven and earth. Nature is not alive and the machinery of nature is not maintained by angels; on the other hand, matter is not ultimate. It is the creation of God.

Wink was very impressed by a book by Dorothy Maclean. She and her colleagues apparently had spectacular success with their gardens in Scotland, and the alleged secret was that she had learned to communicate with the angels of her plants. "She would get centered on her higher self through meditation and then address a question to the angel of a particular species of plant." She found that "the being behind the garden pea held in its consciousness the archetypal design of all pea plants" in a "sort of inner energy stream of divinity."[12] Wink cites *1 Enoch* in support of her ideas. He admits that the Bible says "very little" about nature angels ("nothing" would be more accurate), but he still finds the idea very attractive and compares it to the nature spirits of Native Americans. He still prefers to think of nature angels as "the numinous interiority of created things," but he says that they can help us through our ecological crisis.[13]

He finally muses to himself, "How then did it come to pass that I, who had some few years ago conceived this study as a thoroughgoing demythologization of the Powers in social science categories, now find myself speaking realistically of angels? Having set sail in pursuit only of scholarly thoroughness and the desire to leave no stone unturned, I through no intention of my own have quite sailed off the map of our two-dimensional universe, into a universe that is *alive*."[14]

Actually, it is not all that surprising. Having treated spiritual beings strictly in terms of immanence and having forgotten the doctrine of creation and the lesson that the biblical heaven transcends earth, the road to the old gods was broad and easy.

The Tie that Binds— ## Evangelical Spiritual Warfare

An emerging force in evangelical theology is "spiritual warfare," the notion that direct conflict with Satan and demonic forces is at the very heart of the Christian life. This approach to Christianity argues that demons control nations, cities, and individuals and that they even inhabit objects. It claims that the Christian who does not directly confront, rebuke, and bind the demons has little hope of overcoming sin in personal life or of having meaningful success in evangelism and missions.

Confronting demons has therefore become the centerpiece of much of mission strategy. The basic idea is that "territorial demons" govern all the nations, cities, and tribes of the world. As long as these demons go unchallenged, efforts to reach people with the gospel will largely be weak and ineffective. These powers that govern the world are no demonic small-fry, however. They are high, powerful, and can only be cast down by "strategic level" prayer and confrontation. Being territorial, however, they are limited by national boundaries, city limits, and the like. In other words, if you pray into submission the demon of Minneapolis, you can be effective there—but you will lose all your power when you step over into St. Paul.[15]

Thus, in order to evangelize Mississippi, one must first tackle the demon of Mississippi, and then perhaps also the demon of Tupelo in order to work in that city. The local pastor, after a period of prayer and fasting, should proclaim, "I bind you, spirit of Tupelo, in Jesus' name!" or something like that. Then he can get about the business of reaching the people. Should he fail to do this, the demon of Tupelo could frustrate efforts to proclaim Christ.

Positive Emphases

Several emphases commend this theology. First, the spiritual warfare movement regards sustained prayer to be a prerequisite to evangelism. Too often, Christian preaching lacks power and effect because Christians have not adequately sought God's Spirit to work with and through us. Second, it accentuates the importance of personal holiness for anyone involved in ministry. Again, we should not think that we can sway people to a fear of God and personal integrity if we lack it ourselves. Third, this approach calls people to a new boldness about proclaiming the faith. The sense that proclaiming Christ is part of a larger, spiritual struggle gives greater urgency to the task.

No longer is witnessing a private matter that involves only me and my neighbor, but it is a great battle in which I am on the side of the angels. Another helpful teaching of the movement, one that many contemporary churches could stand to hear, is that evangelism and church growth comes first of all by seeking the face of God rather than by new techniques and programs.

The spiritual warfare movement also calls on missionaries and preachers to take seriously the context in which they work. Missionaries must recognize that real demons are behind the religion of the tribes to whom they preach. They must expect to face genuine conflict with the spirits, pray intelligently and seriously for the breaking of the demonic power, and be prepared to face hostile reactions from the devotees of spirits.

Pastors in North America, moreover, should learn all they can about the history of the city in which they work, and in particular they should reckon with the spiritual legacy of that city. Does the city have any spiritual awakenings in its history? Does it suffer heavily under pornography or gambling? Through these and similar questions, a local pastor can understand his spiritual environment.

Finally, the spiritual warfare movement has called Christians back to recognize that paganism and sin are essentially demonic at heart.

Christians must take seriously the heavenly dimension of the earthly situation.

Problems and Questions

A Theological Novelty? At the same time, the movement has many excesses and many notions that must be challenged. To begin with, even its adherents admit that this is a new approach to evangelism.[16] This is not insignificant; after two thousand years of church history and missions, we should be wary of theological innovations. For centuries before us, Christians have invaded new lands, evangelized pagan tribes, and confronted gods and demoniacs. Missionaries have broken and still break the power of superstition and free entire tribes and nations from idols, gods, and spirits through the simple message of the gospel.

In a word, they have plundered Satan's domain without making use of the "power encounter" (direct conflict with a demon, often a "territorial spirit"). Why do we suddenly need to start casting out the demons of cities and states and nations? For C. Peter Wagner, the "power encounter" is in many cases "the key to the spread of the gospel."[17] How was the church able to get so far and evangelize so many without this essential secret to missionary success?

Converting the Missionaries. At times, one cannot avoid the feeling that the spiritual warfare movement has descended to the level of pagan superstition. Advocates frequently warn us about the dangers of areas and objects that demons supposedly inhabit. More than that, they often uncritically accept the teachings of pagans. Vernon J. Sterk, for example, gives the following account of the beliefs of the Tzotzil tribes: "All of the Tzotzil tribes, with whom we worked for more than 20 years, can identify specific tribal deities which act as guardian spirits (saints and ancestral gods), and they can also name specific evil spirits that are in charge of the various kinds of evil in their culture. The *Yajval Balamil* or 'Earth Owner' controls sickness and curing through 'soul loss and redemption.' There are many demons, like the *Poslom* which takes the form of a ball of fire and attacks people at night to cause severe swelling. The *J'ic'aletic* or 'Blackmen' are looters and rapists who commit indiscriminate attacks of all kinds of evil."[18]

As far as I can tell, Sterk accepts the Tzotzil theology at face value. He certainly does not repudiate it. Sterk goes on to observe that it is helpful to know the names of these demons in order to confront them and adds that the Tzotzil think it is very important to know the names of their animal spirit companions.[19] But should we believe the Tzotzil or any other pagan theology? Does the *Poslom* really take the form of a ball of fire and attack people? Missionaries through the last century have liberated many tribal peoples from superstition by teaching them how living in unsanitary conditions and drinking polluted water has made them easy prey for parasites and disease. Sterk apparently prefers that they attribute their diseases to *Yajval Balamil.*

Wagner apparently ascribes floods in Bangladesh to the god Rudra, attributes the exploitation of the Amazon rain forest to the goddess Iara, and agrees with native Hawaiian religion that the volcano goddess Pele rules on the Big Island.[20] I had always thought that God was in control of nature.

I am not suggesting that we dismiss tribal beliefs as so much nonsense, but surely we should hesitate about being converted to their religion! While demons may stand behind many of their gods, that does not mean that the local interpretation of the gods is true or helpful to us. We should not approach shamanistic beliefs about territorial spirits as secular skeptics, but neither should we delve deeply into pagan beliefs or accept their worldview. Being prepared to confront demons and believing that pagan religion can have a powerful hold over people does not imply that we should join them in their fear of the spirits. In Isaiah 44, the prophet mocks idols as nothings. Should we allow ourselves to be filled with dread at what the prophets mocked?

Sterk's analysis of the riot in Ephesus illustrates how far he takes this theology. According to Acts 19:21–41, Paul had been preaching there and making many converts, but the people rioted when they realized that every new convert to Christ was a lost devotee of Artemis and lost customer for her idol makers. Sterk regards Artemis as a living goddess, a "principality" who stirred up opposition to Paul's ministry in Ephesus.[21] The Apostle Luke, by contrast, attributes all the problems in Ephesus to a greedy silversmith named Demetrius and does not treat Artemis as anything but an idol. Unless we want to claim for ourselves deeper insight into the spiritual dynamics of the events of Paul's life than the Bible itself possesses, I think we should leave the explanation of events where Luke leaves it.

In short, demonism stands behind the pagan gods, but this does not make the pagan gods real beings, nor does it mean that we can identify each "god" as a specific demon or believe the myths of their gods. Paul acknowledged that sacrificing to idols is sacrificing to demons, and thus Christians should avoid contact with pagan temples. But he also said that an idol (that is, the god that the idol represents) is "nothing" and that there is but one God and one Lord (1 Cor. 8:4–6; 10:14–22).

Along the same lines, spiritual warfare advocates attribute tremendous freedom and power to Satan. Although they confess that he has been "bound in heaven," they still regard him as free on earth. The practical result is that, in many of their anecdotes, Satan seems to be a more real presence on earth for them than God. For this reason, they readily believe that a sorcerer can utter a curse and throw an entire nation into turmoil. Wagner reports that a Macumba high priest cursed Argentina and that all the atrocities and turmoil that followed in the years 1976 to 1981 were the direct result.[22] Is God no longer sovereign over nations? Is it edifying to attribute that kind of power to a Macumba priest? Spiritual warfare advocates raise no questions when a Nigerian former occult leader claims to have had 7,212 demons under his control.[23]

The problem is that we, like everyone else, are prone to be enslaved by fear, superstition, and the apparent power of evil. Believing in pagan religion, even while ascribing it to demons, only adds to its power. One writer claims that a "Board Room of Hell" plans all the world's evil, including drug trade, sexual abuse, and terrorism.[24] This has the power to terrify us and, in some perverse way, titillate us. It is a conspiracy theory raised to a cosmic level. This vision does not encourage or strengthen us; it only paralyzes us in the attribution of incredible power to the side of darkness. Are devils real? Yes. Do they corrupt the world? Yes. But fantasizing about demons does us no good at all. It simply makes them seem bigger and God seem smaller.

Fasting Satanists and Other Oddities. As we shall see, some of the principles of the spiritual warfare movement have precious little biblical support. Perhaps as a result of this, leaders of the movement rely heavily upon a few often repeated anecdotes that somehow lose force with repetition. These concern power encounters of various kinds, in which a demon kills someone or is himself thwarted, and evangelism either flourishes or languishes as a result.

Some anecdotes are meant to jolt Christians into an awareness of the conflict with Satan and his followers. One concerns a Christian (variously described as a man or a woman) who was on a plane next to someone who refused the meal that the flight attendant offered. The Christian asked this person why he had not taken a meal, and he replied, "I am a Satanist, and I am fasting in order to hasten the breakup of the marriages of Christian pastors." I have heard this anecdote so many times, with so many variations, that I am forced to conclude either that we will never know if anything like this ever really happened or that the airlines are overflowing with fasting Satanists.

Another strange feature of spiritual warfare is the willingness to claim victories for nonevents. According to Steven Lawson, John Dawson was one day meditating on the warning of Leviticus 26:31 that God would destroy cities and began to wonder if the text was talking about Los Angeles (it is actually talking about Israel). He and others began to pray for the city out of a sense that some terrible disaster was about to overtake it. Dawson believed that some unspecified disaster in Los Angeles was averted through the prayers of Christians that summer in 1984.[25]

You will recall that we have seen similar claims from New Age angelphiles, except that their claims tended to be more specific, as when they claimed that a French nuclear reactor would have had a catastrophic meltdown had they and their angels not intervened. Those of us who are Christian may want to accept the Christians' claims and reject those of the New Age angelphiles, but objectively we have no grounds for doing so. In both cases nothing happened, and Dawson does not even know what did not happen.

Praying for our nations and cities is important, and it may be that in heaven we will see how our prayers averted disasters of which we never were aware. Meanwhile, we can hardly go around saying that we prayed and thanks to our prayers we don't know what did not happen. During the days of Hezekiah of Judah, the Assyrian army besieged Jerusalem. Hezekiah prayed for rescue, and the angel of the Lord killed thousands of Assyrian soldiers in a single night. The next morning, the dead bodies were there for all to see (Isa. 36–37). Now that was a deliverance.

The (Evil) Spirit of St. Louis. Spiritual warfare advocates often claim that it is important to discern the nature of the ruling demon over a city in order to pray intelligently for that city. If we know what that demon specializes in, and especially if we know his name, then our prayers will be much more effective in undoing his work. In order to achieve this, they often call upon a special gift of discernment. Some of the leaders of the movement claim that when they come to a new location they can discern in the unseen realm the nature of the territorial spirit in charge there. Their "discernment," however, can be quite lame, often no more than what anybody on the street could tell you. The dominant spirit of New York is "greed" (no real shock, since Wall Street and most major financial institutions are there), and the spirit of Los Angeles (home of the film industry) turns out to be "pornography." The territorial spirit of Washington, D.C. is (who would have guessed it?) "power."[26] But, of course, greed and arrogance and lust are found in all of these cities in full measure anyway.

Behind this approach to bagging demons is the idea that people can get special words from God to tell them what demons they need to exorcise. Wagner explains that through a "word of knowledge" one can find out the name and work of some specific demon and then bind him.[27] Strangely, Wagner admits that in his experience the "word of knowledge" and subsequent "binding" fails to work more often than it does. He explains that high-ranking demons sometimes simply have too much power or that the Christians involved have not submitted enough to the Lordship of Christ.[28] This has the same "heads-I-win, tails-you-lose" ring to it that we saw in the New Age angelphilia when it sought to explain why alleged messages from angels often do not come true. If it works, that proves that our message is right. If it does not work, then you did something wrong. Again we note that the biblical standard for prophets is that the prophet's words never fail (Deut. 18:21–22).

Feel the Power. The rising emphasis on spiritual warfare, fueled by novels such as those by Frank Peretti and others, is having bizarre results. I know of one case involving the funeral of a Christian man, in which the congregation was asked if anyone had something to share. A man stood and announced that God had told him why the individual had died: Gabriel and Michael were in the middle of some particularly difficult battles with Satan, and they needed the now-deceased individual to come up and help them in their combat.[29]

The leaders of this movement also regularly tell us of personal encounters with Satan and demons, but the details are often rather odd. Larry Lea, for example, claims that while flying in an airplane he saw in a vision a black cloud of demons hovering over a city and then hovering over every city in America.[30]

I find it troubling that they make so much of the concept of power. They attribute great power to demons and by the same token acclaim the tremendous power that Christians gain through prayer. I see two dangers here. First is that the yearning for power may actually add to the fascination with demons. If power is what we are after, and if we perceive the demons and those who serve them to have overwhelming power, then the demonic itself becomes attractive. "Feel the power of the Dark Side!" Darth Vader exhorts young Luke Skywalker in *Star Wars*. Put another way, the quest for power is itself demonic. We should recall that Christ's power is made perfect in weakness and that the weakness of the cross overcame the works of the devil. Paul, who does frequently speak of Christ's power within us, learned that lesson firsthand (2 Cor. 12:9).

Second, the visions, power encounters, and alleged triumphs wrought by the leaders in this movement naturally lead to a spiritual elitism. "Brother X must be a mighty man of prayer—he has seen the devil!" The average Christian may feel he has no right to question a man who has bound Satan, seen visions, and regularly hears the voice of God. This does indeed lead to a kind of power over people, but it is not necessarily of God.

Name It and Bind It. The sheer amount of attention this movement gives to devils is troubling. This comes out in their desire to be able to name demons in power encounters. Wagner, for example, gives us a list of names of the devil and demons because he thinks this will "expose them and make them more vulnerable to attack."[31] The notion that one must know the names of spirits in order to deal with them is itself of pagan origin, and we have already seen how mystical books like the *Testament of Solomon* went to great lengths to name all the significant demons as well as the angels that thwart them. In the New Testament, by contrast, the names of demons is a matter of indifference. The only example we have of anything like a name is in the Gerasene demoniac episode, in which the demons identified themselves as "Legion, for we are many" (Mark 5:9). This is hardly a detailed list of demon names, and Jesus did not use the name "Legion" in casting out the demons. Elsewhere, neither He nor the apostles concern themselves with demonic names at all.

By contrast, a contemporary author says, "I cannot be too emphatic. In dealing with the princes and rulers of the heavenlies, they must be identified. Even the ancient Greeks knew how to approach their gods (whom we now identify as 'principalities')."[32] Once again we see that the teachings of paganism have become normative for Christian practice. Other modern writers publish detailed lists of the supposed names of demons they have confronted.[33]

This fixation on demons goes so far that some leaders address demons in their prayer time. Larry Lea preaches that we should stand up in the courage of God and cry out, "Give up, enemies to the North, everything God has for me, for my family, for my church."[34] I think that God is in control of all that He has for me and that the "enemies to the North" do not have the power to hold back or give up anything. Apart from that, being a good Protestant, I do not speak to Mary, the saints, or the angels in my prayer time—and I am sure that I am not going to start yelling at demons while at prayer!

The Bible and Spiritual Warfare

Territorial Spirits or Guardian Angels? Biblical support for the excesses of the spiritual warfare movement is flimsy. Advocates cite a few passages in support of the notion of "territorial spirits." In 1 Kings 20:23, for example, the Syrians say that the Israelite gods are gods of the hills, but that theirs are gods of the plains. Some claim this as evidence of territoriality among the spirits. But this is merely the Bible reporting what the pagans believed; it does not endorse the opinion. The whole point of the text is that God rules the whole earth (v. 28).

The Bible does imply in a few texts that spirits are over the nations, but it does not necessarily claim that these spirits are demonic. In reality, most Christian interpreters have seen these to be something like guardian angels for the nations. This view goes back as far as the ancient Greek translation of Deuteronomy 32:8: "When the Most High divided the nations, when he separated the sons of Adam, he appointed the bounds of people according to the number of the angels of God." If this version of the text is correct, it might be taken to mean that God assigned guardian angels over the nations (even this is not certain; the only thing it explicitly says is that the separation of the nations somehow corresponds to the number of angels). But the verse in no way implies that the nations are under territorial demons.

The Jewish thinker Philo knew of the notion that the nations had guardian angels, and early Christian theologians readily accepted it. Clement of Alexandria, for example, wrote that "the angels have been apportioned among the nations according to an ancient and divine decree."[35] Origen thought that the Macedonian who asked for help in the vision of Paul (Acts 16:9) was the angel of Macedonia.[36] Eusebius believed that the angels to whom God had entrusted the nations turned the eyes of peoples up to the starry heavens, not in order to persuade them to worship the stars but to draw them into contemplation of the God behind the stars.[37] In short, they believed that these angels had the task of leading the nations to the one true God. That they failed was not the fault of the angels but of the stubbornness of the people with whom they worked.

The Church Fathers believed that the vestiges of truth remaining in pagan religions reflected the activity of the angels. Some thought that the best of Greek philosophy showed the influence of lesser angels, and Origen thought that Hinduism contained remnants of the truth because of the activity of their angels. Of course, the Church Fathers did not deny that demons had influence on the nations as well. They especially saw the hand of the devil in the rise of idolatry, and many believed that succumbing to idol worship allowed demons to usurp angels in the position of governance of the nations.[38] Still, we must recognize that many Christians believed that the "powers" over the nations were not necessarily demonic.

Some modern advocates of spiritual warfare admit that the Bible may speak of the nations as being under good angels, but they speculate that these angels came to feel proud of their power and fell from grace. Apart from the unorthodox view of angels implied here (that angels are continuing to fall), it sounds a little like these interpreters are trying to improve on the biblical account or at least add to it. Indeed, one exponent of the movement considers the dualism of the Jewish apocalyptic literature to be an advance over the Old Testament.[39]

Daniel and the Prince of Persia. The Old Testament text on this subject that they most like to cite is Daniel 10:13–14, in which an angel appears. He says that the "prince of the kingdom of Persia" opposed him for three weeks, but that the angel Michael came and helped him. Spiritual warfare advocates see here definitive proof that demons govern the nations by specific assignment from Satan. They also observe that some very tough fighting goes on between angels and these territorial spirits and that the spirits can hinder the messages of God as they come down to earth, and they look to Daniel's prayerfulness as a type for how we ought to engage in the battle.

On close inspection, however, all is not as it seems. First, it is not at all clear that the "prince of the kingdom of Persia" is a demon—he could just as easily be a guardian angel over Persia striving to protect the interests of Persia. The text goes on to prophesy how the Persian empire will soon collapse and be replaced by the Greek empires. In seeking to hinder the angel from taking his message to Daniel, the "prince" of Persia could be taken as a spirit loyally contending for the nation under his charge. Also, although Daniel was fasting for three weeks, the text does not imply that he challenged the prince of Persia to any kind of "power encounter." Daniel never contacted the prince of Persia at all; he only heard of him through another angel.

Was the prince of Persia an angel or a demon? Actually, we do not know because the text is silent on that question. All we know is that he is a spirit who somehow represented Persia, an empire whose days were numbered. This ambiguity about the nature of the powers over the nations continues into the New Testament in the letters of Paul.

Powers and Spirits in the New Testament. We have seen how Paul frequently speaks of powers, principalities, thrones, and the like. We have also seen that there is a studied ambiguity and that we have no grounds for discerning a hierarchy of angels in these terms. Some interpreters, however, believe that all or almost all of the references to powers and the like actually describe high-ranking demons.[40] Several passages, however, do not readily admit to this interpretation.

In 1 Corinthians 2:8, Paul says that if the "rulers of this age" had understood the wisdom of God, "they would not have crucified the Lord of glory." Some people argue that Paul means that God outwitted Satan into doing just what He wanted, namely, crucifying Jesus. I doubt that, but regardless I do not believe we can exclude from Paul's meaning the humans who actually crucified Jesus. After all, it was the very Jewish and Gentile leadership, whose "wisdom" Paul rejects, who carried out the crucifixion. We may even have a reflection of Jesus' own words on the cross, "Father, forgive them, *for they do not know what they are doing*" (Luke 23:34, emphasis added).

One can always contend that the "powers" in 1 Corinthians 2 must be demons and not human rulers since verse 6 says they are being destroyed, and this seems more appropriate for spirits than human rulers.[41] This, however, is too facile an interpretation. Paul's main concern was not with any individuals, be they demonic or human, but that the "wisdom" of this age has been destroyed by the "foolishness" of God. Christ's cross has destroyed the ideology—the religious and philosophic underpinning—of both Jew and Gentile. The cross has swept away Jewish religious authority, Greek philosophy, Roman militarism, and every other power or ideal. It is for this reason that Paul could describe the powers as "doomed to perish." Their very "wisdom" has been shown to be folly and their legitimacy has collapsed. To interpret this passage simply to say that at the cross Jesus defeated the demons, however true that might be, is to miss almost entirely Paul's sweeping vision of Christ's triumph over every institution, every ideology, every philosophy, every religion, every king, every spirit, and every form of power, be it of earth or of heaven.

In some passages the "powers" are strictly human governments, as in Titus 3:1. The prime example is Romans 13, in which Paul tells us to submit to every power. Clearly, though, Paul does not want us to submit to demons! Notwithstanding the clever (and at times ridiculous) attempts by some scholars to see spiritual forces here,[42] we should not read beyond the plain meaning of the text. Words that come across to us in some English translations as exotic, mysterious sounding entities such as "powers" or "principalities" often meant to Greek readers no more than "authorities" (policemen, tax collectors, mayors, and the like). The New Testament scholar Herman Ridderbos emphatically makes the point that he sees no angels or demons here.[43]

In Colossians 1:16, Paul says that all things in heaven and on earth, including "thrones and powers," were created in and for Christ. We have already seen that "visible or invisible" and "in heaven or on earth" tells us that both angelic and human power is in view. We should also observe that these heavenly powers are primarily, if not exclusively, angelic and not demonic. This is because they were created "in and for" Christ. While one might argue that the demons were originally created for Christ but that they fell from grace, that interpretation hardly seems to be the point of this verse; it forces something extraneous upon it. One would not normally speak of demons as created "for Christ."

Some contend that since the powers of Colossians 2 are demons, then the powers of Colossians 1 must be demons too.[44] This does not follow. Paul used the words like "powers" in several different ways, and no single meaning dominates.[45] At times, Paul deliberately used ambiguous language. (We do the same thing; we can say "spirits" and depending on the context mean angels or demons or both.)

Apart from that, it is not clear that the powers of Colossians 2 are demonic or at least not exclusively so. We should recall that Paul was warning the Colossians not to become involved in any doctrine that teaches people to try to escape the bondage of this world by avoiding certain defiling substances ("Do not handle, Do not taste, Do not touch," v. 21) or by seeking the help of angels and spirit guides (v. 18). Paul's response—that Christ has taken captive all the powers and is Lord of them all—might be paraphrased like this: "Listen, Colossians! It doesn't matter what 'powers' or 'authorities' there may be! Christ has taken all captive and all have bowed to Him! You are wasting your time if you think those 'powers' can do you any good! All they will do is pull you away from Christ!"

We need to bear in mind that in almost all paganism, Gnosticism, and New Age and Christian angelphilia, people do not turn to wicked spirits for help, at least not knowingly so. Instead, they turn to angels whom they believe to be good in order to gain their help. If the powers in Colossians 2 were demons, Paul does not explicitly say so. To the contrary, he warns the Colossians about worshiping angels (v. 18).

If Paul had said, "You must not seek the aid of devils!" the Colossians would have replied, "Well, of course not! We don't seek the demons. We worship the angels so that they will protect us from demons." Like their modern counterparts, they had no interest in entering the service of Satan. If the Colossians had been doing something as alarming and appalling as knowingly serving demons, no doubt an astounded Paul would have challenged this in the boldest terms. But the Colossians were not Satanists.

Also, Paul did not waste his time trying to prove that the spirits to whom they were turning were not good angels but were really demonic. Had he done that, he would have implied that turning to good angels was acceptable: the Colossians just needed to be sure that their spirits really were good. No, Paul simply said that Christ has taken captive all the powers, whatever they may be, and declared that Christians should never turn to any spirit, power, or angel for help. Christ is the only savior.

In short, the notion that the "powers" are always demonic and that these demonic forces govern the territories of the earth is neither the clear teaching of the Bible nor the historic understanding of the Church. Such a notion seriously misses the point of various passages in the Bible.

Does that mean that "powers" can never refer to demonic forces? Not at all. The classic text in which they are certainly demonic is Ephesians 6:12: "For our struggle is not against enemies of blood and flesh, but against the rulers, against the authorities, against the cosmic powers of this present darkness, against the spiritual forces of evil in the heavenly places." Here, Paul warned about powers that are heavenly (and not of this world) and plainly said that they are "spiritual" and "evil." He also said that we must resist these forces by putting on the "armor of God," which includes the helmet of salvation, the shield of faith, and so forth.

Ephesians 6 has all of the elements of conflict—swords, armor, and flaming arrows from the devil. If this is not spiritual warfare, what is? Perhaps the better question would be, What is spiritual warfare? Is it exorcising demons and going into hand-to-hand combat with the devil, or is it something a bit less spectacular but no less significant or important?

Paul did not say a word about confronting, binding, or exorcising demons. Instead, he gave us the spiritual, heavenly side of the normal, day-to-day struggle that every Christian faces. If he had meant that we were to put on the armor of God specifically to exorcise a demon, he would not have had to explain that our real battle is against spiritual forces in high places. That much would have been obvious.

Rather, he told the Ephesians that every day as they sought to do the will of God, were faithful to Christ, and resisted temptation, they were in a spiritual battle with satanic powers. Paul exalted the ordinary Christian life to a higher level than we could imagine and so gave our apparently petty and mundane struggles dignity and significance. Have we resisted temptation to be peevish toward a colleague? Did we fight off the desire to react with anger against someone who cut us off on the freeway? Did we turn away from a magazine that might have drawn us into lust? Have we restrained our lips from uttering profanity? In doing so, we have struck a blow against the angels of hell. But we should be sure that our spiritual armor is firmly strapped on. After all, it is a constant, daily battle.

Some say that Christ is the spiritual warrior we should imitate.[46] Just as He overcame the power of demons and exorcised them, they argue, so should we. When we think about it, however, Christ's encounters with demons can hardly be called "battles." He simply appeared on the scene, and they shrieked with terror and begged for mercy. His position over the demons is that of sovereign God, not combatant. The only places where we saw Him engaged in real spiritual battle were the wilderness, where He encountered Satan, and in Gethsemane. In both cases, He was not binding demons but *resisting temptation.* If one should care to add the crucifixion to this list of battlegrounds, Christ won His victory not by a power encounter with Satan but by submission to death.

I am hardly proposing a novel interpretation of Ephesians 6. To the contrary, this is the view of the text that Christians have always taken. One of the greatest expositions of this chapter by one of the greatest preachers of any generation is that by D. M. Lloyd-Jones. His two volumes of sermons on 6:10–20 take up 736 pages. He used the biblical text to warn us against cults, heresies, intellectual delusion, mysticism, and the arrogance of mere intellectual knowledge about the Bible. He dealt with the emotional struggles of life, with issues surrounding the nature of true faith, with sentimentalism, and with true and false zeal. He examined at length the troublesome question of assurance of salvation. He exhorted us in the areas of discouragement, temptation, and quenching the Spirit of God. In all of these he saw the "wiles of the Devil" in action, and he takes the devil very seriously. He also encouraged us that the battle is the Lord's and that He has given us the means to spiritual victory.[47] But you will have to look long and hard to find Lloyd-Jones encouraging us to "bind" demons as the key to Christian living and evangelism. The reason, plain and simple, is that exorcising demons is not what Ephesians 6 is all about.

Some spiritual warfare advocates also look to Revelation 12 as a picture of the conflict that goes on between angels and demons. But we have already seen that the real point of this text is that because of the cross, the accuser no longer has any ground on which to stand. It points to our redemption in Christ, not to battles with devils.

But does the New Testament say nothing about binding the devil? Yes, it does. In Matthew 12:29, Jesus says, "Or how can one enter a strong man's house and plunder his property, without first tying up the strong man? Then indeed the house can be plundered."

In this passage, the Jewish opposition accused Jesus of being a sorcerer who cast out demons through an allegiance with Satan himself (v. 24). Jesus, in rabbinical fashion, responded with several counter arguments: First, if Satan's forces opposed one another, their power would collapse (vv. 25–26). Second, their own people engaged in exorcism too, but were not accused of being in league with the devil (v. 27). Third, if He cast out demons by the power of God, they should see this as evidence that the kingdom of God had come (in other words, that Jesus is the Messiah; v. 28). Fourth, one must first bind Satan in order to plunder him (v. 29). Finally, in verses 30–32, He warned them that they were in mortal danger for rejecting the work of God.

Jesus "binds the strong man" in order to take away his possessions—that is, the people whom Satan has held captive. Jesus could not minister to demon-possessed persons without first casting out their devils. He did not attempt to teach the Gerasene demoniac while he was still raving and howling. Also, the sight of Jesus going about delivering people possessed by devils was powerful evidence that God had come into the world, and the Jewish leaders should have paid heed.

Does Jesus imply that one must always exorcise demons or bind territorial spirits before evangelizing or when entering a new territory? If so, He did not practice it Himself. Nowhere did He cast out a territorial spirit, and He frequently evangelized without exorcising. In the episode of the "woman at the well," for example, He entered Samaritan territory without concerning Himself with the "dominant spirit" of the region, and He evangelized the woman and the rest of the village without casting out any demons (John 4).

The same is true of the apostles. They did not focus on exorcism, and they never bound territorial spirits. The best example of an exorcism is that of the girl in Acts 16:16–18, who followed Paul for "many days" as she cried out that he was a servant of the Most High God. Finally, in exasperation at the nuisance, Paul turned to her and commanded the demon to depart. That does not sound like a man who made exorcism the hallmark of his work!

Even where we read in passing of large numbers of people being delivered from demons (for example, Acts 19:11–12), the Bible implies that these were miracles that God did in order to validate Paul's message

(v. 10). They were not power encounters that cleared away the territorial spirits.

It is indeed strange that, if binding territorial spirits is crucial to success in missions, Paul neither practiced it nor said anything about it. In Acts we follow him as he evangelized Asia Minor and Greece and even see him as a survivor of a shipwreck among the superstitious pagans of Malta. Nowhere does he pause to "discern" whether the territorial spirit of any place was "Lust" or "Fear" or "Greed." We search his letters in vain for information on how to recognize and bind a local demon. Can it be that the Apostle to the Gentiles was ignorant of this spiritual secret to successful missions? I do not think so—for Paul, the "strong man" was already bound. God bound the powers at the cross and has taken captivity itself captive (Eph. 4:8), and now the way is open for every nation, tribe, and language to turn from idols to the living God.

One of the most overused metaphors of New Testament scholars in this regard compares the conflict with the powers to the European campaign in World War II. The cross, it is said, was like "D-Day," when the decisive victory was won, but we have not yet come to "V-Day," the day of the final victory over the powers. We still have to slug it out with a determined enemy as we march to the final objective. But for the apostle Paul, the cross is not merely the assurance that victory is ahead; it is the victory. If any military analogy is appropriate, it is that we are to plunder the defeated foe (by rescuing the nations with the gospel). We are not to secure the final victory, since that has already occurred.

To summarize, three things stand out in biblical teaching in regard to spiritual warfare. First, demons are real and sometimes Christians must exorcise them. Second, all Christians struggle with evil powers in the sense that the Christian life is a struggle for holiness against the world, the flesh, and the devil. Third, in regard to freeing the world from bondage to the powers, Christ has already won the victory in its entirety. The path is open to take the gospel to every nation.

There is, however, one other aspect of spiritual warfare we need to consider: the sovereignty of God.

The Sovereign God

I have heard it said that if your worldview does not include the devil, then when something goes wrong that you will either blame God or yourself. My worldview includes the devil, but I find that idea troubling. In fact, it is a throwback to a dualistic view of God and Satan in which God is locked in a battle with Satan and I am caught in the middle. If something goes wrong, it is because Satan did it. How quickly we forget that in the Bible, the devil is always under God's authority. It seems that many Christians would rather have a nearly omnipotent Satan than a truly sovereign God.

Spiritual warfare advocates often ascribe their trials and temptations to Satan. With perverse logic, many of Jimmy Swaggart's followers claimed that his scandalous behavior proved what a spiritual giant he was: Why else would the devil give him so much attention? Those who specialize in "deliverance ministry" claim that there are specific demons for specific sins and that the experienced practitioner recognizes the signs of their departure. For example, a demon of tobacco departs with an audible exhale. R. C. Sproul rightly calls this kind of thinking "unmitigated nonsense."[48]

A pastor may believe that when a series of crises hits his church—such as moral problems, personal conflicts, or the death of a key member—he is experiencing "spiritual warfare" and is under the attack of the devil. While it may well be that the devil is behind some of his troubles, we must recall that the devil is under the authority of God. We must remember Job. What he endured can hardly be called "warfare" with the devil. God simply allowed the devil to afflict Job. Also, the main reason church members sin is not that the devil is powerful but that they are sinners.

Imagine how different World War II would have been if Eisenhower could have issued orders to Hitler and his generals and if the German forces had no choice but to obey. They could only attack when and where Eisenhower permitted, they had to retreat or surrender whenever they were told, and they could not take a single Allied prisoner or inflict a single casualty without his express permission. We would hardly call that a war! And yet that is precisely how the Bible portrays the relationship between God and the devils. It is no contest: they are entirely under His control.

The notion of "warfare" is only one way of looking at the spiritual situation, and it only applies to us, and that not so much when we cast out demons but when we resist temptation. From God's perspective, the devils are no threat whatsoever. Satan could not touch a hair of

Job's head or for that matter a hair on one of Job's cows' heads unless God allowed it. Perhaps it is in its diminution of the sovereignty of God and its acceptance of a dualistic theology that the spiritual warfare movement is most thoroughly unbiblical, misguided, and dangerous.

Regard not them that have familiar spirits, neither seek after wizards, to be defiled by them: I am the LORD your God.
LEVITICUS 19:31, KJV

Familiar Spirits

Concluding Thoughts on Angels and the New Spirituality

ANGELS ARE REAL. SOME PEOPLE HAVE SEEN THEM. They continue to influence human life. They can and do protect people. If all this is so, why should anyone have concerns about the new interest in angels?

We need to review what we have learned. The Bible describes angels and devils in *functional* terms. That is, it gives us some examples of what they have done, but it says little or nothing about their origin, their nature, or in the case of the devils, their fall. It does, however, place great stress on the sovereignty of God over the entire host of heaven. It exhorts us to recognize that Christ is the only savior, that He fulfills our need for spiritual growth, that He alone is our mediator, and that only He and never the angels can identify with us.

We have seen that angels have captured the imagination of people through the ages, however, and that angels especially come into prominence in sects and heresies of Judaism and Christianity. We have seen in the Pseudepigrapha and in the Gnostics, for example, attempts to identify the good and bad angels by name, to catalog the powers of the spirits, to find out what maladies individual demons cause, and to find the names of angels who thwart those demons. We have observed gross distortions of the Bible in the doctrines of emanations, reincarnation, dualism, and monism. We have seen how people fantasized freely about the spirits and invented in great detail stories to fill in the gaps of the biblical record. We have found that many people believed that the goal of the soul was to achieve a return to heaven, or a kind of deification, and we have seen that angels often appeared as guides in the spiritual quest.

And yet, as if in a grand demonstration of the proverb that "what goes around comes around," we have seen all the bizarre features of the old angelphilia come back upon us in the strange world of the new spirituality. Once again, people are (supposedly) contacting angels and giving us a new revelation of how the universe works. Once again, we are being exhorted to find our way back to the Source, the One, or the Ineffable Being. Once again, we are told to look to the angels as our guides. Like time travelers we again see people in God's name trying to identify demons everywhere so that they can exorcise them. Once again, people attribute every problem to devils and assert that we need to know the names of the devils in order to deal with them. Like reruns of some forgotten television shows, new religious novels and fantasies again tell of the strange happenings among the angels and demons. Everywhere we look, we see evidence of a resurgence not of spiritual *life* but of spiritual *decadence*.

The biblical injunctions are plain: have nothing to do with familiar spirits or with those who claim to know them (Lev. 19:31), and do not seek after secret knowledge or the things God has hidden (Deut. 29:29; 1 Tim. 4:7; 1 Cor. 4:6). Notice that Leviticus 19:31 does not say, "Avoid evil spirits, but it's all right to get to know the good angels." Rather, we are to avoid seeking contact with the spirits altogether. It is not just that we might be deceived or that the angel might turn out to be a devil. All fascination with angels and every desire to get to know them is a distraction from Christ. Karl Barth puts contemporary angelphilia in its place: "[Angels] cannot save, redeem or liberate the earthly creature. They cannot forgive even the smallest sin, or remove even the slightest pain. They can do nothing to bring about the reconciliation of the world.

They did not create it. They can neither be wrathful nor gracious toward it. They did not establish the covenant between God and man, and they cannot fulfill, maintain, renew or confirm it. They do not overcome death."[1]

Thus, to seek the companionship of the angels is to deny the sufficiency of God. Any angel who takes on the role of instructor, guide, or savior is not functioning as an angel at all. Barth was right: True angels are fully subordinate to the message of Christ.

Also, something else in Leviticus 19:31 stands out: "Do not turn to mediums or wizards; do not seek them out, to be defiled by them: *I am the* LORD *your God*" (emphasis added). We have but one God and Savior. The notion that an angel can be your close companion and guide and yet not become your god is delusion. The spiritual being you love, from whom you learn, and who gives you protection is surely your *god* whether you call him that or not.

At the beginning of this book, I cited Deuteronomy 29:29: "The secret things belong to the LORD our God, but the revealed things belong to us and to our children forever, to observe all the words of this law." We know very little about the nature of the angels, their names and functions, or the origin of evil. God has not chosen to tell us these things, and we do not need to know them. But God has told us His name, and the name of His Son, and the way of redemption, holiness, and true spirituality. That way, that truth, and that life is Jesus Christ alone. Anything else is a silly myth (1 Tim. 4:7) and goes beyond what is written (1 Cor. 4:6).

The Church in a Not-so-secular Society

This study of angels has taught me a great deal—not so much about the angels as about *us*. Now as never before in my lifetime, people want spirituality in their lives. The baby-boomers have come of age and that big chill called death is on their horizon. Upscale cars and homes do not satisfy. Like the Romans of the first century, who eagerly went after every cult and mystery religion, people are greeting the end of one millennium and dawn of another with a profound sense of need for their souls.

We are in the post-modern age. The secular age is over. One pastor reports that people in his area "*assume* the reality of the supernatural," but that the dominant religion is now New Age.[2] The November 28, 1994, edition of *Newsweek* documented the sense of spiritual emptiness that drives people away from the barren towers of the secular city. It quotes Emory University anthropologist Charles Nuckolls: "We've stripped away what our ancestors saw as essential—the importance of religion and family . . . . People feel they want something they've lost. But it has left a gaping hole."[3]

Sadly, the church has not caught on. Perhaps understandably, Christians view the new religions with alarm and fear, but we should recognize that they also represent a new opportunity. Rather than try to suppress this spiritual quest, we need to show that Jesus Christ is the fulfillment of spiritual hunger. We need to recall that it was in that confused, demonic, and decadent era of the first century that the gospel of Jesus Christ first came forth and captured men and women all over the Roman world. We need to read again the words of Paul, who rejoiced to see how in every place people turned from idols to serve the living and true God (1 Thess. 1:9). Unfortunately, we cannot carry this message or draw people in as long as our own spirituality, morality, and compassion seem so evidently lacking.

I think it is probably obvious to you that Christians will have trouble attracting people to churches as long as we are plagued by scandal, consumed with quarreling among ourselves, and living in most respects like everyone else. But there is more. People want more than honest, decent Christians: they dabble in the *new* spirituality because they want *real* spirituality. They do not want only to *hear* about holiness and transcendence and power beyond themselves; they want to *experience* these things. The standard evangelical answer—going back to Augustine's remark that the soul is restless until it rests in God—is that God is the something that fills the void in the soul. This is true, but if our view of God and our expressions of devotion to Him have nothing of mystery and holiness about them, we should not be surprised that people walk away still hungry.

Perhaps the most telling critique of the barrenness of contemporary Christian worship comes from *Ski* magazine. In an article describing the Vallée Blanche in the Chamonix area of France, it cites one man's appraisal of the experience of being there: "The valley is a huge, vaulted space, the floor of God's winter palace, a dwarfing place, a place so unrelentingly breathtaking that you have to find a bar or café at the bottom in order to sit down, gather your thoughts and reassess your importance in the universe. It's what going to church is supposed to be like."[4] Indeed. Going to church *is* supposed to impress upon us the grandeur of God, awe our cynical and jaded spirits, and drive us to our knees. Clever manipulation will not accomplish this.

We cannot continue to "do church" without reckoning with its primary purpose—the adoration of God. Churches cannot function as places of spiritual narcissism and expect the presence of God to be conspicuous. Too often our "worship" focuses entirely on ourselves. We view the church service as a time of challenging people or making them feel guilty or encouraging them or even "uplifting" them. At best, people praise the preacher because he is a powerful orator, a good teacher, or a good wordsmith. At worst, the preacher pretends to preach and the people pretend to listen. But in the end it matters not whether the people go away feeling "filled" or "empty," since their attention and that of the service has always been on themselves.

This is not to say that New Age spirituality is doing any better. To the contrary, angelphilia is perhaps the most thorough form of spiritual narcissism. On the other hand, the rapid growth of the movement speaks loudly of people's desire for ritual, sacredness, and something beyond themselves. How much better it would be if our churches would offer the one thing that is never found in the New Age: communion with the living God in a place that is truly holy. Then, as the Scripture says, those who visit would have to say, "God is really among you" (1 Cor. 14:25).

By the way, this draws into question the whole idea of "seeker services," if by that we mean services that are as nonsacred as possible. When we jettison sacred music and times of common prayer and reading and instead try to be as secular as possible, how will that attract a seeker? A seeker is by definition someone who is seeking spiritual meaning! Yet we feel we are doing them a favor by turning our church services into social club meetings and by avoiding everything that might seem "religious."

This is not the place to develop a theology of worship, and I do not think that one size fits all. People and cultures are different, and we cannot simply prescribe a single formula that will work for everybody. I have been in churches in Korea where I could feel the presence of God as soon as I walked in the door, but I do not think that a single model for a church service, be it Korean or whatever, works for every church.

The basic principle is surprisingly simple. We must focus on God and not ourselves. We cannot fake spirituality, and we cannot achieve it by looking into our own navels to see if we are feeling spiritual. Nor do we gain it by exhorting people to be more devout or by manipulating their emotions. We achieve it when everything we do in worship has the goal not of lifting up ourselves but of honoring God.

It may seem strange to you that I close this book with a call to Christian worship. In fact, that is where this book has been heading from the start. This modern trend I call angelphilia is no more and no less than a yearning for God. Every time a man or woman calls on a guardian angel, meditates, or speaks longingly of the angels, he or she is really expressing a desire for heaven, worship, and God. Every time a person shudders in fear of devils and looks for ways to combat them, that person is really confessing the absence of God in his or her life. People want spiritual life.

The Place of Angels in the Christian Faith

But what of the angels themselves? What part can they play in our lives? We should not seek the angels themselves. If God wills it, we will encounter an angel in this world; if not, we have not missed out on the best God has to offer. Still, they are important. I began this book by asking if I have been missing something due to my previous neglect of angels. The answer to that question is yes, I have.

The angels are another part of the glory of heaven that we see by faith. They are, as Barth has said, an expression of the earthward movement of heaven. By believing in the angels, we understand in a deeper way that there is a realm that is higher and greater than our own. We understand that there is another glory that far surpasses anything in this world, and we long to join the choirs of heaven in praising God.

Does God "need" angels? Could He not get along without them? I am sure He could, but heaven is a richer place because they are there. God is not a God of an impoverished and meanly furnished kingdom; His realm has riches beyond all our imaginings. The angels add glory to heaven the same way the mountains, the trees, the great beasts of the field, and even we humans add glory to earth. If we try to do without the angels, then our faith, our heaven, and our God become smaller.

Faith in angels also helps us on earth. In our church services, we should not forget that angels are present and that we join with them in the worship of God. If our meetings really are sacred occasions and if we acknowledge that angels from the realms of glory are here among us, how can we not direct our worship services toward God and away from ourselves? If, on the other hand, we view church as a strictly human affair, perhaps with God merely casting a sideways glance at us from on high, we naturally will begin to seek things in church that titillate us.

We should not forget that angels are our guardians and servants. Some time after I began to research this book, I went to the Calgary Zoo with my son who was then five years of age. Leaving him with his sister, I turned away for a few moments to look at some animals with my other daughter. When I looked back, he was gone. His sister who had been with him had no idea where he was. In the frantic search that followed, I did what any fretful, incompetent-feeling father would do. I prayed. Only this time, I did not just pray as I would have before, "God, protect my son." I prayed, "God, send your angels to protect my son." I had learned that the same angels who encamped around Elisha could also encamp around my son. It is not that God "alone" was unable to protect him; it is that the angels are another tool in His hands whereby He is strong to save. Viewed in this way, subordinate to God and never as beings we relate to apart from God, angels add to God's glory and power. (By the way, we eventually found my son.)

Finally, angels add to our sense of mystery about life under God. We contemplate them and their many works, and we realize that we, too, may someday be surprised by a heavenly visit. Life filled with awe and the sense that God may act in an unanticipated way should never be dull. After all, some have entertained angels without knowing it.

Notes

Chapter 1

1. Sophy Burnham, *A Book of Angels* (New York: Ballantine, 1990), 198–202.
2. Ibid., 201.
3. This information was given to me by Mario Toneguzzi, a reporter for the *Calgary Herald*, in private conversation on October 21, 1994.
4. Karl Barth, *Church Dogmatics*, vol. 3, pt. 3, trans. G. W. Bromiley and R. J. Ehrlich (Edinburgh: T. and T. Clark, 1960), 416.

Chapter 2

1. Archibald Robinson and Alfred Plummer, *A Critical and Exegetical Commentary on the First Epistle of St. Paul to the Corinthians*, International Critical Commentary (ICC) (Edinburgh: T. and T. Clark, 1911), 86.
2. For a good yet brief discussion of these issues, see Leon Morris, *The First Epistle to the Corinthians*, Tyndale New Testament Commentaries (TNTC) (Grand Rapids: Eerdmans, 1958), 151–56. For more detailed studies, see for example Peter J. Tomson, *Paul and the Jewish Law* (Minneapolis: Fortress Press, 1990), 131–49, and David W. J. Gill, "The Importance of Roman Portraiture for Head-Coverings in 1 Corinthians," *Tyndale Bulletin* 41 (1990), 244–60.
3. For a good, brief discussion of Galatians 3:19, see Timothy George, *Galatians*, New American Commentary (NAC) (Nashville: Broadman & Holman, 1994), 255–57.

---

4. See J. Alec Motyer, *The Prophecy of Isaiah* (Downers Grove, Ill.: InterVarsity, 1993), 76, note 3. Motyer comments that the word *seraphim* would have the definite article if it were a title.

5. Only in one place, Matthew 1:24, does the article appear. In that instance, the article does not imply that some specific angel called "the angel of the Lord" is meant; it merely refers to the same angel mentioned in Matthew 1:20.

6. Barth, *Church Dogmatics*, 490.

7. For further discussion of this issue, see William George Heidt, *Angelology of the Old Testament* (Washington, D.C.: Catholic University of America Press, 1949), 69–101.

8. See Craig L. Blomberg, *Matthew*, NAC (Nashville: Broadman Press, 1992), 276.

9. I cannot bring myself to accept the solution of D. A. Carson, *Matthew*, Expositor's Bible Commentary (Grand Rapids: Zondervan, 1984), 400–401, that the angels here are the spirits of deceased children rather than actual angels.

Chapter 3

1. For a development of this thesis, see Peggy L. Day, *An Adversary in Heaven* (Atlanta: Scholars Press, 1988).

2. I. Howard Marshall, *Commentary on Luke*, New International Greek Testament Commentary (NIGTC) (Grand Rapids: Eerdmans, 1978), 788.

3. John Polhill, *Acts*, NAC (Nashville: Broadman Press, 1992), 351.

4. Robinson and Plummer, *First Corinthians*, 99–100.

5. R. V. G. Tasker, *The Second Epistle of Paul to the Corinthians*, TNTC (Grand Rapids: Eerdmans, 1958), 173–77.

6. This is a rabbinical tradition found in the Life of Adam and Eve, 13f.

7. Merrill F. Unger, *Biblical Demonology* (Chicago: Scripture Press, 1952), 52.

8. For a good discussion of the structure of the Book of Isaiah, see Christopher R. Seitz, *Zion's Final Destiny* (Minneapolis: Fortress Press, 1991).

9. See Ludwig Koehler and Walter Baumgartner, *The Hebrew and Aramaic Lexicon of the Old Testament* (Leiden: E. J. Brill, 1994), 244.

10. J. Alec Motyer, *The Prophecy of Isaiah*, 144–45, and John N. Oswalt, *The Book of Isaiah: Chapters 1–39*, New International Commentary on the Old Testament (NICOT) (Grand Rapids: Eerdmans, 1986), 322–23.

11. James B. Pritchard, *Ancient Near Eastern Texts Relating to the Old Testament* (Princeton, N.J.: Princeton University Press, 1969), 164–65, 307.

12. Walther Eichrodt, *Ezekiel*, Old Testament Library (OTL) (Philadelphia: Westminster, 1975), 393–95, and John Taylor, *Ezekiel*, Tyndale Old Testament Commentary (TOTC) (Downer's Grove, Ill.: InterVarsity, 1979), 196–97.

13. See Bruce M. Metzger, *Breaking the Code: Understanding the Book of Revelation* (Nashville: Abingdon, 1993), 72–74.

14. Gordon J. Wenham, *Genesis 1–15*, Word Biblical Commentary (Dallas: Word, 1987), 138–43. Also Victor P. Hamilton, *The Book of Genesis: Chapters 1–17*, NICOT (Grand Rapids: Eerdmans, 1990), 261–71.

15. "[The identity of the 'sons of God'] is clear from their frequent occurrence in biblical and West Semitic lore. They are the lesser gods who meet in Yahweh's assembly (Job 1:6; 2:1; Ps. 29:1; 89:7 with the older form bn 'lm [compare the Ugaritic *bn ilm*]). They were present with Yahweh at the dawn of creation (Job 38:7), and they were shortly thereafter apportioned among the nations (Deut. 32:8, Q: *bny 'lhym*). The *bn il* or *bn ilm* occur dozens of times in Ugaritic mythology, with a similar range of functions as their Israelite counterparts. The chief god of the pantheon, El, is called *'ab bn il*, 'father of the sons of El,' which indicates that the term *bn il* originally included the notion of the patrimony of El. The bn 'lm are also mentioned in the Phoenician inscriptions of Arslan Tash . . . and Karatepe . . .and in the Ammonite inscription from the Amman Citadel . . . ." Ronald S. Hendel, "Of Demigods and the Deluge: Toward an Interpretation of Genesis 6:1–4," *Journal of Biblical Literature, (JBL)* 106:1 (March 1987), 16, n. 16.

16. For example, Billy Graham, *Angels: God's Secret Agents* (New York: Doubleday, 1975), 19.

17. See 1 Peter 3:19–20. The meaning of this text is disputed, but it appears to me that the "spirits in prison" are the sons of God of Genesis 6:1. They did not "keep their first place" in the sense that they abandoned the angelic realm for the human. Christ announced to them that human redemption is accomplished and their fate is sure.

18. Matthew 6:13b may be translated either as "deliver us from evil" or "deliver us from the evil one." I think that the latter is more likely.

Chapter 4

1. T. K. Abbott, *The Epistle to the Colossians*, ICC (Edinburgh: T. and T. Clark, 1979, reprint ed.), 268.

2. C. F. D. Moule, *The Epistles to the Colossians and to Philemon*, Cambridge Greek Testament (London: Cambridge University Press, 1958), 92. Also, Walter Wink, *Naming the Powers: The Language of Power in the New Testament* (Philadelphia: Fortress Press, 1984), 67.

3. For a good discussion of this issue, see Eduard Schweizer, "Slaves of the Elements and Worshipers of Angels: Gal. 4:3 and Col. 2:8, 18, 20," *JBL* 107 (1988): 455–68.

4. Barnabas Lindars, *The Theology of the Letter to the Hebrews* (Cambridge: Cambridge University Press, 1991), 37–39.

5. See George H. Guthrie, *The Structure of Hebrews: A Text-Linguistic Analysis* (Leiden: E. J. Brill, 1994). Guthrie summarizes his position as follows: "Simply put, the purpose of the book of Hebrews is to exhort the hearers to endure in their pursuit of the promised reward, in obedience to the word of God, and especially on the basis of their new covenant relationship with the Son."

6. For various options here, see F. F. Bruce, *The Epistle to the Hebrews*, New International Commentary on the New Testament (NICNT) (Eerdmans: Grand Rapids, 1964), 15–17.

Chapter 5

1. On the pantheon as a mirror of city-state bureaucracy, see Lowell K. Handy, *Among the Host of Heaven* (Winona Lake, Ind.: Eisenbrauns, 1994).

2. For a photograph of the statue, see Peter Lamborn Wilson, *Angels* (New York: Pantheon Books, 1980), 84.

3. On the last notion, see Hershel Shanks, "Is the Vatican Suppressing the Dead Sea Scrolls?" in Hershel Shanks, ed., *Understanding the Dead Sea Scrolls* (New York: Random House, 1992), 275–90.

4. For a good survey of the Dead Sea Scrolls and their interpretation, see James C. VanderKam, *The Dead Sea Scrolls Today* (Grand Rapids: Eerdmans, 1994).

5. Maxwell J. Davidson, "Angels at Qumran: A Comparative Study of 1 Enoch 1–36, 72–108" and "Sectarian Writings from Qumran," *Journal for the Study of Pseudepigrapha*, series 11 (Sheffield, England: Sheffield Academic Press, 1992), 144–62.

6. Davidson, *Qumran*, 187–211.

7. See Carol Newsome, *Songs of the Sabbath Sacrifice: A Critical Edition* (Atlanta: Scholars Press, 1985), 23–38.

8. Davidson, *Qumran*, 212–34. Davidson mentions on page 233 that certain Old Testament passages speak of sons of Belial and the like (for example, Deut. 13:13–14), but none of these occurrences is really the same as what we see in the War Scroll.

9. *1 Enoch* 15:8–10, translation by E. Isaac, in Charlesworth 1.21–22.

10. *1 Enoch* 69:6–7, in Charlesworth 1.47–8.

11. *1 Enoch* 89:59ff. See D. S. Russell, *The Method and Message of Jewish Apocalyptic*, OTL (Philadelphia: Westminster, 1964), 246–47.

12. All citations of *2 Enoch* below are from the longer version in the Charlesworth edition.

13. *2 Enoch* 4–6, translated by Francis I. Andersen, in Charlesworth 1:110, 112.

14. *Anchor Bible Dictionary*, s.v. "Enoch, Third Book of," by Philip S. Alexander, 2.523–24.

15. A. Cohen, *Everyman's Talmud* (New York: Schocken, 1975), 52.

16. Morris B. Margolies, *A Gathering of Angels: Angels in Jewish Life and Literature* (New York: Ballantine, 1994), 81.

17. *3 Enoch* 1–15. *3 Enoch* 16 also tells how Metatron was dethroned and humbled, but this chapter is probably a later addition since it contradicts the tone of the rest of the book. See vol. 1, p. 268, n. a, of the Charlesworth edition.

18. *3 Enoch* 35:1–2, translated by P. Alexander, in Charlesworth 1.288.

19. *3 Enoch* 47:2, translated by P. Alexander, in Charlesworth 1.300.

20. *Testament of Reuben*, 2:1–5:6.

21. *Testament of Judah*, 15:5–6, translated by H. C. Kee, in Charlesworth 1.799.

22. *Testament of Dan*, 6:2. See Russell, *Method and Message*, 242.

23. *Testament of Job*, 46:9, translated by R. P. Spittler, in Charlesworth 1.864.

24. This summary is based on the translation by D. C. Duling, found in Charlesworth, 1.960–87.

25. Gershom Scholem, *Kabbalah* (New York: Meridian, 1974), 5.

26. Fischel Lachower and Isaiah Tishby, *The Wisdom of the Zohar*, trans. David Goldstein (London: Oxford University Press, 1989), 2:554, citing Zohar Hadash, Bereshit 7d.

27. Lachower and Tishby, *Wisdom*, 2:447–70.

28. *Zohar* I, III; Lachower and Tishby, *Wisdom*, 2:540–42.

29. Ibid., *Wisdom*, 2:630.

30. Ibid., *Wisdom*, 2:628–32.

31. Cohen, *Everyman's Talmud*, 47–58.

32. Moses Maimonides, *The Guide to the Perplexed*, trans. Shlomo Pines (Chicago: University of Chicago, 1963), 263.

33. Jean Danielou, *The Angels and Their Mission*, trans. David Heimann (Dublin: Four Courts Press, 1957), 48–50.

34. See Barth, *Church Dogmatics*, 370.

35. Augustine develops his angelology especially in *City of God* 11, 9–15. Over against the massive bulk of the work, this is a tiny portion indeed.

36. Gregory of Nazianzus, *Or. 38. 9.*

37. Anselm of Canterbury, *Cur Deus Homo*, 1.16–18.

38. Harold O. J. Brown, *Heresies* (New York: Doubleday, 1984), 39.

39. Werner Foerster, *Gnosis: A Selection of Gnostic Texts*, trans. R. McL. Wilson (London: Oxford University Press, 1972), 1:48–58.

40. Robert Haardt, *Gnosis: Character and Testimony* (Leiden: E. J. Brill, 1971), 184.

41. Haardt, *Gnosis*, 193.

42. In another version, it is by five lights in the form of Yaldabaoth's angels.

43. Foerster, *Gnosis*, 13–7.

44. Giovanni Filoramo, *A History of Gnosticism*, trans. Anthony Alcock (Oxford: Basil Blackwell, 1990), 183–84. On the bridal-chamber, see Foerster 2:87–92 and Kurt Rudolph, *Gnosis: The Nature and History of Gnosticism*, trans. Robert McLachlan Wilson (San Francisco: Harper and Row, 1985), 245–50.

45. Frederick Copleston, *A History of Philosophy*, vol. II, *Medieval Philosophy: Augustine to Scotus* (London: Burns and Oates Limited, 1964), 100.

46. Kenneth Scott Latourette, *A History of Christianity*, rev. ed. (New York: Harper and Row, 1975), 1:210.

47. Copleston, *History*, 100.

48. Dionysius the (Pseudo-) Areopagite, *The Celestial Hierarchies* 1 (Surrey, England: The Shrine of Wisdom, 1949), 21.

49. Ibid., 22.

50. Dionysius, *Celestial Hierarchies* 2, 24–28.

51. David Connolly, *In Search of Angels* (New York: Perigee, 1993), 85–87.

52. Dionysius, *Celestial Hierarchies* 7, 38–39.

Chapter 6

1. St. Thomas Aquinas, *On the Truth of the Catholic Faith; Summa Contra Gentiles, Book Two: Creation*, trans. James F. Anderson (New York: Doubleday, 1956), 312–16.

2. St. Thomas Aquinas, *Summa theologica,* trans. the Fathers of the English Dominican Province, rev. by Daniel J. Sullivan, Great Books of the Western World 19 (Chicago: Encyclopædia Britannica, 1952), 1:278–80.

3. St. Thomas Aquinas, *On the Truth of the Catholic Faith: Summa Contra Gentiles, Book Three: Providence,* trans. Vernon J. Bourke (New York: Doubleday, 1956), 44.

4. Thomas rejected the notion of universal matter that the scholar Avicebron had advocated. Many Christian scholars of his day were drawn to the idea, but Aquinas saw both the logical errors and dangerous tendencies of the system. See James Collins, *The Thomistic Philosophy of Angels,* Catholic University of America Philosophical Studies 89 (Washington, D.C.: Catholic University of America, 1947), 42–74.

5. *Summa theologica,* LXV.4.

6. For a full discussion, see Collins, *Thomistic,* 257–91.

7. All the quotes from Calvin in this section are from *The Institutes of the Christian Religion,* 1.14, trans. Henry Beveridge (Grand Rapids: Eerdmans, 1972), 1.144–48.

8. John Milton, *Paradise Lost and Paradise Regained,* ed. Christopher Hicks (New York: Signet Classics, 1982), 47.

9. Milton, 80.

10. Milton, 82.

11. C. S. Lewis, *A Preface to Paradise Lost* (New York: Oxford University Press, 1961), 108–15, misses the most important point when he sets out to prove that Milton and his contemporaries probably believed that angels were in some sense corporeal, and that therefore Milton's depictions of angels are acceptable. The real problem is not corporeality in itself but that Milton's heaven is really earth and his angels are really humans.

12. For a good defense of the view that Milton's Satan and his demons are really evil, see Lewis, *Preface,* 94–107.

13. Notwithstanding Lewis' skill in finding moral lessons in the poem.

14. Sig Synnestvedt, *The Essential Swedenborg* (New York: The Swedenborg Foundation, 1970), 168.

15. Ibid., 171.

16. *Encyclopædia Britannica,* 1988, s.v. "Swedenborg, Emanuel."

17. Synnestvedt, *Essential Swedenborg,* 104–118.

18. Emanuel Swedenborg, *Angelic Wisdom Concerning Divine Love and Wisdom,* trans. John C. Ager (New York: Citadel, 1965), 88–89.

19. Ibid., 190–91.

20. Barth, *Church Dogmatics,* 371–72.

21. Ibid., 391.

22. Ibid., 410–11.

23. Ibid., 451.

24. Ibid., 467–76.

25. Ibid., 477–83.

26. Ibid., 486.

27. Ibid., 493–99.
28. Ibid., 499–511.
29. Ibid., 500.
30. Ibid., 514–15.
31. Ibid., 494.
32. Ibid., 401–404.
33. Geddes MacGregor, *Angels: Ministers of Grace* (New York: Paragon, 1988).
34. Many books by reputable biologists either challenging or at least voicing concerns over evolution are available. See, for example, Lane P. Lester and Raymond G. Bohlin, *The Natural Limits to Biological Change* (Grand Rapids: Zondervan, 1984) and Pattle P. T. Pun, *Evolution* (Grand Rapids: Zondervan, 1982).
35. See Hugh Ross, *The Creator and the Cosmos* (Colorado Springs, Colorado: NavPress, 1993).

Chapter 7

1. C. S. Lewis, *Miracles: A Preliminary Study* (New York: Macmillan, 1947), 84.
2. MacGregor, *Angels: Ministers of Grace*, 130.
3. My analysis of the philosophical argument for the existence of angels is dependent on Mortimer J. Adler, *The Angels and Us* (New York: Collier Books, 1982), a book which I heartily recommend, and James Collins, *The Thomistic Philosophy of Angels*, Catholic University of America Philosophical Studies 89 (Washington, D.C.: Catholic University of America, 1947), 16–41.
4. While Aquinas was to some degree following the Neoplatonic thought of Pseudo-Dionysius, he took pains to reject any notion of emanations.
5. Adler, *Angels*, 131–32, has an interesting anecdote on this point.
6. For example, Douglas Connelly, *Angels Around Us* (Downer's Grove, Ill.: InterVarsity, 1994), 37–38.
7. Connelly, *Angels*, 141.
8. Eileen Elias Freeman, *Touched by Angels* (New York: Warner Books, 1993), 34–35.
9. *Summa theologica*, 1.63.7 (volume 1, page 331 of the Great Books edition).
10. Basil, *Adv. Eun.*, 3.1, cited in Jean Danielou, *The Angels and Their Mission*, trans. David Heimann (Dublin: Four Courts Press, 1957), 68.
11. *Shepherd of Hermas* 2, 6, 2. Cited from Alexander Roberts and James Donaldson, *The Ante-Nicene Fathers* (Grand Rapids: Eerdmans, 1983), 2:24.
12. Gregory of Nyssa, *Life of Moses*, cited in Danielou, *Angels and Their Mission*, 81.
13. Origen, *Sel. Ps.*, 37, cited in Danielou, *Angels and Their Mission*, 77.
14. Ibid., 77.
15. Ambrose, *de Vid.*, 9.
16. Origen, *Hom. in Num.* 25, 5, cited in Danielou, *Angels and Their Mission*, 100.
17. Danielou, *Angels and Their Mission*, 99.
18. *Const. ap.*, 8,41, cited in Danielou, *Angels and Their Mission*, 98.

19. Barth, *Church Dogmatics*, 457.

Chapter 8

1. For a survey of New Age attitudes toward Jesus, see Douglas Groothuis, *Revealing the New Age Jesus* (Downer's Grove: InterVarsity Press, 1990).

2. For surveys of the history and teachings of the New Age movement, see Russell Chandler, *Understanding the New Age* (Dallas: Word, 1988); James W. Sire, *The Universe Next Door*, 2nd ed. (Downer's Grove, Ill.: InterVarsity, 1988), 156–208; and Douglas R. Groothuis, *Unmasking the New Age* (Downer's Grove: InterVarsity, 1986).

3. Sire, *Universe*, 204.

4. Alma Daniel, Timothy Wyllie, and Andrew Ramer, *Ask Your Angels* (New York: Ballantine Books, 1992).

5. Burnham, *A Book of Angels*.

6. Terry Lynn Taylor, *Guardians of Hope* (Tiburon, California: H. J. Kramer, 1992).

7. Rosemary Ellen Guiley, *Angels of Mercy* (New York: Pocket Books, 1994).

8. John Randolph Price, *The Angels Within Us* (New York: Fawcett Columbine, 1993).

9. Burnham, *Book of Angels*, 81–192.

10. Guiley, *Angels of Mercy*, 38, 57.

11. Ibid., 191.

12. Daniel, Wyllie, and Ramer, *Ask Your Angels*, 88.

13. Guiley, *Angels of Mercy*, 161.

14. Ibid., 101.

15. Ibid., 157–58.

16. Price, *Angels Within*, 9, 45–51.

17. Daniel, Wyllie, and Ramer, *Ask Your Angels*, 61–63.

18. Guiley, *Angels of Mercy*, 66.

19. Daniel, Wyllie, and Ramer, *Ask Your Angels*, 114.

20. Ibid., 114–26.

21. Taylor, *Guardians*, 92.

22. Ibid., 144, emphasis original.

23. Ibid., 145.

24. Price, *Angels Within*, 98.

25. Ibid., 63.

26. Daniel, Wyllie, and Ramer, *Ask Your Angels*, 67; see also 219, 277.

27. Guiley, *Angels of Mercy*, 195.

28. Taylor, *Guardians*, 18.

29. Ibid., 16.

30. Daniel, Wyllie, and Ramer, *Ask Your Angels*, 98.

31. Ibid., 79.

32. Guiley, *Angels of Mercy*, 212–215.

33. Daniel, Wyllie, and Ramer, *Ask Your Angels*, 39–55, 337.

34. Guiley, *Angels of Mercy*, 74.

35. Daniel, Wyllie, and Ramer, *Ask Your Angels*, 339.
36. Ibid., 337.
37. Price, *Angels Within*, 14.
38. Daniel, Wyllie, and Ramer, *Ask Your Angels*, 213.
39. Burnham, *Book of Angels*, 240–51.
40. Rosemary Gardner Loveday, as cited in Guiley, *Angels of Mercy*, 64.

Chapter 9

1. See Taylor, *Guardians*, xvii.
2. Price, *Angels Within*, 16.
3. Ibid., 52.
4. Ibid., 218.
5. Ibid., 38–39.
6. The GRACE process is described in Daniel, Wyllie, and Ramer, *Ask Your Angels*, 102–209.
7. Ibid., 241–43, 274.
8. Taylor, *Guardians*, 8–17.
9. Ibid., 140.
10. Guiley, *Angels of Mercy*, 80–81.
11. Taylor, *Guardians*, 20.
12. Daniel, Wyllie, and Ramer, *Ask Your Angels*, 222–23.
13. Taylor, *Guardians*, 33, 35.
14. Daniel, Wyllie, and Ramer, *Ask Your Angels*, 256.
15. Taylor, *Guardians*, 81.
16. Daniel, Wyllie, and Ramer, *Ask Your Angels*, 281.
17. Taylor, *Guardians*, 85.
18. Daniel, Wyllie, and Ramer, *Ask Your Angels*, 128–33.
19. Taylor, *Guardians*, 101; Daniel, Wyllie, and Ramer, *Ask Your Angels*, 231.
20. Price, *Angels Within*, 63–64.
21. Taylor, *Guardians*, 12.
22. Ibid. 121.
23. Ibid., 27, 44.
24. Daniel, Wyllie, and Ramer, *Ask Your Angels*, 144–45, 157. See also Burnham, *Book of Angels*, 138, on drug addiction.
25. Taylor, *Guardians*, 175.
26. Daniel, Wyllie, and Ramer, *Ask Your Angels*, 75.
27. Ibid., 171.
28. Guiley, *Angels of Mercy*, 192.
29. Daniel, Wyllie, and Ramer, *Ask Your Angels*, 215.
30. Ibid., 98.
31. Ibid., 91.
32. Ibid., 96.
33. Ibid., 163–64.
34. Price, *Angels Within*, 127.
35. Daniel, Wyllie, and Ramer, *Ask Your Angels*, 323–24.

36. Ibid., 92.

37. Taylor, *Guardians*, 142.

38. Ibid., xviii.

39. See, for example, Daniel, Wyllie, and Ramer, *Ask Your Angels*, 299.

40. See Taylor, *Guardians*, 63.

41. See Daniel, Wyllie, and Ramer, *Ask Your Angels*, 208–9.

42. Ibid., 353.

43. Price, *Angels Within*, 3–5.

44. Daniel, Wyllie, and Ramer, *Ask Your Angels*, 25.

45 Ibid., 75.

46. Ibid., 86.

47. Ibid., 80–81.

48. Guiley, *Angels of Mercy*, 9.

49. Daniel, Wyllie, and Ramer, *Ask Your Angels*, 238.

50. Taylor, *Guardians*, 161, 165.

51. Daniel, Wyllie, and Ramer, *Ask Your Angels*, 340.

52. Guiley, *Angels of Mercy*, 87–89.

53. See Daniel, Wyllie, and Ramer, *Ask Your Angels*, 184ff, and Taylor, *Guardians*, 93–94.

54. Daniel, Wyllie, and Ramer, *Ask Your Angels*, 69.

55. Ibid., 66.

56. Ibid., 97.

57. Guiley, *Angels of Mercy*, 62.

58. Taylor, *Guardians*, 118.

59. Price, *Angels Within*, 70, 93, 187.

60. Daniel, Wyllie, and Ramer, *Ask Your Angels*, 29.

61. Guiley, *Angels of Mercy*, 73.

62. Ibid., 103–104; see also 181, 203, and Burnham, *Book of Angels*, 71.

63. Daniel, Wyllie, and Ramer, *Ask Your Angels*, 73.

64. Guiley, *Angels of Mercy*, 123–34.

65. Taylor, *Guardians*, 106.

66. Ibid., 17, 59, 13.

67. Price, *Angels Within*, 16.

68. Guiley, *Angels of Mercy*, 194.

69. Daniel, Wyllie, and Ramer, *Ask Your Angels*, 253, 282, 286, and 293.

70. Guiley, *Angels of Mercy*, 194. Price, *Angels Within*, 12, similarly says that the "Causal Powers are extensions of the Spirit of God within each individual."

71. Burnham, *Book of Angels*, 136.

72. Taylor, *Guardians*, xxi.

73. Guiley, *Angels of Mercy*, 221–22.

74. Daniel, Wyllie, and Ramer, *Ask Your Angels*, 28.

75. Price, *Angels Within*, 215–17.

Chapter 10

1. *Encyclopedia Judaica*, s.v. "Angels and Angelology," 2:976.

2. Margolies, *A Gathering of Angels*, 10.

3. Ibid., 41.

4. Ibid., 26.

5. Ibid., 135.

6. Margaret Barker, *The Great Angel: A Study of Israel's Second God* (Louisville: Westminster, 1992), has argued that the Israelites believed that the High God El-Elyon had a heavenly council with whom he consulted and which included Yahweh, the son of El-Elyon. For this reason, she contends, the Jewish followers of Jesus were able to accept him as the Son of God—the notion was not nearly as alien to them as we have been led to believe. Although I find aspects of Barker's analysis untenable, I believe that the main point, that the Israelites did not have unitarian monotheism, to be deserving of further study. At any rate, it is clear that the Israelites did not believe that God was the sole inhabitant of heaven.

7. Barth, *Church Dogmatics*, vol. 3, pt. 3, 448.

8. Georges Huber, *My Angel Will Go Before You*, trans. Michael Adams (Dublin: Four Courts Press, 1983), 18.

9. Ibid., 23.

10. Ibid., 36.

11. Ibid., 36.

12. MacGregor, *Angels: Ministers of Grace*, 13.

13. *Catechism of the Catholic Church* (Ottawa: CCCB, 1994), 79.

14. Huber, *My Angel Will Go*, 59.

15. Ibid., 100.

16. Freeman, *Touched*.

17. Ibid., 2–8.

18. Ibid., 13–18.

19. Ibid., 18–24.

20. Ibid., 69–70.

21. Ibid., 147.

22. Ibid., 34.

23. For example, see Ibid., 189: "only God can be at the center of attention, because only God is at the center, only God *is* the center" (emphasis original).

24. Ibid., 157, emphasis original.

25. Ibid., 164–88.

26. Ibid., 188, emphasis original.

27. Ibid., 64.

28. Ibid., 160.

29. Ibid., 155.

30. For this survey, I am dependent on Heinz Gstrein, *Engelwerk oder Teufelsmacht* (Mattersburg-Katzelsdorf: Edition Tau, 1990), 11–52.

31. Ibid., 60.

32. Ibid., 15.

33. Ibid., 57–58, 63.

34. Ibid., 255.

35. Ibid., 63–64.

36. Ibid., 59.

37. Ibid., 258–59, translated from German.

38. Ibid., 59.

39. Ibid., 64.

40. Ibid., 64, translated from German.

41. Ibid., 257, translated from German.

42. Ibid., 65.

43. Translated from the Latin document "Decretum de doctrina et usibus particularibus consociationis cui nomen 'Opus Angelorum,'" *Acta Apostolicae Sedis* 84 (August 3, 1992): 805.

44. *Acta Apostolicae Sedis*, 84:806; translated from Latin.

45. Graham, *Angels: God's Secret Agents.*

46. Ibid., 49.

47. Ibid., 50–51.

48. Ibid., 99–109.

49. Marilynn Carlson Webber and William D. Webber, *A Rustle of Angels* (Grand Rapids: Zondervan, 1994).

50. Ibid., 15–16. William Webber also feels that he was saved by an angel when he fell off a scaffold (pp. 17–18).

51. Ibid., 160, emphasis original.

52. Ibid., 169–73.

53. Ibid., 175–78. They take Revelation 12 to be a description of "Lucifer's sin" and do not see that it has to do rather with his role of accuser.

54. Ibid., 180. A similar list appears in Timothy Jones, *Celebration of Angels* (Nashville: Thomas Nelson, 1994), 191–213.

55. Webber and Webber, *Rustle*, 166–67.

56. Landrum Leavell, *Angels, Angels, Angels* (Nashville: Broadman, 1973); C. Fred Dickason, *Angels: Elect and Evil* (Chicago: Moody Press, 1975); Connelly, *Angels Around Us*, 38–41, 73.

57. St. Augustine, *The City of God* 11.13, trans. Henry Bettenson (London: Penguin, 1972), 445.

Chapter 11

1. Personal correspondence from Micki Stella, retired Southern Baptist missionary to South Korea, dated January 17, 1995.

2. V. Raymond Edman, "I, Too, Saw an Angel," *Bulletin of Wheaton College* (Dec. 1959), cited in Timothy Jones, *Celebration of Angels* (Nashville: Thomas Nelson, 1994), 117–23. The story is also repeated in Joan Wester Anderson, *Where Angels Walk* (New York: Ballantine, 1992), 108–11.

3. Anderson, *Where Angels Walk*, 58–59.

4. Ibid., 60–62.

5. Guiley, *Angels of Mercy*, 106.

6. Burnham, *Book of Angels*, 231–37.

7. Ibid., 572–74.

8. The "man in Christ" he speaks of here (12:2) was undoubtedly himself.

Chapter 12

1. C. S. Lewis, *The Screwtape Letters* (New York: Macmillan, 1953), 131.
2. Ibid., 111.
3. Ibid., 41.
4. Ibid., 22.
5. Ibid., 66–67.
6. Ibid., 47.
7. Ibid., 49.
8. Steven Lawson, "Defeating Territorial Spirits," in *Engaging the Enemy*, C. Peter Wagner, ed. (Ventura, Calif.: Regal, 1991), 29. Lawson also states, "These fictionalized accounts tell how packs of demons have taken over complete towns, infesting government, education, and even churches."
9. Frank E. Peretti, *This Present Darkness* (Wheaton: Crossway, 1986), 240–44. In fairness to Peretti, other characters with demons in his book are not so easily handled.
10. Ibid., 370–73.
11. Roger Elwood, *Stedfast* (Dallas: Word, 1992), 7.
12. Ibid., 39.
13. For example, ibid., 63, 186.
14. Ibid., 30.
15. Ibid., 30–31.
16. Ibid., 70–71, 176.
17. Ibid., 53–63.
18. Ibid., 75.
19. Ibid., 143.
20. Lewis, we should add, perpetuates the same notion in *The Screwtape Letters*, but as we have already observed, Lewis's overall picture is so unrealistic that the reader is probably not inclined to take this seriously either.
21. Elwood, *Stedfast*, 141.
22. Ibid., 33.
23. Ibid., 32, emphasis original.
24. Ibid., 33, 185–86.

Chapter 13

1. Walter Wink, *Naming the Powers* (Philadelphia: Fortress, 1984), *Unmasking the Powers* (Philadelphia: Fortress, 1986), and *Engaging the Powers* (Philadelphia: Fortress, 1986).
2. Wink, *Unmasking*, 13–14; emphasis original.
3. Ibid., 25; emphasis original.
4. Ibid., 41–68.
5. Ibid., 66–67.
6. Wink, *Engaging*, 55–56.
7. Wink's views on the atonement are in *Engaging the Powers*, 139–55. He is heavily influenced by René Girard's theories of mimesis and the scapegoat. Wink admits that Paul "gives credence" to the notion of a sacrificial atonement

in various places and concludes that Paul was "unable fully to distinguish the insight that Christ is the end of sacrificing from the idea that Christ is the final sacrifice whose death is an atonement to God." "And," Wink adds, "Christianity has suffered from this confusion ever since" (pp. 153–54.).

8. Wink himself does not classify his view as the example theory of the atonement but as the "Christus Victor" view. But as far as I can tell, in Wink's analysis, the death of Christ put an end to sacrifice only in the sense that it was a rejection of the legitimacy of violence. It did not end the Domination System in any way. Also, Wink gives numerous historical anecdotes of how following the example of nonviolence has broken the power of violent political oppression. His is an example theory by any other name. Also, I do not believe that the Christus Victor model is as opposed to substitutionary atonement as Wink implies.

9. For a full and helpful study of this issue, see Stanley J. Grenz and Roger E. Olson, *Twentieth Century Theology* (Downer's Grove, Ill.: InterVarsity, 1992).

10. Wink, *Unmasking*, 126. Wink's discussion of the gods is in *Unmasking*, 108–27.

11. Wink's discussion of the elements is in *Unmasking*, 128–52.

12. Ibid., 157.

13. Ibid., 153–71.

14. Ibid., 170, emphasis original.

15. Timothy M. Warner, "Dealing with Territorial Demons," in Wagner, *Engaging the Enemy*, 53.

16. For example, Steven Lawson, "Defeating Territorial Spirits," in Wagner, *Engaging the Enemy*, 32. On page 29, Wagner describes this as "some of the new things the Spirit is saying to the churches."

17. Wagner, "Territorial Spirits," in Wagner, *Engaging the Enemy*, 43.

18. Vernon J. Sterk, "Territorial Spirits and Evangelization in Hostile Environments," in Wagner, *Engaging the Enemy*, 149.

19. Ibid., 159–60.

20. C. Peter Wagner, *Warfare Prayer* (Ventura, Calif.: Regal, 1992), 143–47. On Pele, for example, he says that "few visitors have not been informed that the principality over the Big Island is the volcano goddess, Pele," and he gives no indication of doubt about the accuracy of this belief.

21. Sterk, "Territorial," 153–54. John Dawson, "Foreword," in Wagner, *Engaging the Enemy*, xiv, similarly states that the gods of Olympus were "powerful demons."

22. Wagner, "Territorial Spirits," 46.

23. Lawson, "Defeating," 35–36.

24. Thomas B. White, "Understanding Principalities and Powers," in Wagner, *Engaging the Enemy*, 62.

25. Lawson, "Defeating," 39–40.

26. Dawson, "Foreword," xi, and Lawson, "Defeating," 32.

27. C. Peter Wagner, "Spiritual Warfare," in *Engaging the Enemy*, 15–17.

28. Ibid., 18–19.

29. This anecdote was related to me by Don Dilmore on Jan. 25, 1995.

30. Larry Lea, "Binding the Strongman," Wagner, *Engaging the Enemy*, 86.

31. Wagner, *Warfare Prayer*, 146–47.

32. Dick Bernal, *Storming Hell's Brazen Gates*, 57, cited in Sterk, "Territorial," 159.

33. Wagner, "Territorial Spirits," 48.

34. Lea, "Binding," 94–95.

35. Clement of Alexandria, *Strom.* 6.17, cited in Jean Danielou, *The Angels and Their Mission*, 15.

36. Origen, *Hom. In Luc.* 12, cited in Danielou, *Angels and Their Missions*, 17.

37. Eusebius, *Dem. Ev.* 4, 7–8, cited in Danielou, *Angels and Their Missions*, 19–20.

38. See Danielou, *Angels and Their Missions*, 14–23.

39. White, "Understanding," 61.

40. For example, Clinton E. Arnold, *Powers of Darkness* (Downer's Grove, Ill.: InterVarsity, 1992).

41. Thus, Arnold, *Powers*, 103.

42. For example, Oscar Cullmann, *Christ and Time*, trans. Floyd V. Filson (London: SCM Press, 1951), 195–96, follows Gnostic exegesis to conclude that the authorities are angelic.

43. Herman Ridderbos, *Paul: An Outline of His Theology*, trans. John Richard de Witt (Grand Rapids: Eerdmans, 1975), 326.

44. Arnold, *Powers*, 141–42.

45. Richard R. Melick, Jr., *Philippians, Colossians, Philemon* (Nashville: Broadman, 1991), 219, holds that the powers of Colossians 2 are demonic but says that those of chapter 1 are ambiguous.

46. Robert J. Schwartzbeck, "Divine Warrior Typology in Ephesians 6:10–20: A Neglected Element in the Study of Spiritual Warfare," (M.A. Thesis, Trinity Evangelical Divinity School, 1991).

47. D. M. Lloyd-Jones, *The Christian Warfare* (Grand Rapids: Baker, 1977) and *The Christian Soldier* (Grand Rapids: Baker, 1978).

48. R. C. Sproul, *Pleasing God* (Wheaton, Ill.: Tyndale, 1988), 91.

Chapter 14

1. Barth, *Church Dogmatics*, 460.

2. Stanley J. Grenz, "Proclaiming God in a World of Many Gods," *Christian Week* (Sept. 20, 1994), 5, emphasis original.

3. "In Search of the Sacred," *Newsweek* (Nov. 28, 1994), 55.

4. Neil Stebbins, "The World on High," *Ski* (Jan. 1995), 120.

Selected
Bibliography

Abbott, T. K. *The Epistle to the Colossians. ICC. Reprint edition.* Edinburgh: T. and T. Clark, 1979.

Adler, Mortimer J. *The Angels and Us.* New York: Collier Books, 1982.

Anderson, Joan Wester. *Where Angels Walk.* New York: Ballantine, 1992.

Arnold, Clinton E. *Powers of Darkness.* Downer's Grove, Illinois: InterVarsity, 1992.

Barker, Margaret. *The Great Angel: A Study of Israel's Second God.* Louisville: Westminster, 1992.

Barth, Karl. *Church Dogmatics.* vol. 3, pt. 3. Translated by G. W. Bromiley and R. J. Ehrlich. Edinburgh: T. and T. Clark, 1960.

Blomberg, Craig L. *Matthew.* NAC. Nashville: Broadman Press, 1992.

Brown, Harold O. J. *Heresies.* New York: Doubleday, 1984.

Bruce, F. F. *The Epistle to the Hebrews.* NICNT. Eerdmans: Grand Rapids, 1964.

Bubeck, Mark I. *The Adversary: The Christian Versus Demon Activity.* Chicago: Moody, 1975.

Burnham, Sophy. *A Book of Angels: Reflections on Angels Past and Present and True Stories of How They Touched Our Lives.* New York: Ballantine, 1990.

Catechism of the Catholic Church. Ottawa: CCCB, 1994.

Chandler, Russell. *Understanding the New Age.* Dallas: Word, 1988.

Charlesworth, James H., ed. *The Old Testament Pseudepigrapha.* 2 vols. New York: Doubleday, 1983.

Cohen, A. *Everyman's Talmud.* Reprint ed. New York: Schocken Books, 1975.

Collins, James. *The Thomistic Philosophy of Angels.* Catholic University of America Philosophical Studies 89. Washington, D.C.: Catholic University of America, 1947.

Congregatio pro Doctrina Fidei. "Decretum de doctrina et usibus particularibus consociationis cui nomen 'Opus Angelorum.'" *Acta Apostolicae Sedis* 84(August 3, 1992): 805.

Connelly, Douglas. *Angels Around Us.* Downer's Grove, Ill.: InterVarsity Press, 1994.

Connoly, David. *In Search of Angels: A Celestial Sourcebook for Beginning Your Journey.* New York: Perigee Books, 1993.

Copleston, Frederick. *A History of Philosophy.* Volume II, *Medieval Philosophy: Augustine to Scotus.* London: Burns and Oates Limited, 1964.

Cullmann, Oscar. *Christ and Time.* Translated by Floyd V. Filson. London: SCM Press, 1951.

Daniel, Alma, Timothy Wyllie, and Andrew Ramer. *Ask Your Angels.* New York: Ballantine, 1992.

Danielou, Jean. *The Angels and Their Mission.* Translated by David Heimann. Dublin: Four Courts Press, 1957.

Davidson, Maxwell J. "Angels at Qumran: A Comparative Study of 1 Enoch 1–36, 72–108 and Sectarian Writings from Qumran," *Journal for the Study of Pseudepigrapha* Series 11. Sheffield, England: Sheffield Academic Press, 1992.

Day, Peggy L. *An Adversary in Heaven.* Atlanta: Scholars Press, 1988.

Dickason, C. Fred. *Angels: Elect and Evil.* Chicago: Moody Press, 1975.

Eichrodt, Walther. *Ezekiel.* OTL. Philadelphia: Westminster, 1975.

Elwood, Roger. *Stedfast: Guardian Angel.* Dallas: Word, 1992.

Encyclopædia Britannica, 1988, s.v. "Swedenborg, Emanuel."

Filoramo, Giovanni. *A History of Gnosticism.* Translated by Anthony Alcock. Oxford: Basil Blackwell, 1990.

Foerster, Werner. *Gnosis: A Selection of Gnostic Texts.* Two volumes. Translated by R. McL. Wilson. London: Oxford University Press, 1972.

Freeman, Eileen Elias. *Touched by Angels.* New York: Warner Books, 1993.

George, Timothy. *Galatians.* NAC. Nashville: Broadman, 1994.

Gill, David W. J. "The Importance of Roman Portraiture for Head-Coverings in 1 Corinthians." *Tyndale Bulletin* 41 (1990).

Gilson, Etienne. *The Philosophy of St. Thomas Aquinas.* Translated by Edward Bullough. New York: Dorset Press, n.d.

Ginzberg, Louis. *The Legends of the Jews*. Translated by Henrietta Szold. Philadelphia: The Jewish Publication Society of America, 1920.

Grenz, Stanley J., and Roger E. Olson. *Twentieth Century Theology*. Downer's Grove, Ill.: InterVarsity, 1992.

Groothuis, Douglas R. *Revealing the New Age Jesus*. Downer's Grove: InterVarsity Press, 1990.

———. *Unmasking the New Age*. Downer's Grove: InterVarsity, 1986.

Gstrein, Heinz. *Engelwerk oder Teufelsmacht*. Mattersburg-Katzelsdorf: Edition Tau, 1990.

Guiley, Rosemary Ellen. *Angels of Mercy*. New York: Pocket Books, 1994.

Guthrie, George. *The Structure of Hebrews. Supplements to Novum Testamentum LXXIII*. Leiden: E. J. Brill, 1994.

Hamilton, Victor P. *The Book of Genesis: Chapters 1–17. NICOT*. Grand Rapids: Eerdmans, 1990.

Handy, Lowell K. *Among the Host of Heaven*. Winona Lake, Indiana: Eisenbrauns, 1994.

Heidt, William George. *Angelology of the Old Testament*. Washington, D.C.: Catholic University of America Press, 1949.

Helmbold, Andrew K. *The Nag Hammadi Gnostic Texts and the Bible*. Grand Rapids: Baker, 1967.

Hendel, Ronald S. "Of Demigods and the Deluge: Toward an Interpretation of Genesis 6:1–4." *Journal of Biblical Literature* 106:1 (March 1987).

Hooper, Walter, ed. *The Collected Poems of C. S. Lewis*. London: HarperCollins, 1994.

Huber, Georges. *My Angel Will Go Before You*. Translated by Michael Adams. Dublin: Four Courts Press, 1983.

Hughes, Graham. *Hebrews and Hermeneutics*. Cambridge: Cambridge University Press, 1979.

Jones, Timothy. "The Trouble with Angels." *Today's Christian Woman*. (November-December, 1994): 108–13.

———. *Celebration of Angels*. Nashville: Thomas Nelson, 1994.

Kinnaman, Gary. *Angels: Dark and Light*. Ann Arbor, Michigan: Servant Publications, 1994.

Koehler, Ludwig, and Walter Baumgartner. *The Hebrew and Aramaic Lexicon of the Old Testament*. Leiden: E. J. Brill, 1994.

Lachower, Fischel, and Isaiah Tishby. *The Wisdom of the Zohar*. Translated by David Goldstein. London: Oxford University Press, 1989.

Latourette, Kenneth Scott. *A History of Christianity*. Revised edition. New York: Harper and Row, 1975.

Leavell, Landrum P. *Angels, Angels, Angels*. Nashville: Broadman, 1973.

Lester, Lane P. and Raymond G. Bohlin. *The Natural Limits to Biological Change*. Grand Rapids: Zondervan, 1984.

Lewis, C. S. *Miracles: A Preliminary Study*. New York: Macmillan, 1947.

————. *A Preface to Paradise Lost.* New York: Oxford University Press, 1961.

————. *The Screwtape Letters.* New York: Macmillan, 1953.

Lindars, Barnabas. *The Theology of the Letter to the Hebrews.* Cambridge: Cambridge University Press, 1991.

Lloyd-Jones, D. M. *The Christian Soldier.* Grand Rapids: Baker, 1978.

————. *The Christian Warfare.* Grand Rapids: Baker, 1977.

MacGregor, G. H. C. "Principalities and Powers: The Cosmic Background of Paul's Thought." *New Testament Studies 1* (1954): 17–28.

MacGregor, Geddes. *Angels: Ministers of Grace.* New York: Paragon House, 1988.

Maimonides, Moses. *The Guide of the Perplexed.* Translated with an introduction by Shlomo Pines. Chicago: University of Chicago Press, 1963.

Margolies, Morris B. *A Gathering of Angels: Angels in Jewish Life and Literature.* New York: Ballantine, 1994.

Marshall, I. Howard. *Commentary on Luke.* NIGTC. Grand Rapids: Eerdmans, 1978.

Melick, Richard R., Jr. *Philippians, Colossians, Philemon.* NAC. Nashville: Broadman, 1991.

Metzger, Bruce M. *Breaking the Code: Understanding the Book of Revelation.* Nashville: Abingdon, 1993.

Milton, John. *Paradise Lost and Paradise Regained.* Edited by Christopher Hicks. New York: Signet Classics, 1982.

Morris, Leon. *The First Epistle to the Corinthians.* TNTC. Grand Rapids: Eerdmans, 1958.

Motyer, J. Alec. *The Prophecy of Isaiah.* Downers Grove, Illinois: InterVarsity, 1993.

Moule, C. F. D. *The Epistles to the Colossians and to Philemon.* Cambridge Greek Testament. London: Cambridge University Press, 1958.

Newport, John P. *Demons, Demons, Demons.* Nashville: Broadman, 1972.

Newsome, Carol. *Songs of the Sabbath Sacrifice: A Critical Edition.* Atlanta: Scholars Press, 1985.

Osborn, Lawrence. "Entertaining Angels: Their Place in Contemporary Theology." *Tyndale Bulletin* 45.2 (1994): 273–96.

Peel, Doris. *A Gathering of Angels.* Boston: Fleetwood Press, 1979.

Peretti, Frank E. *This Present Darkness.* Wheaton, Illinois: Crossway Books, 1986.

Polhill, John. *Acts.* NAC. Nashville: Broadman, 1992.

Price, John Randolph. *The Angels Within Us.* New York: Ballantine, 1993.

Pritchard, James B. *Ancient Near Eastern Texts Relating to the Old Testament.* Princeton, N.J.: Princeton University Press, 1969.

Pun, Pattle P. T. *Evolution.* Grand Rapids: Zondervan, 1982.

Ridderbos, Herman. *Paul: An Outline of His Theology.* Translated by John Richard de Witt. Grand Rapids: Eerdmans, 1975.

Roberts, Alexander, and James Donaldson. *The Ante-Nicene Fathers.* Grand Rapids: Eerdmans, 1983.

Robinson, Archibald, and Alfred Plummer. *I Corinthians.* ICC. Edinburgh: T. and T. Clark, 1911.

Ross, Hugh. *The Creator and the Cosmos.* Colorado Springs, Colorado: NavPress, 1993.

Rudolph, Kurt. "Gnosticism." In *The Anchor Bible Dictionary.* Vol. 2. Edited by David Noel Freedman. New York: Eerdmans, 1992.

Russell, D. S. *Divine Disclosure: An Introduction to Jewish Apocalyptic.* Minneapolis: Fortress Press, 1992.

———. *The Method and Message of Jewish Apocalyptic.* Philadelphia: Westminster Press, 1964.

Scholem, Gershom. *Kabbalah.* New York: Meridian, 1974.

Schwartzbeck, Robert J. "Divine Warrior Typology in Ephesians 6:10–20: A Neglected Element in the Study of Spiritual Warfare." MA Thesis, Trinity Evangelical Divinity School, 1991.

Schweizer, Eduard. "Slaves of the Elements and Worshippers of Angels: Gal 4:3 and Col 2:8, 18, 20." *Journal of Biblical Literature* 107 (1988): 455–68.

Seitz, Christopher R. *Zion's Final Destiny.* Minneapolis: Fortress Press, 1991.

Sire, James W. *The Universe Next Door.* Second edition. Downer's Grove, Illinois: InterVarsity, 1988.

Sproul, R. C. *Pleasing God.* Wheaton, Illinois: Tyndale, 1988.

St. Augustine. *The City of God.* Translated by Henry Bettenson. London: Penguin, 1972.

St. Thomas Aquinas. *Summa theologica.* Translated by the Fathers of the English Dominican Province. Revised by Daniel J. Sullivan. Great Books of the Western World 19. Chicago: Encyclopædia Britannica, 1952.

———. *On the Truth of the Catholic Faith. Summa Contra Gentiles. Book Two: Creation.* Translated by James F. Anderson. New York: Doubleday, 1956.

———. *On the Truth of the Catholic Faith. Summa Contra Gentiles. Book Three: Providence.* Translated by Vernon J. Bourke. New York: Doubleday, 1956.

Stewart, James S. "On a Neglected Emphasis in New Testament Theology." *Scottish Journal of Theology* 14 (1951): 292–301.

Stone, Eden. "Are There Angels Among Us?" *New Age Journal* (April 1994), 88–93, 147, 149–51.

Swedenborg, Emanuel. *Angelic Wisdom Concerning Divine Love and Wisdom.* Translated by John C. Ager. New York: Citadel, 1965.

Synnestvedt, Sig. *The Essential Swedenborg.* New York: The Swedenborg Foundation, 1970.

Tasker, R. V. G. *The Second Epistle of Paul to the Corinthians.* TNTC. Grand Rapids: Eerdmans, 1958.

Taylor, John. *Ezekiel.* TOTC. Downer's Grove, Illinois: InterVarsity, 1979.

Taylor, Terry Lynn. *Guardians of Hope: The Angels' Guide to Personal Growth.* Tiburon, California: H. J. Kramer Inc., 1992.

ten Boom, Corrie, with John and Elizabeth Sherrill. *The Hiding Place.* Washington Depot, Connecticut: Chosen, 1971.

Tomson, Peter J. *Paul and the Jewish Law.* Minneapolis: Fortress Press, 1990.

Torrance, Thomas F. "The Spiritual Relevance of Angels." In *Alive to God.* J. I. Packer and Loren Wilkinson, ed., Downer's Grove, Illinois: InterVarsity, 1992.

Unger, Merrill F. *Biblical Demonology.* Chicago: Scripture Press, 1952.

VanderKam, James C. *The Dead Sea Scrolls Today.* Grand Rapids: Eerdmans, 1994.

Wagner, C. Peter. *Engaging the Enemy: How to Fight and Defeat Territorial Spirits.* Ventura, California: Regal Books, 1991.

———. *Warfare Prayer.* Ventura, California: Regal Books, 1992.

Ward, Theodora. *Men and Angels.* New York: Viking, 1969.

Webber, Marilynn Carlson, and William D. Webber. *A Rustle of Angels.* Grand Rapids: Zondervan, 1994.

Wenham, Gordon J. *Genesis 1–15.* Word Biblical Commentary. Dallas: Word, 1987.

Whitehouse, W. A. "God's Heavenly Kingdom and His Servants the Angels." *Scottish Journal of Theology* 4 (1951): 376–82.

Wilson, Peter Lamborn. *Angels.* New York: Pantheon Books, 1980.

Wink, Walter. *Engaging the Powers.* Philadelphia: Fortress, 1986.

———. *Naming the Powers.* Philadelphia: Fortress, 1984.

———. *Unmasking the Powers.* Philadelphia: Fortress, 1986.

Yates, Roy. "The Powers of Evil in the New Testament." *Evangelical Quarterly* 52 (1980): 97–111.